A Singular Woman

A Singular Woman

The Untold Story of Barack Obama's Mother

JANNY SCOTT

RIVERHEAD BOOKS

a member of Penguin Group (USA) Inc.

New York

2011

RIVERHEAD BOOKS
Published by the Penguin Group
Penguin Group (USA) Inc., 375 Hudson Street, New York, New York 10014, USA •
Penguin Group (Canada), 90 Eglinton Avenue East, Suite 700, Toronto, Ontario M4P 2Y3,
Canada (a division of Pearson Penguin Canada Inc.) • Penguin Books Ltd, 80 Strand, London
WC2R 0RL, England • Penguin Ireland, 25 St Stephen's Green, Dublin 2, Ireland (a division of
Penguin Books Ltd) • Penguin Group (Australia), 250 Camberwell Road, Camberwell,
Victoria 3124, Australia (a division of Pearson Australia Group Pty Ltd) • Penguin Books
India Pvt Ltd, 11 Community Centre, Panchsheel Park, New Delhi–110 017, India •
Penguin Group (NZ), 67 Apollo Drive, Rosedale, North Shore 0632, New Zealand
(a division of Pearson New Zealand Ltd) • Penguin Books (South Africa) (Pty) Ltd,
24 Sturdee Avenue, Rosebank, Johannesburg 2196, South Africa

Penguin Books Ltd, Registered Offices: 80 Strand, London WC2R 0RL, England

Lyrics from "Bésame Mucho," by Consuelo Velázquez, are used by permission of Promotora
Hispano Americana de Música S.A. Administered by Peer International Corporation.
All rights reserved.

Library of Congress Cataloging-in-Publication Data
Scott, Janny.
A singular woman : the untold story of Barack Obama's mother / Janny Scott.
        p.   cm.
ISBN 978-1-59448-797-2
1. Dunham, S. Ann (Stanley Ann).   2. Mothers of presidents—United States—Biography.
3. Obama, Barack—Family.   I. Title.
E909.D86S36   2011   2010054195
        973.932092—dc22
            [B]

Printed in the United States of America
3   5   7   9   10   8   6   4   2

BOOK DESIGN BY AMANDA DEWEY

While the author has made every effort to provide accurate telephone numbers and Internet addresses
at the time of publication, neither the publisher nor the author assumes any responsibility for errors, or
for changes that occur after publication. Further, the publisher does not have any control over and does
not assume any responsibility for author or third-party websites or their content.

I think sometimes that had I known she would not survive her illness, I might have written a different book—less a meditation on the absent parent, more a celebration of the one who was the single constant in my life.

—BARACK OBAMA, *Dreams from My Father,*
preface to the 2004 edition

For Joe

Prologue

*I am the son of a black man from Kenya
and a white woman from Kansas.*

—BARACK OBAMA, MARCH 18, 2008

The photograph showed the son, but my eye gravitated toward the mother. That first glimpse was surprising—the stout, pale-skinned woman in sturdy sandals, standing squarely a half-step ahead of the lithe, darker-skinned figure to her left. His elastic-band body bespoke discipline, even asceticism. Her form was well padded, territory ceded long ago to the pleasures of appetite and the forces of anatomical destiny. He had the studied casualness of a catalog model, in khakis, at home in the viewfinder. She met the camera head-on, dressed in hand-loomed textile dyed the color of indigo, a silver earring half hidden in the cascading curtain of her dark hair. She carried her chin a few degrees higher than most. His right hand rested on her shoulder, lightly. The photograph, taken on a Manhattan rooftop in August 1987 and e-mailed to me twenty years later, was a revelation and a puzzle. The man was Barack Obama at age twenty-six, the community organizer from

Chicago on a visit to New York. The woman was Stanley Ann Dunham, his mother. It was impossible not to be struck forcefully by the similarities, and the dissimilarities, between them. It was impossible not to question, in that moment, the stereotype to which she had been expediently reduced: the white woman from Kansas.

The president's mother has served as any of a number of useful oversimplifications. In the capsule version of Obama's life story, she is the white mother from Kansas coupled alliteratively with the black father from Kenya. She is corn-fed, white-bread, whatever Kenya is not. In *Dreams from My Father,* the memoir that helped power Obama's political ascent, she is the shy, small-town girl who falls head over heels for the brilliant, charismatic African who steals the show. In the next chapter, she is the naive idealist, the innocent abroad. In Obama's presidential campaign, she was the struggling single mother, the food stamp recipient, the victim of a health-care system gone awry, pleading with her insurance company for coverage as her life slipped away. And in the fevered imaginings of supermarket tabloids and the Internet, she is the atheist, the Marxist, the flower child, the mother who "abandoned" her son or duped the state of Hawaii into issuing a birth certificate for her Kenyan-born baby, on the off chance that he might want to be president someday.

The earthy figure in the photograph did not fit any of those.

A few months after receiving the photo, I wrote an article for *The New York Times* about Dunham. It was one in a series of biographical articles on then Senator Obama that the *Times* published during the presidential campaign. It was long for a newspaper but short for a life, yet people who read it were seized by her story and, some said, moved to tears. As a result of the article, I was offered a chance to write a book on Dunham, and I spent two and a half years following her trail. I drove across the Flint Hills of Kansas to the former oil boomtowns where her parents grew up during the Depression. I spent many weeks in Hawaii, where she became pregnant at seventeen, married at eighteen, divorced and remarried at twenty-two. I traveled twice to Indonesia, where she brought her son, at six, and from whence she sent him back, alone, at age ten, to her parents in Hawaii. I visited dusty villages in Java where, as a young anthropologist, she did fieldwork for her Ph.D. dissertation on peasant blacksmithing. I met with bankers in glass towers in Jakarta where, nearly two decades before Muhammad Yunus and Grameen Bank shared the Nobel Peace Prize for their work with microcredit, Dunham worked on the largest self-sustaining commercial microfinance program in the world. I combed through tattered field notebooks, boxes of personal and professional papers, letters to friends, photo albums, the archives of the Ford Foundation in Midtown Manhattan, and the thousand-page thesis that took Dunham fifteen years to complete. I interviewed nearly two hundred colleagues, friends, professors, employers, acquaintances, and relatives, including her two children. Without their generosity, I could not have written this book.

To describe Dunham as a white woman from Kansas is about as illuminating as describing her son as a politician who likes golf. Intentionally or not, the label obscures an extraordinary story—of a girl with a boy's name who grew up in the years before the civil rights movement, the women's movement, the Vietnam War, and the Pill; who married an African at a time when nearly two dozen states still had laws against interracial marriage; who, at age twenty-four, moved to Jakarta with her son in the waning days of an anti-communist bloodbath in which hundreds of thousands of Indonesians are believed to have been slaughtered; who lived more than half of her adult life in a place barely known to most Americans, in an ancient and complex culture, in a country with the largest Muslim population in the world; who spent years working in villages where an unmarried, Western woman was a rarity; who immersed herself in the study of a sacred craft long practiced exclusively by men; who, as a working and mostly single mother, brought up two biracial children; who adored her children and believed her son in particular had the potential to be great; who raised him to be, as he has put it jokingly, a combination of Albert Einstein, Mahatma Gandhi, and Harry Belafonte, then died at fifty-two, never knowing who or what he would become.

Had she lived, Dunham would have been sixty-six years old on January 20, 2009, when Barack Obama was sworn in as the forty-fourth president of the United States.

Dunham was a private person with depths not easily fathomed. In a conversation in the Oval Office in July 2010, President Obama described her to me as both naively idealistic and sophisticated and smart. She was deadly serious about her work, he said, yet had a sweetness and generosity of spirit that resulted occasionally in her being taken to the cleaners. She had an unusual openness, it seems, that was both intellectual and emotional. "At the foundation of her strength was her ability to be moved," her daughter, Maya Soetoro-Ng, once told me. Yet she was tough and funny. Moved to tears by the suffering of strangers, she could be steely in motivating her children. She wept in movie theaters but could detonate a wise-crack so finely targeted that no one in earshot ever forgot. She devoted years of her life to helping poor people, many of them women, get access to credit, but she mismanaged her own money, borrowed repeatedly from her banker mother, and fell deeply in debt. In big and small ways, she lived bravely. Yet she feared doctors, possibly to her detriment. She was afraid of riding the New York City subway system, and she never learned to drive. At the height of her career, colleagues remember Dunham as an almost regal presence—decked out in batik and silver, descending upon Javanese villages with an entourage of younger Indonesian bankers; formidably knowledgeable about Indonesian textiles, archaeology, the mystical symbolism of the wavy-bladed Javanese kris; bearing a black bag stuffed with field notebooks and a Thermos of black coffee; a connoisseur of delicacies such as tempeh and *sayur lodeh,* an eggplant stew; regaling her colleagues with humorous stories, joking about one day being reincarnated as an Indonesian blacksmith, and protesting slyly all the while that she was "just a girl from Kansas."

There is little evidence in the papers she left behind and in the accounts of friends and colleagues that Dunham set out to change the world. She was admirably, movingly, sometimes exasperatingly, human. Her life was not simple, which may help explain why it has been misunderstood or misrepresented or was relegated to the shadows. It involved tensions and choices that will be recognizable to readers, especially women. It was an improvisation, marked by stumbles and leaps. "I am not such a harsh critic after all, having screwed up royally a few times myself," she wrote cajolingly to a friend at age thirty, already divorced from her first husband, separated from her second, and on her way to becoming a single parent of two. She was resilient. As one friend of hers put it, Dunham kept "dislocating the center." She lived by strong values, which she passed on to her children. She was idealistic and pragmatic. She was not a visionary or a saint; she believed that people's lives could be made better, and that it was important to try. Directly or indirectly, she accomplished more toward that end than most of us will.

Then suddenly, in midstream, she was gone. "She had no regrets about any of her choices," Maya told me. "She just wanted more time. More time to make mistakes, more time to do good things . . ."

Anyone writing about Dunham's life must address the question of what to call her. She was Stanley Ann Dunham at birth and Stanley as a child, but she dropped the Stanley upon graduating from high school. She was Ann Dunham, then Ann Obama, then Ann Soetoro until her second divorce. Then she kept her second husband's name but modernized the spelling to Sutoro. In the early 1980s, she was Ann Sutoro, Ann Dunham Sutoro, S. Ann Dunham Sutoro. In conversation, Indonesians who worked with her in the late 1980s and early 1990s referred to her as Ann Dunham, putting the emphasis on the second syllable of the surname. Toward the end of her life, she signed her dissertation S. Ann Dunham and official correspondence (Stanley) Ann Dunham. Beginning in the first chapter of this book, I've chosen to take her lead and use whatever name she was using at any given time.

During the presidential campaign, people who had known Dunham well were perplexed by what they felt were the caricatures of her that emerged. In a supermarket checkout line, one friend of Dunham's, Kadi Warner, wept at what seemed to her the injustice of a tabloid newspaper headline: "Obama Abandoned by His Own Mother!" Her friends were certain they could see her in Obama's intellect, his temperament, and his humor—not to mention his long chin, the toothiness of his smile, the angle of his ears. Yet he, who had already written a book centered on the ghost of his absent father, seemed to say more about his grandparents than he did about his mother. Some thought they could guess at some of the reasons. "He's running for election in America, not Indonesia," a former colleague of Dunham's, Bruce Harker, told me two weeks before the election. "Americans spend what percent of our gross national product on foreign assistance? Do you really think he can get elected by saying, 'My mother was more Indonesian than American'? He plays the hand he has to play: 'I was raised by a single mother on food stamps; I was raised by my grandmother— like a lot of black folks.'

"To talk about his mother as a do-gooder foreign-assistance peacenik anthropologist in Indonesia?" he added, stopping to make sure that I understood he was being sarcastic. *"Where's Indonesia? Is that near India?* No way."

This is not a book about President Obama, it is a book about his mother. But she shaped him, to a degree he seems increasingly to acknowledge. In the preface to the 2004 edition of *Dreams from My Father,* issued nine years after the first edition and nine years after Dunham's death, Obama folded in a revealing admission: Had he known his mother would not survive her illness, he might have written a different book—"less a meditation on the absent parent, more a celebration of the one who was the single constant in my life." Two years later, in *The Audacity of Hope,* he returned to the subject. Only in retrospect, he wrote, did he understand how deeply her spirit "invisibly guided the path I would ultimately take." If his ambitions were fueled by his feelings about his father, including resentment and a desire to earn his father's love, those same ambitions were channeled by his mother's faith in the goodness of people and in the value of every life. He took up the study of political philosophy in search of confirmation of her values, and became a community organizer to try to put those values to work. He dedicated that book, his second, "to the women who raised me"—his maternal grandmother, Tutu, "who's been a rock of stability throughout my life," and his mother, "whose loving spirit sustains me still."

That would have pleased her. Dunham, for whom a letter in

Jakarta from her son in the United States could raise her spirits for a full day, surely wondered about her place in his life. On rare occasions, she indicated as much—painfully, wistfully—to close friends. But she would not have been inclined to overstate her case. As she told him, with a dry humor that seems downright Kansan, "If nothing else, I gave you an interesting life."

One

Dreams from the Prairie

I n the late winter of 2009, Charles Payne reluctantly agreed to allow me to visit him in Chicago. He was eighty-four years old, the eldest of the three siblings of Madelyn Payne Dunham, the indomitable grandmother who famously helped raise Barack Obama and went on to live long enough to follow his two-year presidential campaign from her Honolulu apartment before expiring at age eighty-six, two days before the election. Her brother, a pioneer in the computerization of library data who had retired in 1995 as assistant director of the library at the University of Chicago, had chosen to ignore both a letter I had FedExed to his home and a message on his phone. When he slipped up one morning and answered the phone when I called, he said he had made a vow to himself not to talk to people like me. On the handful of occasions when he had made an exception, he said, he had gotten in trouble. We talked for ten minutes, circling each other. Then he said I could come, assuring me that the visit would probably not be worth my time. So, on a cold February morning when the wind barreled off Lake Michigan and snow lined the embankments along the rail line from O'Hare Airport, I was met at the door to Mr. Payne's apartment on Lake Shore Drive by a slim, silver-haired, youthful-looking octogenarian (who had recently solved the problem of creeping weight gain, he later informed me, by eliminating lunch from his life). He had a pleasant but skeptical look on his face. It was the look of someone too civil by temperament and training to tell a nosy visitor to take a hike.

We sat across from each other at a round table in his spotless and clutter-free kitchen. The apartment was unique in the building, thought to have been custom-designed by the architect as a jewel box and a nest for himself; men who had come to restore the living room mantelpiece had once told Mr. Payne it appeared to be European and hundreds of years old. Mr. Payne began with a cautionary tale. In 2000, he said, he had thrown himself a seventy-fifth birthday party at the urging of his son, and had invited his three siblings. It was the millennium, after all; they had last all been together at their mother's funeral, thirty-two years before. Madelyn, the retired bank vice president, arrived from Honolulu; Arlene, the retired university researcher in education and statistics, arrived from Chapel Hill, North Carolina; Jon, the former city planning director, arrived from Littleton, Colorado. Mr. Obama, then the Illinois state senator from the Thirteenth District, came with his wife, Michelle, and their daughter, Malia. "What I was struck by was that after all these years, the memories of our childhood were very different—memories of the same incident," Mr. Payne told me. "Madelyn would remember one thing; Arlene would remember another thing. And neither one of them was correct, according to the way I remembered it." He had noticed the same thing some years earlier while reading an oral history of the work of a Library of Congress task force that developed the first machine-readable standard for bibliographic data—a task force on which he had served. "I was just struck by how totally distorted people's memories of that were," he said. "And what I was particularly amused by was that each of them that I listened to turned out to be, more or less, the hero of the story: They innovated this, it was their idea to do this and that, they were the leader in so and so."

He paused, looking at me evenly. Was he making himself clear?

"All of this is just to tell you: Don't trust memory."

It is impossible to reconstruct the earliest years of Stanley Ann Dunham and the stories of her parents, Stanley Armour Dunham and Madelyn Lee Payne, without trusting the memories of people who knew them. There is no authoritative history of the Dunham and Payne families and of the events that led them to the Flint Hills of Kansas in the first decades of the twentieth century. Genealogists have traced their ancestors back over two centuries to Indiana, Missouri, Virginia, Arkansas, the Oklahoma Territory, Ohio, Kentucky, Tennessee, New Jersey, Pennsylvania, Delaware, and Massachusetts. But the reliability of those family trees is uncertain. There are newspaper birth announcements, baptism records, high school annuals, military registration cards, marriage licenses, census records, city directories, newspaper articles, obituaries, death notices, funeral announcements. But the public record offers only a frame without color, texture, or emotion, like the vestigial adhesive corners left behind in old albums after the photographs have faded or fallen away. There is President Obama's sweet and lyrical account of his grandparents' story in his 1995 memoir, *Dreams from My Father,* woven from tales he was told as a child, retold with the discretion a son and grandson might bring to their telling at a time when his mother and grandmother were still alive. There are a few distant relatives with memories like attics stuffed with family lore, and former classmates, in dwindling numbers, with fragmentary memories of coming of age in the Sunflower State during the Great Depression. At the time of the writing of this book, Stanley Ann's parents were no longer living. Her mother, Madelyn, agreed in September 2008 to be interviewed—on the condition that the interview would occur after the presidential election. Stanley Ann's father, Stanley, died of prostate cancer in 1992. All of their siblings were alive, however, and spoke in detail about what they remembered. Their help has made it possible to take a stab at the story of the family that produced, on a wintry day in Wichita in November 1942, Stanley Ann.

There is something fresh and quintessentially American about the family tree that extends its branches through and around Stanley Ann's son, President Obama. Yes, there was the white mother from Kansas and the black father from Kenya. Then there was the Javanese stepfather, Lolo Soetoro, with whom Mr. Obama lived for four years in Jakarta as a small child; there is President Obama's African-American wife, Michelle, a descendant of slaves. There is his half-Indonesian half sister, Maya Soetoro-Ng; her Chinese-Canadian husband, Konrad Ng; and the president's Kenyan and half-Kenyan half siblings scattered across the globe in places such as Nairobi and Beijing. The family that gathered in Washington, D.C., for the inauguration of the first black president of the United States in January 2009 seemed both uniquely American and at the same time brand-new. In its mixing of races, ethnicities, nationalities, and cultures, it seemed to embody at once the aspirations of the founding fathers to create a place of opportunity for all people, the country's promise as a beacon for immigrants in an increasingly global culture, and progress in the ongoing struggle to move beyond the United States' racial history.

Less well known, but classically American in an older sense, is the family tree that spawned Stanley Ann Dunham. Her ancestors were farmers, teachers, abolitionists, Methodist ministers, Baptists, Civil War veterans, veterans of two world wars. They were long-lived people, many of whom lasted into their eighties and early nineties. They were named for patriots and poets: Ralph Waldo Emerson Dunham, Christopher Columbus Clark and George Washington Clark (brothers of Thomas Jefferson Clark and Francis Marion Clark). Going back several generations, they put their faith in education to an unusual degree. At a time when few Americans were educated beyond high school, both of Stanley Ann's grandfathers on her paternal side went to college, according to her uncle, Ralph Dunham. For generations, members of both sides of the family have been teachers. There have long been rumors, unproven, of Cherokee blood. According to family lore, a great-great-grandfather of Madelyn Payne Dunham is said to have married an aunt of Wild Bill Hickok. Her grandfather is reputed to have shaken the hand of President Lincoln from his father's shoulders and seen his brother shot by bushwhackers in southern Missouri a half-dozen years later. Her aunt, Ruth McCurry, a schoolteacher, is said to have taught Mickey Mantle in Commerce, Oklahoma. Ralph Dunham remembered, as a small child, spending the night in the home of William Allen White, the Sage of Emporia, after Dunham's father, an employee of the El Dorado Garage, delivered to Mr. White his Pierce-Arrow. Charles Payne served in the 89th Infantry Division that liberated Ohrdruf, a sub-camp of Buchenwald and the first Nazi concentration camp liberated by U.S. troops in Germany in April 1945. The family has been around long enough, and was interested enough in history, to have accumulated a lot of stories. "You're probably aware that we're related to the Bushes, to Dick Cheney," Ralph Dunham told me matter-of-factly. "Also, Mark Twain is a distant relative. If you want to go far enough back, we're tied in with some royalty back up the line. And another thing: I'm a first cousin times removed of Jefferson Davis. You see, my great-grandfather Clark's mother was a Davis, and she was a first cousin to Jefferson Davis. . . ." For all the efforts to make Barack Obama appear exotic, even alien, he can claim a heritage that could hardly be more American. There is even something American, in the best sense of the word, in the swift march of those generations over the last century and a half from small farms to medium-size towns to big cities and sprawling metropolitan areas and finally across oceans and vast cultural distances to places like Jakarta, Yogyakarta, and Kalimantan.

As a small boy in Augusta, Kansas, Charles Payne, Stanley Ann's uncle, knew both his grandfathers. His grandfather on his mother's side, Thomas Creekmore McCurry, had a farm in Peru, Kansas, which was a town of about one hundred people near the southern edge of Chautauqua County on the Oklahoma line. His paternal grandfather had a farm in Olathe, the seat of Johnson County in northeastern Kansas. They worked the land the way it had traditionally been done—without plumbing, electricity, or tractors. Thomas C. McCurry prided himself on the straightness of the rows he cut with his horse-drawn plow, his daughter Leona McCurry Payne used to tell her children. He planted his potatoes, she used to say, "in the dark of the moon." Each set of grandparents raised half a dozen children, more or less. Those children grew up, flocked to towns, found jobs, and did not grow their own food. Their children, in turn, went off to college, left Kansas behind, and ended up in pleasant metropolitan areas all across the United States. The four Paynes—Madelyn, Charles, Arlene, and Jon—had no more than one or two children each. Two of those children became anthropologists who did fieldwork in Indonesia. Richard Payne, the son of Charles Payne, and a younger first cousin of Stanley

Ann's, spent several years in the Indonesian part of Borneo, now called Kalimantan. On the final night of the Democratic National Convention in Denver in August 2008, Richard Payne and his father got a ride back to their hotel in a sport-utility vehicle with Maya Soetoro-Ng, President Obama's half sister, and other family members. "Somehow Maya and Richard got to talking in Bahasa Indonesia," Charles Payne recalled, referring to the Indonesian national language. "They carried on quite a conversation. When they were finished with that—showing off, of course—Maya said to Richard, 'You have kind of a yokel accent.' He said, 'Yeah, I know.'"

Kalimantan is a far cry from Kansas, the state where Stanley Ann's story begins. But Kansas is a far cry from the stereotype that its name may conjure up. It is more complex, contradictory, and surprising—a place of extremes. Craig Miner, a historian and author of *Kansas: The History of the Sunflower State, 1854–2000,* has described it as a place of thousand-mile-diameter storms and aviator-dazzling summer clouds "triple the height of Pikes Peak." It long held the title for having the largest hailstone on record. It has had the highest number of F5-intensity tornadoes of any state since 1880. At times, Miner has written, the night sky is brilliantly clear: The Andromeda Galaxy, more than two million light-years away, appears as obvious as the moon. But the dust on the ground has been so thick that on occasion people have driven with their headlights on in broad daylight. The summer that Stanley Ann's mother, Madelyn, was eleven, the temperature in Augusta, her hometown, hit 121 degrees Fahrenheit on July 18—the hottest on record. The varnish on the pews in the Methodist church softened, and parishioners' clothes had to be yanked free. The all-time low is forty degrees below zero. Kansas is a place where prairie idealism has sometimes coexisted, Miner has written, with elements of anti-Semitism, anti-intellectualism, isolationism, and the Ku Klux Klan. On the issue of slavery, Kansans were bitterly split. The state entered the Union in 1861 after four years of small-scale but brutal guerrilla warfare, including massacres, raids, the destruction of printing presses, the ransacking of homes. The state's motto is *Ad astra per aspera:* To the stars through difficulties. It is an idea that Stanley Ann's forebears would have understood.

Had she lived to see the presidential election of 2008, Stanley Ann might have thought of it, too.

There is a cast of mind that some say is distinctly Kansan. A month before Barack Obama sewed up the Democratic nomination, Craig Miner suggested to me that Obama's "kind of high-minded idealism" was a descendant of the "practical idealism" promoted by William Allen White, the reform-minded newspaper editor and politician from Emporia. Historically, the people of Kansas have been idealistic, progressive, and pragmatic. They tried to do things that other people just talked about, and they believed in the possibility of change. "Of course, Kansans disagree violently about what 'better' is," Miner said. "They tended to extremes on the left and right—all of those based on believing strongly that you can make things better. So we had the biggest circulating Socialist paper in the United States, published in Girard, Kansas. You think of Kansas as a Republican state, and largely it was, but it was the very liberal wing of the Republican party, the Theodore Roosevelt Republicans." The state experimented early on with corporate regulation in the form of one of the early railroad regulatory commissions. The state Normal School at Emporia minted teachers, dispatching them like missionaries to small towns. Kansas may have been, for a time, the state with the highest percentage of residents able to read and write, Miner said. Even Prohibition, pursued longer and more vigorously in Kansas than elsewhere, came from an idealistic impulse to fix problems such as crime and domestic abuse by tackling the underlying problem of drunkenness. "The rest of the country said, 'You can't do that. People won't change,'" Miner told me. "I sometimes say Kansans are not the people who say, 'I'm okay, you're okay.' They say, 'You're not okay, I'm not okay, and I know how to fix it. I can make some of this better.'"

Stanley Ann's parents came from the Flint Hills, a two-hundred-mile-long band of grassland that is the largest unplowed vestige of the tallgrass prairie that once dominated North America's midsection. Left behind when the inland seas disappeared, giving birth to the Great Plains, the hills were named by Zebulon Pike for the flintlike chert, a type of silica-containing quartz, in the soil, which makes it impossible to plow. The place is a rolling ocean of wildflowers and grasses—Indian grass, buffalo grass, eight-foot-tall Big Bluestem, "the redwood of grasses." There are hundreds of wildflower species, one hundred and fifty bird species, ten million insects per acre. For at least eight thousand years, the region was occupied by Native Americans who hunted the abundant bison, elk, moose, and antelope. In the early nineteenth century, wagon trains came through, followed later by railroads. Settlers from the eastern United States put down roots around the trading post in Augusta, where Madelyn's family would eventually settle, and along the Walnut River in El Dorado, where Stanley's family came to live. The settlers tried planting corn, but it stripped the nutrients from the soil and died during repeated droughts. There were livestock epidemics and dust storms. In Augusta, on August 8, 1874, grasshoppers blanketed the ground, a foot deep in places. They ate clothes off clotheslines, mosquito netting out of windows, bark off trees, wooden handles of tools. Everything but the onions, it was said.

The Flint Hills were tough to cultivate but they made ideal pasture. Cowboys drove cattle overland from Texas to Kansas for summer grazing, then on to railroad cattle towns for shipping to feedlots and eventual slaughter. As the railroads expanded, small towns became shipping points for cattle to be loaded on trains to Kansas City and Chicago. Cow towns such as Wichita, thirty miles west of El Dorado, flourished. In 1886, Butler County discovered kaffir corn, a tropical African variety of sorghum used to feed cattle and poultry, and ideally suited to the Kansas climate. Kaffir corn was drought- and heat-resistant, and thrived in dry warmth. As Butler County farmers turned increasingly to cattle raising, the price of kaffir corn soared. By 1911, nearly sixty thousand acres were planted with kaffir corn. To celebrate, the Knights of Mapira, a fraternal order, organized the first Kaffir Corn Carnival, a three-day celebration in downtown El Dorado that included parades, pageants, and contests. A triumphal arch made of kaffir corn and other crops spanned the first block of East Central Avenue. Twenty-nine townships in the county built booths decorated with animals, township maps, and the seal of Kansas, all out of kaffir corn. Men competed in fence-building, nail-driving, and hog-calling contests. Women did chicken calling, geese picking, butter churning. There was turtle racing and a float competition. In October 1926, the title of Miss El Dorado for that year's carnival went to Stanley Ann's great-aunt Doris Evelyn Armour, a 1923 graduate of El Dorado High School and a former student at Kansas State Teachers College in Emporia, whom the local newspaper described as "a genuinely beautiful girl, with dark brown bobbed hair, brown eyes and a delicate coloring that is entirely natural and most becoming."

Butler County had another resource, even better than kaffir corn and far more unsettling. A few years before the births of Stanley Dunham and Madelyn Payne, a massive oil strike upended the economy of the region almost overnight. In the porous stone along the eastern edge of the Nemaha Ridge in southeastern Kansas, there were pools of oil and natural gas. On October 7, 1915, the Wichita Natural Gas Company struck oil on land owned by John Stapleton about five miles northwest of El Dorado. It was one of the largest oil strikes of the time. Oil companies and entrepreneurs thundered in. In 1918, the year Stanley was born, the El Dorado field produced 29 million barrels, a figure that Craig Miner says was more than nine times the total output for Kansas three years earlier. El Dorado was the largest-producing single field in the United States. It was wartime, too, so oil prices were high. There were more strikes near Towanda and Augusta. Derricks and tank farms sprung up. Soon there were eight refineries in towns such as El Dorado, Augusta, Wichita, and Potwin. The population of El Dorado and the surrounding township soared to 14,459 in 1920 from 3,262 in 1915, more than quadrupling in five years. Hundreds of one-room shacks and tents were thrown up, as El Dorado home owners leased their backyards and gardens, and built houses in vacant lots to rent out. Oil companies rolled out instant towns, with names such as Oil Hill and Midian, replete with tennis courts, swimming pools, baseball teams, and horseshoe pits. Oil-field lease houses—with walls made of compressed wood pulp, no indoor plumbing or electricity, and heat from a single stove—rented for an average of seven dollars a month. Oil-field employees worked twelve-hour shifts around the clock. Drugstores stayed open late into the night. Then the storm passed. In 1925, the year Madelyn turned three and her family moved from Peru to Augusta, the boom peaked. By the 1930s, the oil companies had turned their attention elsewhere. The population of Butler County dwindled. Left in the boom's wake was the memory of a bonanza that had barreled through town like a westbound train.

In December 2008, I visited Ralph Dunham, the brother of Stanley Dunham and uncle of Stanley Ann, in a retirement community in Springfield, Virginia, where he was living with his wife, Betty. Stanley Dunham had been dead for sixteen years, so I had turned to Ralph, his only sibling, for help. Ralph, whose full name is Ralph Waldo Emerson Dunham, told me that his grandfather, who had studied at Kansas State University to become a pharmacist, had been an admirer of Emerson. So he named his son Ralph Waldo Emerson Dunham, who in turn passed the name on to his eldest son. Ralph told me that his mother admired Henry Morton Stanley, the journalist and explorer who found David Livingstone beside Lake Tanganyika in 1871. So she named her second son Stanley. Ralph, a year and a half older than Stanley, was the more studious and less flamboyant of the two Dunham brothers. He graduated from El Dorado High School in 1934, intending to become a teacher. He majored in math at Kansas State Teachers College in Emporia and got a Ph.D. in educational psychology from UC Berkeley in 1950. He taught in colleges in the South, then worked for the U.S. Naval Personnel Research Activity, doing training and qualifications for the Polaris program, then the Federal Aviation Agency, then the Office of Education, which later became the Department of Education. He served as a lieutenant in the Army during World War II and was in Normandy and the Rhineland after D-Day, remained in the Reserve afterward, and retired as a lieutenant colonel. While being trained in rapid fire with an Enfield, he stunned the sergeant by firing his two clips of ammunition in about thirty-five seconds and hitting the bull's-eye every time. At age seven, he had learned from his father how to fire a single-shot, bolt-action .22 rifle.

The dark secret in the Dunham boys' childhood involved a hunting trip with their father. The elder Ralph Dunham, born in Argonia, Kansas, in 1894, had arrived in Wichita at age twenty and married Ruth Lucille Armour the following year. According to their marriage license, filed with the probate court in Sedgwick County in October 1915, Ruth was eighteen. But her gravestone at Sunset Lawns Cemetery in El Dorado, where she was buried eleven years later, gives the year of her birth as 1900. If the gravestone is correct, she was no more than sixteen when she married. Her eldest son, Ralph, was born in 1916; Stanley followed a year and a half later in 1918. Their father was dashing, it was said in the family. His occupational history suggests he was restless. In a military registration card filled out in June 1917, he described himself as a self-employed café owner in Wichita. In 1923, he was listed in the El Dorado city directory as working in sales at the El Dorado Garage. A few years after that, he owned an automobile dealership, repair shop, and garage in Topeka. When that failed, he ran a drugstore in Wichita with his parents. His obituary in *The Wichita Eagle* in 1970 described him as a retired Boeing Company employee. It was a pattern not unlike the one that his younger son, Stanley, would follow some years later. Perhaps it was a distant antecedent to the wanderlust that Maya Soetoro-Ng would one day say she inherited from her adventurous mother, Stanley Ann.

On Thanksgiving in 1926, the young Dunham family, Ralph and Ruth Dunham and their two boys, traveled from their home in Topeka to Melvern to hunt and spend the holiday with a sister and brother of Ralph Sr.'s. A detailed account of the day appeared on the front page of *The Topeka State Journal* the following afternoon. Ralph Sr. and Ruth had "a disagreement" after arriving in Melvern, the article stated. When Ralph Sr. and his brother left the house with the boys to go hunting, Ruth Dunham, the boys' mother, departed for Topeka. She made her way to a drugstore near the Dunhams' home and near her husband's garage. She told the owner, George W. Lawrence, that a dog had been run over by a car and that she wanted to buy something to kill it. "Lawrence recommended chloroform," the newspaper reported. "Mrs. Dunham said that she didn't want that, as the smell of chloroform made her sick. She finally persuaded Lawrence to sell her ten grains of strychnine. She stayed in the store for several minutes, Lawrence said, seemingly in the best of spirits and joking with the proprietor."

Later that evening, the owner of an auto-painting shop in the same building as Ralph Dunham's garage noticed Ruth in the office, apparently writing, when he went to put away his car. A half-hour later, George Lawrence, who also parked in the garage, saw her, too. Back in Melvern, Ralph had returned from hunting and learned that his wife had left. He returned to Topeka, found no one at home, and began a search. Shortly before two a.m., he found his wife's body on the garage office floor, the article stated. Though an ambulance took the body to St. Francis Hospital, the newspaper quoted the county coroner as having said Ruth Dunham had been dead for anywhere between a few minutes and two hours, and that the death was a suicide. She had written a letter saying she had taken poison because her husband no longer loved her, the newspaper reported. She was twenty-six years old.

A rather different version of Ruth's death appeared on the same day on the second page of the newspaper in El Dorado, where her parents, Harry and Gabriella Armour, lived with Ruth's sister, Doris, the recently named Miss El Dorado. According to that account, put forward from that time on for public consumption, Ruth died of ptomaine poisoning at home in Topeka. She had spoken by telephone with her parents just hours before, the newspaper reported, "and was apparently in the best of health." An article in *The Wichita Eagle* went one step further: "Mrs. Dunham had been feeling well up to a late hour Thursday night and it is believed that food eaten at a Thanksgiving dinner was responsible for her death."

Stanley Dunham, at age eight, and his brother, Ralph, age ten, went to live with their maternal grandparents—just as Stanley's grandson, Barack Obama, at age ten, would do forty-five years later. Stanley and Ralph's father moved to Wichita to run a drug-store with his father; he lived next door to his parents in an apart-ment above the store. Apparently, the boys inquired as to why they were not living with their father. "My father's answer to that was that my grandparents dearly loved us and that he wasn't about to take us away from them," Ralph Dunham told me. "However, the fact was that he was dead broke at the time, and he couldn't afford to take proper care of us. And my grandfather had a good job." After their father remarried and had two more children, Stanley and Ralph barely saw him. "Well, we did once in a while if we were in Wichita or something like that," Ralph said. "We'd see him. But very rarely." Asked if he and Stanley had known their half sisters at that time, he said, "No, not at all."

Recalling that period eighty years later, Ralph skated quickly past his mother's death and made no mention of suicide. His mother passed away, the Depression happened, his father's business collapsed, and he and Stanley moved in with their grandparents in El Dorado. When I described the article in the Topeka newspaper, he said simply, "I was only ten years old. Of course, I was told the ptomaine-poisoning story. But that could have been possible." He knew his mother had left a note, but, he said, he never knew what it said. He seemed to have retained a small child's distorted mem-ory of that day—small details magnified, central drama swept into the shadows. "Actually, she went to the hospital and died in the hospital, I know that," he said. "My grandparents came down. Of course, we were glad to see them. We didn't realize my mother was in the hospital or anything like that. We had seen a game—I can remember it was a board game, and the game was Uncle Wiggily. They gave us some money to go down to the drugstore to buy this

Uncle Wiggily game. And when we came back from that, then they told us that my mother had died."

The boys moved into what became, with their arrival, a four-generation household. It included their grandparents, the boys' Aunt Doris, and their great-grandfather, Christopher Columbus Clark, a Civil War veteran, then in his early eighties. The Armours had been teachers, Ralph Dunham said. But Mr. Armour, a lover of math and math puzzles, had discovered that he could make more money as an oil-field pumper, using his math skills to calculate the oil levels in tanks. He worked twelve-hour shifts, seven days a week. A few years after Stanley and Ralph moved in, the Armours moved the family, minus Aunt Doris, to an oil lease eight miles from El Dorado by gravel road. Ralph, who said he inherited his interest in math and teaching from his grandparents, recalled life in the reconfigured family fondly. His grandmother, about forty years old when her daughter died, was young enough to be her grandsons' mother—just as Madelyn would be when her grandson would first move in with her and Stanley in Honolulu in 1971. Doris Armour was young enough to be the boys' sister. Stanley and Ralph developed a passion for games, particularly checkers, from their grandfather and great-grandfather. Many years later, when Stanley and Madelyn had become grand masters in duplicate bridge in Hawaii, he would want to play checkers on his occasional visits to Ralph's home in Virginia. The last time they played, it was getting late, Ralph was tired, and Stanley had a flight to catch. Ralph suggested they quit, but Stanley was one game behind. "He insisted he wasn't going to quit," Ralph recalled. "So I really concentrated, and I beat him the next three games. Then he would go."

Stanley was dark-haired and handsome, like his father. He matured earlier than Ralph and prided himself on his looks. At twenty-three years old, he was nearly six feet tall and weighed one hundred and sixty-five pounds, according to his military records. The most striking feature on his large head was a powerful, elongated chin—which Stanley Ann would inherit and pass on to her son. In the head shots in the 1936 El Dorado High School annual, *The Gusher,* Stanley's chin looks twice as long as anyone else's. Thick black hair rolls back off his forehead in glistening waves. His mouth is compact. On occasion, he had a slightly quizzical tilt to his head—a familial trait I had first noticed one day while watching Stanley Ann in a video made a few years before her death. At that moment, I remembered seeing that tilt in Obama. "I'll tell you one thing," Ralph Dunham said of his great-nephew. "When he makes a speech, as Madelyn says, 'He looks just like Stanley, only he's black.'"

As a boy, Stanley did not fit the mold: That is the way Ralph put it. Ralph was the Boy Scout, the future scoutmaster who graduated at the top of his class at El Dorado Junior College. Stanley, a year and a half younger, was, Ralph said, "a Dennis the Menace type." He liked to do unusual things, Ralph said, maybe because he wanted attention. At three years old, he ran away from home with the boy next door. He had a knack for getting into trouble. "He was a nonconformist, I'd say," Ralph said. "He didn't like to follow rules just because they were rules. He liked to have a reason for them. He liked to be a little bit daring." For a teenager in small-town Kansas, Stanley was a flamboyant dresser. He struck some as a born salesman: He could strike up a conversation with almost anybody, it seemed. He was opinionated, occasionally even pompous and overbearing. He had a temper. "If people disagreed with him, he could be very unpleasant," Ralph said. "He could make it very uncomfortable." He was a great teller of stories, some of which appeared to be intended to demonstrate his worldliness and sophistication. He was not above embroidering his tales, even making a few up. Take the one about the time he and a friend bummed a ride from the president, Herbert Hoover. Hoover was visiting El Dorado while en route to the West Coast, and the whole town turned out to watch. The way Stanley and his friend told the story later, they skipped the parade and were walking down the highway when the president's car stopped and picked them up. After they got settled, Stanley's friend lit a cigarette. According to the story, Ralph Dunham told me, Hoover leaned over and laid dibs on the remainder when Stanley's friend was finished. The president, according to Stanley, said, "Butts on that."

Ralph said he had doubts about another Stanley story, recounted in *Dreams from My Father*. According to that story, Stanley was thrown out of high school by the time he was fifteen for punching the principal in the nose, and spent the next three years living off odd jobs, hopping railcars to Chicago and California and back home, and "dabbling in moonshine, cards, and women." Ralph Dunham remembered all that rather differently. He said Stanley dropped out of the El Dorado High School class of 1935 in his senior year, most likely because he was not doing well academically, and returned some years later to graduate. "I won't say that he hadn't been in trouble and maybe had seen the principal," Ralph said. "But I think that's a story that was made up. My brother could have told Barack that, of course. My brother wasn't always truthful about stuff like that."

STANLEY ANN'S MATERNAL grandmother, Leona, was the sixth of seven children of Margaret Belle Wright and Thomas Creekmore McCurry. Leona grew up on the McCurry farm in Peru and became a teacher, as did her unmarried sister, Ruth, who taught school for fifty years in Kansas and in Commerce, Oklahoma.

Thomas and Margaret McCurry, great-grandparents of Ann Dunham, in Peru, Kansas

Their brother, Frank W. McCurry, who climbed derricks as a child in Peru and went on to become a pharmacist, a chemical engineer, and an oil company vice president, acquired a certain degree of fame, as an adult, for an unusual hobby. Over forty-five years, he built, fine-tuned, and continually updated a fully functioning scale model of an oil refinery, made largely out of glass. The model refinery, which had two catalytic cracking units and actually produced gas from oil, traveled to high schools and colleges all across the country. Frank McCurry's daughter, Margaret McCurry Wolf, told me on a sweltering summer day in her kitchen in Hutchinson, Kansas, "Next to godliness and cleanliness, my dad was for education."

Leona's mind, too, ranged far beyond the four walls of the little house in Augusta where she and her husband, Rolla Charles Payne, raised Stanley Ann's mother, Madelyn, and her three siblings in the 1930s and 1940s. To her children, Leona seemed uncommonly bright. She took them outside under the vast night skies and taught them the constellations. She stocked the house with good books and planned car trips during her husband's monthlong summer vacation—trips to Civil War battlefields in Missouri; to Yellowstone Park; to the Black Hills; to Arkansas, Kentucky, Tennessee, Mississippi, and Louisiana; to Washington State. In the summer of 1934, in the midst of the Depression and before the youngest Payne was born, the family drove to Chicago, along with two schoolteacher maiden aunts, to see the World's Fair. "I think that World's Fair was a transforming event for all three of us kids," Charles Payne, Madelyn's brother, said. "It was so far beyond the experience of Augusta, Kansas, that it was a true eye-opener. We were exposed to art, anthropology, intellectual stuff. I remember eating lunch at a German beer garden—all the dancing girls with German accents. At the Swedish pavilion, we watched them make a ceramic sugar bowl and creamer in a sleek, modern design. We still have them, and they're damn good-looking. I remember seeing models of ships—was the Field Museum open then?—in such fine detail, down to bolts and knobs, and marveling at the fact that anybody could do that. There was probably a drive, for all three of us after that, to get out of small-town Kansas and into a more cosmopolitan setting. I remember trying to tell some friends about it and finding I was not able to convey the magnificence of it verbally."

That trip, he said, probably helped ensure that he and his siblings left Augusta behind them "almost as soon as we could."

Madelyn's father, Rolla Charles Payne, had grown up on his family's farm in Olathe and had gone to work for the Sinclair Oil and Gas Company as a bookkeeper and later as district clerk in Augusta. (The name Rolla, which rhymes with "wallah," is said to have ranked among the top five hundred most popular boys' names for a time near the end of the nineteenth century. Rolla Payne, however, did not love it. He went by the initials R.C. or simply Payne, the name by which Leona addressed him.) A veteran of World War I, R. C. Payne appears to have met Leona McCurry in Independence, where they were living and working. They received a marriage license in December 1921, and their first child, Madelyn Lee, was born on October 26, 1922, in Peru. By the time Charles and Margaret Arlene were born several years later, the family had moved to Augusta, another former farming community transformed by oil, eighteen miles southwest of El Dorado. By the end of World War I, there were three refineries in Augusta and ten thousand people living within a five-mile radius—from the families of oil company executives to laborers on the oil leases and a small community of Mexicans employed by the Atchison, Topeka, and Santa Fe Railway and living in an enclave bounded by the Walnut River, South Osage Street, and the Santa Fe tracks. A two-lane brick highway to Wichita opened in 1924, the year a twister roared into town, tore a corner off the high school, and demolished a Catholic church. Jon Payne, the youngest of the four Payne children, who spent his entire childhood in Augusta until his parents moved during his senior year in high school to a tiny oil-field community called Thrall, said he had never met a black person until he went away to college at the University of Kansas.

Butler County was almost entirely white and Christian when Madelyn Payne was growing up in Augusta and Stanley Dunham in El Dorado in the 1920s and 1930s. Recruiters for the Ku Klux Klan moved into the county in the early 1920s, billing the Klan as a patriotic Christian benevolent association. Roxie Olmstead, who grew up in Butler County and later did some research on the Klan, found that the organization advanced north from Oklahoma, recruiting what it called "native born, white, Protestant, Gentile, American" citizens. Klan chapters met in churches, held initiation ceremonies in robes and on horseback, and burned crosses. The focus was moral issues, Roxie Olmstead reported in a paper available at the Butler County Historical Society, such as "faithless husbands and wives in Augusta." There was a Klan parade in Augusta in September 1923; a meeting in El Dorado in August 1924 reportedly attracted three thousand people. The name of the Kaffir Corn Carnival was changed, for 1924 only, to the Kaffir Korn Karnival. William Allen White, who had been editorializing against the Klan since 1921 in *The Emporia Gazette,* ran as an independent candidate for governor in 1924 on what for much of the campaign was an anti-Klan platform. He came in third out of three, but historians say his campaign weakened the Klan. The following year, the state supreme court banned it from operating in Kansas.

For much of Madelyn's childhood, the family lived in a single-story wood-frame house owned by the Sinclair Oil and Gas Company, and next door to the office where her father, R. C. Payne, worked. The house had three bedrooms, one bathroom, a living room, a dining room, a kitchen, and a screened-in back porch, where Charles sometimes slept on a cot. Space was tight. Aunt Ruth McCurry, the teacher, came to stay every summer, bunking in the girls' room. Stanley Ann, as an infant and toddler, lived there during World War II while her father was in the Army and her mother commuted to Wichita for work. Out back, there was a pipe yard and a net for "moonlight basketball." Baseball was played in a nearby vacant lot. Jon Payne remembered helping his mother wash the laundry in a couple of round Maytag washers equipped with wringers and watching the sheets freeze in winter. It was an easy walk along the tree-lined brick streets into town, where there were drugstores with soda fountains and booths, a couple of them with jukeboxes stocked by the late 1930s with the music of Glenn Miller, Benny Goodman, and Tommy Dorsey, and even a small floor for dancing. In the booths, some of the high school students played bridge. During the Depression, people in Augusta went to the movies several times a week. There were cowboy movies at the Isis Theatre on weekends, and the Augusta Theatre, which opened in the summer Madelyn was twelve, was the first to be lit entirely by neon. People flocked to movies starring Bette Davis, from whom teenage girls picked up a veneer of sophistication and learned how to hold a cigarette for maximum glamorous effect. For a time, an instructor from a dance studio in Wichita came in to teach a dozen children ballroom dancing and the jitterbug on the stage of the theater. On Sundays, the Paynes attended the Methodist church. They were not poor—Mr. Payne worked through the Depression—but there was never a lot of money. Madelyn's brother Charles worked in a grocery store up to twenty hours a week and full-time in summer all through high school. Jon was probably in the eighth grade, he said, before he wore "store-bought pants." Leona made many of her children's clothes. Charles Payne, a lifelong Democrat, told me that his mother's family voted Republican but that his father was a Democrat. He remembered the family listening to radio broadcasts of the inauguration of President Franklin D. Roosevelt in 1933 and later his fireside chats. When Alf Landon, the then governor of Kansas, became the Republican presidential nominee running against Roosevelt in the 1936 election, the Paynes backed him: "We were waving sunflower flags."

Augusta, with a population of several thousand, was not the cul-de-sac that the small-town Kansas stereotype might summon to mind. Mack Gilkeson, who grew up in Augusta and knew both Madelyn Payne as a child and Stanley Dunham as a teenager, went on to become a professor of chemical engineering in California and a consultant in places like Papua New Guinea. As many as half of his high school classmates, he said, eventually moved away. Their teachers encouraged students who were academically gifted. Asked when he had first felt the urge to move beyond Butler County, he said, "I was led on that path." Members of Stanley and Madelyn's generation not only left Augusta behind, they abandoned their parents' political views. Mack Gilkeson's parents were Republicans, as was everybody they knew. When they went to Topeka to visit a relative who worked for the newspaper chain owned by the Republican United States senator from Kansas, Arthur Capper, Mack was under orders not to utter the name Roosevelt. That sort of rigidity did not appeal to him. "I just found it distasteful," he said. "When I encountered it, I would say, 'That's not what I'm going to do.'" Because there were no private or parochial schools, everyone in Augusta went to the same high school—children of bank presidents, oil company executives, doctors, farmers, and oil-field workers. "I suppose that led me to be more egalitarian than I would have been from other circumstances," Gilkeson said. Children reared in Augusta had some understanding of class differences. Virginia Dashner Ewalt, an oil pumper's daughter who grew up on the Sinclair oil lease southeast of Augusta and was in the Augusta High School senior-class play with Madelyn, went to elementary school with twenty other children in a one-room schoolhouse heated by a single large coal-burning stove. "Country kids were a little different," she said. She sometimes felt a distinct chill from some of the crowd that had grown up in Augusta.

Leona and R. C. Payne had expectations for their children. They were to be good, study hard, get good marks, and make something of themselves. "My mother had high aspirations," said Margaret Arlene Payne, who got a bachelor's degree from the University of Kansas, a master's degree from Teachers College of Columbia University, and a Ph.D. from the University of Chicago. The message was, Arlene said, "You're going to college. And there's no question." Jon, Madelyn's youngest brother, said, "I don't think they had an expectation of us staying in Kansas. I think they expected much more out of us—to get to college and then do whatever you could." But the Depression and the shadow of war colored the children's sense of their future. Clarence Kerns, historian for the El Dorado High School class of 1935, said there were so few jobs available when his class graduated that nine of his classmates became ministers. Many others became teachers in one-room schoolhouses across Kansas. Few went straight to college. Long-range planning seemed pointless. "The news month by month was always bad," said Mack Gilkeson, recalling the years leading up to and during World War II. "You'd go out and get the morning paper at seven a.m. and look at the headline. It would be: 'The Germans have invaded Norway. The Germans have invaded Greece. The Allies are retreating. Things are going bad in North

Africa.' The future was very uncertain. So you would make the decision, 'I'm going to do this,' and not worry about what two years from now will bring." Some couples married early, craving permanence. Girls who had expected to go straight to college, instead had to find work. "I can remember Madelyn fretting over the fact that some of her friends, who were more well-to-do than we, were planning to go to some fancy college or other, and she knew she couldn't," Charles remembered. "So the question was: Would she go to the local junior college? Should she go to work? That sort of thing." As for himself, he said, "I knew from about the seventh grade on that there was going to be a war and I was going to be in it. So I never really thought a whole lot about going to college, because I just figured, 'Okay, I'll grow up and I'm going to go off to war.' Truth is, I didn't really expect to survive it."

R. C. Payne had a particular attachment to his firstborn daughter, according to her brother Jon, who was born fifteen years later. She was the only child born in Peru before Mr. Payne's job brought the family to Augusta. A notice published in the *Sedan Times-Star* on November 22, 1922, announced, "Charles R. Payne [*sic*] and wife are rejoicing over the arrival of little Madelyn Lee, an 8 lb daughter." She was bright, lively, and strong-willed. She got good grades if she wanted to, Charles Payne said, but she was not above taking off the occasional school-day afternoon with a friend, precipitating a row with her mother, who wanted her children to do their best at all times, not just when they felt like it. Slender, tidy, and well turned out, Madelyn affected a kind of worldliness, at least toward her siblings. "Madelyn in high school always had boyfriends—usually a couple, maybe three different ones," Charles said. "She was nice-enough-looking, no great beauty, and quite vivacious, lively, and fun. Her various boyfriends bored her, to tell you the truth. They were Kansas boys. She tended to view herself more as a Bette Davis type." By her senior year in high school, with the country stuck in the Depression and war on the horizon, Madelyn's options for higher education may have looked limited, at least in the short run. "I think she was looking for a more exciting life, wanting to escape small-town Kansas," Charles said. "And I think she really didn't see her own future. She didn't see anything other than going to school and getting a teaching certificate, which my mother assumed she would do, because that was what she had done. It was either that or be a clerk in the dry goods store."

Stanley Dunham, flamboyant and seemingly worldly, may have looked like just the ticket. After dropping out of high school, he had hit the road for a time. According to Ralph, Stanley, who was four years older than Madelyn, had gone to California and spent some time with a Kansas friend who later became a Hollywood writer. He returned to Kansas, others said, with grand tales of hobnobbing with John Steinbeck, various playwrights, and other California writers of the 1930s. He seemed to have left the impression, at least with Madelyn, that he had a trunk full of plays and the possibility of a literary future—even if, for the time being, he was doing construction at the Socony refinery in Augusta. "He wrote plays and poetry, and he would come over to our house and read them to us," Arlene Payne remembered. "It was, I'm sure, all very exotic to her." Though El Dorado and Augusta were archrivals in football and baseball, it was not uncommon for El Dorado boys to date girls from Augusta and vice versa. It is unclear exactly how or when Stanley and Madelyn met. When I asked Ralph Dunham what he thought drew Madelyn to his brother, he said, "Well, he was a personable guy and wasn't above telling a—" Stopping in mid-sentence, he changed course: "You know, he was okay." When I asked him what he had been about to say, he continued, carefully, "Well, Stanley didn't always tell things exactly like they were. But

Madelyn and Stanley Dunham

not many people do. And when you're courting, you first try to present a good side of yourself and your hopes and ambitions and all the rest." Asked the same question, Jon Payne said, laughing, "Oh, you know, 1930s Kansas, Dust Bowl, Depression, stuck in Hicksville, USA. I think she was looking at Stanley as a way of getting out of Dodge."

Madelyn's parents were not impressed. Stanley came across to them as a glad-hander, a gadabout—the antithesis of the Paynes, Jon said. As Obama described their attitude in his memoir, using the nickname with which he and Maya addressed their grandmother, "The first time Toot brought Gramps over to her house to meet the family, her father took one look at my grandfather's black, slicked-back hair and his perpetual wise-guy grin and offered his unvarnished assessment. 'He looks like a wop.'" Their disapproval did not escape Madelyn's notice. On the evening of the Augusta High School junior-senior banquet in May 1940, Madelyn, at seventeen years old, and Stanley, at twenty-two, slipped out of the banquet and got married in secret. They kept the marriage quiet until Madelyn graduated the following month—to try to prevent her parents from having it annulled, some of her classmates believed. The news reached Stanley's brother, Ralph, only months later. Charles Payne was away at Boy Scout camp by the time it broke.

"My parents were pretty much crushed that their daughter would go off with someone they didn't really have much respect for," he told me. "But they accepted it." Putting as good a face on it as possible, Leona Payne sent out engraved announcements.

Twenty years later, Madelyn Dunham would surely remember her youthful romantic rebellion, her secret marriage, and her parents' reaction, when her daughter, at age seventeen, learned that she was pregnant with the child of a charismatic older man whom she would marry a few months later. Perhaps Madelyn would be struck by the similarities between herself and Stanley Ann—headstrong teenagers swept away by seemingly worldly charmers promising new horizons, the possibility of adventure, and the certainty of escape. Perhaps she thought, too, of Stanley's dead mother, Ruth Armour, who, at an even younger age, had done something similar. To anyone new to the story, Stanley Ann's infatuation, pregnancy, and precipitous marriage to a black student from Kenya might appear to be an inexplicable break with her family's presumably straitlaced, white-bread Kansas history. But Madelyn and Stanley would have known there was a precedent in Madelyn's own decision to override the reservations of her parents and short-circuit any discussion of her future by marrying Stanley and bolting for the coast.

Paradoxically, it may have been on the rim of the Pacific that it first dawned on Madelyn that life with Stanley might prove less dazzling than she had imagined. As soon as school was out, the newlyweds had headed for California, the obvious place for an aspiring writer with a trunk full of unpublished works. But after settling in the San Francisco Bay Area, Madelyn found herself working odd jobs in various quotidian establishments, including a dry cleaner, to help pay the rent, her brother Charles remembered. In later years, she would come to regret deeply that she had never gone to college. She would make sure that her daughter, faced with a similarly abrupt change in life circumstances, was able to stay in school. Madelyn would be the one, too, who would subsidize the education of her grandchildren in one of Hawaii's most respected private schools. But if she thought during that time in California about going back to school, it was not an option. She needed to make money. What was more, after the bombing of Pearl Harbor on December 7, 1941, she and Stanley were back in Kansas, just eighteen months after leaving. Six weeks after Pearl Harbor and a few months short of his twenty-fourth birthday, Stanley enlisted on January 18, 1942, as a private in the U.S. Army. According to his enlistment records, he gave his education as "four years of high school" and his civilian occupation as "bandsman, oboe, or parts clerk, automobile."

The war jolted southeastern Kansas out of the Depression in much the same way that the oil strike at Stapleton Number One, the discovery well at the oil field in El Dorado, had jolted Butler County a quarter-century earlier. Profits from the oil boom had financed a fledgling aviation-manufacturing industry in Wichita, where aviation pioneers such as Clyde Vernon Cessna, Walter Beech, and Lloyd Stearman had helped win Wichita the title "Air Capital of the World." The Stearman Aircraft Company, then a subsidiary of Boeing, had landed its first major military contract in 1934. Now the attack on Pearl Harbor strengthened the case for decentralizing the defense industry, and Wichita became one of the biggest defense aviation centers in the country. In 1941, the government began construction on a new Boeing plant in Wichita and picked Boeing to produce the B-29 Superfortress, the aircraft later used in the firebombing campaign against Japan. Employment at Boeing soared to 29,795 in December 1943—up from 766 two and a half years earlier, according to Wings over Kansas, a website on Kansas aeronautics. The plant operated around the clock. The population of Sedgwick County nearly doubled over five years. Huge temporary housing complexes with names like Planeview and Beechwood sprang up. Next to the Boeing plant, Planeview alone had a population of twenty thousand. Boeing had fifty-six bowling teams. There was a nine-hole golf course and tennis, badminton, and shuffleboard courts. The company bused in workers from as far away as Winfield, Kansas, and Ponca City, Oklahoma. Others commuted by car pool from places such as El Dorado and Augusta. The defense-aviation boom, like the oil boom, would prove fleeting. In 1945, after the suspension of B-29 production, Boeing laid off sixteen thousand workers in a single day. The new plant closed, and employment at Boeing Wichita dropped to about one thousand. But while the war lasted, wages were high and, with men off at war, nearly half of all the aircraft production workers were women. Nationally, eighteen million women are said to have entered the workforce between 1942 and 1945, many of them because of government campaigns to lure housewives into full-time, war-related work. Women became financially independent and took on male responsibilities, in many cases for the first time. Madelyn Dunham was part of that change.

With Stanley away in the Army, Madelyn moved in with her parents in Augusta and commuted by car pool to a job as an inspector on the night shift at Boeing in Wichita. During his presidential campaign, Mr. Obama described his grandmother in that period as Rosie the Riveter—the icon of wartime womanhood, in overalls, painted by Norman Rockwell for the cover of *The Saturday Evening Post*. The prodigious work ethic that would enable Madelyn decades later to work her way up from a low-level bank employee to vice president of the Bank of Hawaii must have been in evidence at Boeing. She became a supervisor, Charles Payne remembered, and was soon making more money than their father. Madelyn saved her money, but she also occasionally splurged. Like a character in a Bette Davis movie, she bought herself a fur coat.

Davis, who had helped small-town girls like Madelyn while away the Depression, was now one of the country's biggest box-office stars. Her movie *Now, Voyager* became a hit across the country in November 1942, playing to audiences made up mostly of women. The film marked a shift in Davis's image. As the government campaigned to recruit housewives into factory work, Davis shed what Martin Shingler, a film scholar, has described as her previously androgynous look and emerged as "the leading spokesperson for femininity, lipstick and glamour." The transformation had begun six months earlier, Shingler suggested, with the May 1942 release of *In This Our Life,* in which Davis played Stanley Timberlake, a southern belle.

That spring, Madelyn Dunham, age nineteen, was pregnant. On November 29, 1942, one month after her twentieth birthday, she gave birth to a brown-eyed, brown-haired daughter with the same delicate coloring so admired in her great-aunt Doris, Miss El Dorado. In *Dreams from My Father,* Obama writes that his mother was born at Fort Leavenworth, the Army base where Stanley was stationed. But Ralph Dunham said he visited Madelyn and the baby in Wichita Hospital when Stanley Ann was a day or two old. Years later, Ann would say that she had nearly entered the world in a speeding taxi. Rushing to the hospital in a snowstorm, she told Maya, Madelyn almost gave birth in the cab. As Ann told the story to Maya, it had a parallel in Maya's birth twenty-eight years later. On that occasion, Madelyn was arriving in Jakarta by plane, and Maya's father, Lolo Soetoro, had gone to the airport to meet her. It was the eve of Independence Day (the Indonesian one), and Ann, waiting in a Catholic hospital in Jakarta to deliver, grew impatient and walked out into the street to look for her husband and her mother. As she told the story, she was on the verge of hopping into a pedicab, called a *becak,* when Madelyn and Lolo finally pulled up. Though delivered in the hospital, Maya, the inheritor of her mother's wanderlust, was nearly born in a *becak.* And Ann, whose adventuring impulse came by way of her Kansan parents, nearly arrived in the Wichita equivalent.

They named her Stanley Ann.

In the years that followed, the explanation most often given was that her father, Stanley, had hoped for a boy. "One of Gramps's less judicious ideas—he had wanted a son," Obama wrote. But relatives doubted that that story was true. Ralph Dunham said his brother "probably would have settled for any healthy child." Maybe he just liked the name. Or maybe that story originated as a joke, delivered teasingly by the great confabulator himself. The fact was, Madelyn was fully in charge of matters such as the naming and handling of the baby, some of her siblings said. Stanley would not have had veto power. "When I asked my grandmother about it, she said, 'Oh, I don't know why I did that,'" Maya told me. "Because she's the one who named her Stanley. That's all she ever said: 'Oh, I don't know.'"

On at least one occasion, Madelyn seemed to suggest that she had taken the name from the southern belle in the movie that just six months earlier had signaled the transformation in Bette Davis's image on-screen. When asked about the name not long after Stanley Ann's birth, Madelyn said cryptically, "You know, Bette Davis played a character named Stanley."

Two

Coming of Age in Seattle

It wasn't easy to be a girl named Stanley growing up in the wake of a restless father. By her fourteenth birthday, Stanley Ann had moved more often than many Americans in those days moved in a lifetime. At age two, she had moved from Kansas to California, where Stanley Dunham spent two years as an undergraduate at the University of California at Berkeley; then she had moved from California back to Kansas, where, after dropping out of Berkeley, her father signed up for a couple of courses at the University of Wichita; from Kansas to Ponca City, Oklahoma, where he worked as a furniture salesman; from Ponca City to Texas, to sell furniture again; from Texas back to El Dorado; from El Dorado to Seattle; and from Seattle to Mercer Island, Washington, where the family touched down for four years before heading westward once again, this time to Hawaii, where Stanley and Madelyn finally settled. By the time Stanley Ann entered Mercer Island High School as a thirteen-year-old freshman in the fall of 1956, she was accustomed to

Madelyn, Stanley Ann, and Ralph Dunham,
Yellowstone National Park, summer 1947

being the outsider and the perpetual other. She had some of the attributes of children of peripatetic parents: She was adaptable and self-sufficient. Experienced in the art of introducing herself, she had developed a preemptive response to the inevitable follow-up question. "I'm Stanley," she would say. "My father wanted a son, but he got me." The retort, true or not, revealed something about the speaker. By the time she was a teenager, Stanley Ann was witty and self-contained, with a wry sense of humor. She had other outsider qualities: She was curious about people, and she was tolerant, not leaping to judgment. She had an unusual capacity even as a child, Charles Payne told me, to laugh at herself. She also had a contentious relationship with her father. She had figured out early on how to get under his skin.

Physically, she resembled him. She had his elongated chin, his compact mouth, his enviable hair. As a child, she was somewhat ungainly, an asthmatic in a household of smokers. As a teenager, she came to loathe the indignities and the regimentation of high school gym. She lacked the makings of an athlete, but she was bright. When Ralph Dunham was a graduate student in educational psychology at UC Berkeley and living in student housing in Richmond, California, with his brother as well as Madelyn and Stanley Ann, he gave his four-year-old niece an intelligence test. "You're not supposed to give intelligence tests to people you're related to, but I think I was pretty objective," he told me. Asked how Stanley Ann did on the test, he said, with visible pride and admiration, "Very well, indeed." She was curious and lively, with the willfulness of her mother. "She would decide to do something and do it whether anyone wanted her to or not," Charles Payne said. Until Mercer Island, she was rarely in one place long enough to develop enduring friendships. At a time when little girls were given names like Mary, Betty, and Barbara, Stanley Ann was teased about hers.

(She wished she had been named Deborah, she told Maya years later.) She was solitary and bookish, inclined to hole up for hours with back issues of *National Geographic,* "always traveling in her mind," as Maya put it. She was independent-minded—though not so much so as to be spared the anxieties of adolescence and the yearning to fit in. As a teenager, she was self-conscious about her appearance; the year she had braces, one friend said, she rarely risked a smile. She had an eye for absurdity and little tolerance for phoniness and glibness. Her humor was arch, sometimes cutting, but not mean-spirited. A look of wry amusement was often on her face. Toward the back of the 1960 Mercer Island High School annual, there is a snapshot of Stanley Ann and a classmate, Marilyn McMeekin, soliciting a yearbook ad from Petram's Ten Cent Store. Marilyn has presented herself, front and center, next to the cash register and the wire rack of Wrigley's gum. She is smiling eagerly, engaging a cashier somewhere outside the frame. In the background, slightly out of focus, Stanley Ann has been captured by the camera, visibly rolling her eyes. She was good at rolling her eyes, her high school friend John Hunt told me.

Her father, Stanley, struck his daughter's friends as jovial, boisterous, a talker. He could be charming and loud, and his humor often involved teasing. Compared with other Mercer Island parents, he and Madelyn seemed, at least to some, more adventurous and hip. They were sharp-witted and unconventional, if less educated and more middle class than upper-middle class. Madelyn was the brains in the family, by most accounts, and the reliable breadwinner. But Stanley called at least some of the shots. In his white convertible, he ferried Stanley Ann and her friends to and from high school basketball and football games. Occasionally, he would let some of them take the wheel, sitting in his lap. They enjoyed his attention; he enjoyed theirs. "Eventually, he sort of sucked up all the air in the car," Susan Botkin Blake, a classmate and friend of Stanley Ann's, told me. "He was one of those people that, given an audience, he'd take it." He embarrassed his daughter, not least with his familiarity with her friends. He was strict and overprotective, Ralph Dunham said. Behind his back, to friends who called her Stan, she referred to Stanley half mockingly as "Big Stan." Kathy Sullivan, a close friend in high school, remembered Stanley Ann glancing at her sideways in Stanley Dunham's car, out of his view, and making a face. Kathy had her own burden of parental embarrassment. Her mother, who had grown up in a farming community in Illinois, still hung the family's laundry on a clothesline. She did not appear, to her teenage daughter, to know the right way to talk. Her mother did not fit in on Mercer Island, Kathy felt, and neither did Stanley Ann's father. It made Kathy feel better that she and Stanley Ann shared these mortifications. "Stanley hated her father at the time that I knew her," she told me. "She hated her father as only a teenager can hate."

Both the time and the geography of the place shaped the experience of coming of age on Mercer Island in the latter half of the 1950s. When the Dunhams arrived in 1956, Mercer Island was almost rural—a 6.2-square-mile slab of wooded land, the shape of a steak, just east of Seattle in Lake Washington. The population was about eight thousand, mostly scattered along the perimeter in handsome waterfront houses and more modest wood-frame cottages. Everyone, just about, was white. Classmates of Stanley Ann's remembered one black student in the entire high school by the year they graduated. The local paper, the *Mercer Island Reporter,* was dense with news of Parent-Teacher Association smorgasbords, ballroom dancing classes, and Camp Fire Girls' "Dad and Daughter" suppers. Ads in the personal section said things like, "Respectable lady interested in forming a card club." Editorials opined earnestly on topics like "Our Vanishing Morals." When the high school French teacher, Madame White, escorted a group of students to Europe one summer, the girls boarded the plane in hats, pumps, and white gloves. Crime was almost nonexistent. Children could spend the night in sleeping bags down by the water or disappear into the woods for an entire day. Susan Botkin's family, she said, did not even have a key to their house. When they went on vacation, her mother would throw the bolt on the front door, set the button lock on the back door on the way out, and leave one clerestory window ajar for her brother to enter through when they returned. The only direct transportation link to Seattle had been a ferry until 1940, when the "floating bridge" between Seattle and the island opened. Roads on the island were tar and gravel. Mercer Island had a small town center, a few stores, little public transportation, no movie theaters, few televisions. "I can remember going with some of my college buddies to Mercer Island. It was almost a feeling that it was a different country," said Jim Sullivan, who would drive his Alfa Romeo convertible from the University of Washington across the pontoon bridge to pick up his girlfriend, Kathy Powell, Stanley Ann's friend. "There were a lot of subtle controls dictated by geography."

Yet change was coming. The great postwar suburbanization of America was under way, and the communities east of Seattle in the shadow of the Cascade Mountains were expanding. Boeing, with its airplane-manufacturing site in Renton, Washington, was building up its commercial-airliner division for the jet age. King County was booming. On Mercer Island, bulldozers and cement mixers rumbled along Island Crest Way, the road that traced the island's backbone like a zipper. The first big apartment complex opened in 1949, and subdivisions followed. Young professionals were moving in, looking for moderately priced housing, good schools, and an easy commute into Seattle. Many were college-educated, successful and affluent, and committed to creating opportunities for their children. "Newcomers' Club Welcomes Eight Residents," read a headline on an article in the *Mercer Island Reporter* that greeted newly arrived women by their husbands' names: "Mesdames Richard Friedenrich, Paul Hindman," and so on. Kathy Powell's father, who moved his family to Mercer Island the year the Dunhams arrived, was a Lockheed engineer turned insurance company manager; her mother had been trained as a nurse. Chip Wall, who had arrived two years earlier, was the son of the commanding officer of a Nike missile battalion that was setting up a missile perimeter defense for Seattle; his mother had gone to stenography school. Susan Botkin's mother was sent west from Missouri by the Girl Scouts organization, Susan told me, to research how to develop scouting in the area. Beyond Mercer Island, the civil rights movement had begun, the birth-control pill was in development, and John F. Kennedy would announce on January 2, 1960, that he was running for president. "There was change in the air," recalled Bill Byers, a classmate and friend of Stanley Ann's. "And we felt it in high school. We didn't know what we were feeling. But that was at the end of the Eisenhower years, and everything was so extremely stable. It was just too quiet. And young people can't stand it when it gets too quiet."

Mercer Island High School had all the energy and ambition of a brand-new school. Until the mid-1950s, there had been no high school on the island; students had commuted to Bellevue or Seattle. The class of 1958 was the first to graduate from the new school, which sprang up among the Douglas firs near the new subdivision, Mercerwood, close to the center of the island. The faculty tended to be young and committed. "Everything was fresh, everybody wanted to work hard, all the parents wanted it to be good," said

Jim Wichterman, who arrived in the mid-1950s as a part-time social studies teacher and football and track coach. "It was just, 'Let's have a good educational system.'" Maxine Hanson Box, a close friend of Stanley Ann's who went on to teach elementary school in Bellevue and Renton for twenty-seven years, told me the Mercer Island High School curriculum was conceived to be challenging. At the time, individual school districts could raise money from local taxpayers to raise teachers' salaries and build facilities, and Mercer Island taxpayers enthusiastically went along. Parents turned out in force for back-to-school nights. They organized graduation parties and knew whose children had gotten into Harvard. The newspaper carried articles about the latest National Merit semifinalists. Maxine's parents, whose own education had been cut short by the Depression, moved to Mercer Island in 1957 in part for the schools. Like other parents on Mercer Island, they made their expectations clear to their children. "You would do your very best, and you would accept a challenge and do the work to get there," Maxine Box told me. "It made a lot of difference to where the kids applied to go to school, and it broadened their horizons about what they could be. There were no limits."

The Dunhams moved into the Shorewood Apartments before school started in 1956. The first large rental apartment complex on the island, it had opened seven years earlier, designed for middle-class living. Two- and three-story brick and wood-trimmed apartment houses stood on broad lawns sloping down to a meandering private waterfront. The apartments had hardwood floors, crown molding, and views of the Cascades. Front doors opened directly onto lawns. The complex had its own tennis courts, community center, and convenience store. In the two years after Shorewood opened, school enrollment on Mercer Island nearly quadrupled. Newcomers to the island, waiting for houses to be completed, touched down in Shorewood. So did ex-spouses digging out from the rubble of wrecked marriages. Most families on Mercer Island lived in single-family houses—from bungalows and split-level duplexes to waterfront homes where a button embedded in the floor under the dining room table would summon the maid. But Shorewood had its own attractions, including plenty of children. From the Dunhams' two-bedroom apartment on East Lexington Way, it was a short walk to 90th Avenue SE and across SE 40th Street to Mercer Island High School. Chip Wall, a friend of Stanley Ann's, lived in Shorewood. Steve McCord, another friend, lived in a house in the trees near the footbridge connecting Lower and Upper Shorewood. Maxine Hanson lived in Mercerwood, three blocks from school. Like most Mercer Island mothers, Maxine's did not work, so Stanley Ann would often go home with Maxine after school. "I'll never forget your mother's chocolate cake," Stanley Ann wrote on the back of a wallet-size copy of her tenth-grade school photo that she gave to Maxine. "Love + luck, Stanley."

They had met on Maxine's first day at the school, in September 1957, at the welcoming assembly in the gym. In the Mercer Island pecking order, the popular boys tended to be star athletes. They dressed well, had ski boats, and were inclined not to speak up in class. The popular girls were good-looking and svelte, and wore pleated wool skirts and twinsets. Brains were not necessarily a liability. There was a group of smart and funny boys—self-styled intellectuals at odds, albeit ambivalently, with the dominant high school culture—who read books outside the curriculum and assumed that most athletes were morons. One of them, Bill Byers, went on to be voted most likely to succeed. Another, Chip Wall, was voted most talented. Stanley Ann's friends were not easily pigeonholed, but they were more outsiders than insiders. They called her Stanley. On that day in 1957, she was sitting with a group of girls (seven of whom would still be eating dinner together monthly some fifty years later). They invited Maxine to join them—a gesture she told me might not have been unrelated to the fact that her older brother, Bill, was six-foot-nine and destined for basketball stardom. "Stanley had only been here a year before me, so she knew what it was like to be a new person at school," Box remembered. "I think that's one of the reasons that we got to know each other so quickly. I can remember Stanley laughing when she introduced herself and said her name was Stanley. And right then she said, 'My father wanted a son.'"

Laughed how? I asked.

"Well, how you would laugh at yourself when you weren't ashamed of anything," she said.

Stanley Ann's humor was quick, dry, and ironic. The future anthropologist was a participant-observer of the culture of the high school and of its denizens' foibles. Her sense of humor, Chip Wall said, was in the spirit of Peter Sellers and *The Goon Show.* She found things funny that other people simply missed. She could be sarcastic and snide, and had a particular disdain for classmates piping the opinions of their parents. Iona Stenhouse, a classmate, described Stanley Ann's sensibility as a "can-you-believe-this? perspective." She was direct. "She would call our bluff, our intellectual pretense," John Hunt said. "That's the way she was—blunt." She was young for her class—more mature intellectually than socially, more confident of her brains than of her appearance. She had what Steve McCord called a slightly regal bearing: Quiet and composed, she held her chin a half-notch higher than most. She wore the pleated or gored skirts and blouses that were de rigueur, but could resist the impulse to upgrade to high-status brands. "She would probably laugh at me and say, 'Sixty dollars for a skirt?'" said Kathy Powell, who squandered her earnings from her weekend job at the Pancake Corral in Bellevue on Evan Picone skirts. Steve McCord said, "She was not a gum-chewing, blinky-eyed bimbo, a Mercer Island cashmere-sweater-wearing social ding-dong." To him, she seemed nonjudgmental and down-to-earth. She was one of the few friends to whom McCord, a year older and a friend from French club, was comfortable confiding his growing realization that he was gay—a fact of his life that, he said, his loyal, devoted parents believed could be cured. In the company of people she did not know well, Stanley Ann was reticent and loath to call attention to herself. Among friends, she was lively and more outgoing. She kept a low profile in class, but when ideas moved her, she spoke her mind. There was a seriousness about her that made Jim Wichterman, the social studies teacher, remember her a half-century later. She seemed interested in the material, interested in ideas. Neither overtly rebellious nor a joiner, she found her way eventually into that mostly male circle of academically high-achieving nonconformists outside of the force field that surrounded the star athletes. "There was this constant tension in her life," Susan Botkin Blake told me. "It was this sense of needing to fit in and yet be apart."

There were slumber parties, sock hops, ski trips, little drinking, no drugs, little dating, less sex. If there was any sex education in the school, no one I spoke with seemed to remember it years later. Maxine Box said that the students who had been on Mercer Island in middle school "had been told by a teacher, 'If you ever sit on a boy's lap, be sure to sit on a newspaper.'" Parking with your boyfriend and "petting" could lead to other things, girls were told. But who knew what those were? Talking to strangers was said to be risky, but what those risks were went undeclared. It was difficult to talk with your mother about sex, and many girls did not have their first appointment with a gynecologist until they were eighteen or older—or married. It would be another year or two before the birth-control pill was approved by the Food and Drug Administration, and many more before it was widely available in places such as college campuses. The only form of birth control teenagers seemed to know about was the condom. One of the brothers who owned the gas station where Bill Byers had an after-school job bought condoms on behalf of young employees, striding out of the pharmacy with a ribbon of condom packets over his shoulder like

Stanley Ann (left), age fourteen, at a slumber party, summer 1957

a bandolier, intending to be shocking. A Mercer Island girl unlucky enough to become pregnant before graduation faced an unhappy fate: Some disappeared abruptly, shipped off to live with a relative or to finish school elsewhere in anonymity; others hid their pregnancies, some marrying quietly before graduation. When one good-looking and likable jock impregnated an upperclassman, her sudden disappearance did not escape Stanley Ann and Kathy Powell's notice. They were shocked, Kathy Powell Sullivan told me, that the girl had to be sent away and that the boy's family had arranged it. Judy Ware, whose parents were Mercer Island bridge-playing friends of Madelyn and Stanley Dunham's, told me that she became pregnant in her senior year. An abortion, still against the law and often unsafe, would have required making arrangements through intermediaries. Judy, anxious to please her parents, stalled before telling them she was pregnant. They arranged for her to be married secretly—no siblings, few photographs—some distance from Seattle. She graduated at five months pregnant.

"We were growing up in that *Leave It to Beaver*, June Cleaver kind of society," Ware told me. "We just weren't very well prepared."

The Dunhams were not, however, the Cleavers. They may have played bridge with the Hansons and the Farners, but they did not match any Mercer Island template. Steve McCord recalled an evening he spent with the Dunhams in the summer of 1959. A good student, he was not an athlete and never felt that he quite fit in. He would have preferred to have grown up on a farm or someplace where, he imagined, people were "looser and less inhibited, less anxious about themselves." Madelyn and Stanley struck him as more colorful, interesting, liberal-minded. "Closet bohemians, maybe," he said. That evening, they smoked a lot of cigarettes and talked. "He had a slightly rotten sense of humor that I liked, a dirty mind," McCord remembered of Stanley Dunham. "They weren't your run-of-the-mill Ozzie and Harriet by any stretch of the imagination. I remember at one point, the conversation was getting goofy. We talked about a lot of things. I said something about prehensile toes. And Stanley turned it around and said 'pretensile hose,' making sort of a phallic reference. It was a silly little dirty joke. And immediately, I think Madelyn pretended to be offended and hissed, 'Stanley!'" There was some discussion of the possibility that the Dunhams might leave Mercer Island after Stanley Ann's graduation. Didn't Madelyn mind dropping everything and starting over? McCord asked her. In an answer that would strike him years later as prescient in light of what became of Madelyn's daughter, she said, "We Dunhams usually bob to the surface."

That was true of Madelyn, certainly. When Stanley had enrolled at UC Berkeley, she had taken a job in the admissions office at the university while Stanley Ann was still a toddler. Back in Kansas, she had worked in a real estate office in Wichita. Mack Gilkeson, who knew her from Augusta, remembered running into her at a restaurant where she was working as a hostess. In Ponca City, even though Stanley was making enough money that Madelyn no longer needed to be employed, she announced to a relative that she was going back to work. "The evening cocktail hour gets earlier every day," she said. "If I don't work, I'll turn into an alcoholic." She modeled shoes, broadcast community news on the radio, may have worked for a newspaper, and got her first job in banking in Texas, Charles Payne told me. When the family moved to Seattle, she parlayed her banking experience into a job in the escrow department of a savings and loan. She was elegant, slim, and well dressed, and she enjoyed her work. At the same time, she kept close track of Stanley Ann's grades. She seemed interested in enabling her daughter to go well beyond what she and Stanley had accomplished. Madelyn had inherited their mother's intelligence, Charles Payne said. Ralph Dunham described her as brilliant. But if she was smarter than Stanley, some said, she was careful not to overplay that advantage in the interest of keeping the peace.

Stanley had brought the family west so he could take a job selling furniture in a department store in downtown Seattle. But he seemed to be around more than Madelyn. To Stanley Ann's friends, he was handsome and jolly, yet Maxine Box described him "as you would a used-car salesman—blustery, but what is behind it all?" He would go a little too far to make Stanley Ann's friends laugh. She was on the receiving end of a disproportionate share of his teasing. He was not averse to issuing orders. "I can't do that because of my father," Iona Stenhouse remembered Stanley Ann saying. "I have to be home because of my dad." From an early age, she ran circles around him. She would trick him, he would become angry, she would play innocent, he would stomp up and down. "If she wanted to do something, he would say no for no reason," one relative said. "She would say things she knew would irritate him. She was able with a straight face to tease him in a way that he didn't know he was being teased, and he would get furious." In high school, when she wanted to go out with a group of friends, she would enlist John Hunt to pretend to be her date and get her out of the house without too much fatherly interrogation. "When I'd get sucked into a conversation with Stan, she'd roll her eyes: 'Don't!'" John Hunt told me. He said, "Big Stan wanted to know about her life, her friends. She kept him locked off." She was like a lot of her friends, Chip Wall said: "We wanted to get out from under the thumb of our parents." Ralph Dunham was especially fond of his niece, whom he had known well as a small child when they were all living in Richmond, California. Years later, Ralph said, Stanley Ann told him it might have been easier if he had been her father. "He was overprotective," Ralph said of Stanley. He tried to control where she went, what hours she kept, whom she was with. He added, "Stanley was very strict with her—which is probably why she maybe tried to break out of the mold once she got older."

Stanley and Madelyn's marriage was stormy. He could be opinionated and stubborn, and had what Obama described years later as a violent temper. He did not like losing arguments and was not in the habit of agreeing to disagree. It was not unknown for him and Madelyn to ruin a family holiday by waging a protracted argument over a period of hours in the presence of out-of-town relatives. Ralph Dunham told me his brother dropped out of UC Berkeley because of a language requirement, but others said Madelyn complained that she had ended up writing too many of Stanley's term papers while he sprawled on the couch, reading murder mysteries. She pulled the plug on Berkeley, it was said, and he did not forgive her for insisting they return to Kansas. "What can you do if your wife won't support you to get an education?" he complained more than once. In the summer of 1957, Madelyn's parents, her aunt Ruth, and her younger brother, Jon, stopped in Seattle on their annual summer road trip. Jon, a few years older than Stanley Ann and more like a cousin than an uncle, had left the University of Kansas and was scheduled to report to the Air Force the following February. He found a job selling menswear at a department store in Seattle and spent four months sleeping on the Dunhams' couch. To him, Madelyn and Stanley's marriage at that time looked shaky. There was loud arguing, not infrequently about money. Stanley Ann would sometimes bolt from the apartment or shut herself in her room. "I think she maybe just didn't want to hear it," Jon Payne told me. Stanley Ann reached the conclusion early on, Kathy Powell Sullivan said, that her parents' marriage was not a model she intended to follow.

Mercer Island was politically conservative but not extreme. In the spring of 1955, a year before the Dunhams moved to Mercer Island, John Stenhouse, a member of the school board and the father of Iona Stenhouse, who would become Stanley Ann's classmate, was subpoenaed to testify before a subcommittee of the House Un-American Activities Committee investigating communist activity in the Seattle area. Born in China and educated in England, he said he had attended a handful of Communist Party discussion-group meetings in Los Angeles in 1943 and in Washington, D.C., in 1946 but had had no contact with the party since. He had moved to Mercer Island in 1949 and joined the school board in 1951. He worked for an insurance company in Seattle and, with his wife, was active in helping to reclaim land on Mercer Island for parks and in working to establish a health cooperative. That spring, school boards in Bremerton and Tacoma were firing teachers who took the Fifth Amendment when called before the subcommittee, and the state legislature made Communist Party membership a crime. On the Stenhouse case, Mercer Island was split. Marilyn Bauer, a close friend of Iona's, told me that her own father was constantly saying, half teasingly, "We're not having the communist over, are we?" Iona Stenhouse, however, recalled feeling sheltered and protected by the community—spirited away to the beach club by family friends, for example, when reporters or lawyers were at her parents' house. In March, two hundred people turned out for a school board meeting to consider Stenhouse's fate. After a two-hour hearing, the board left the decision to Stenhouse, who decided not to step down. To Jim Wichterman, arriving not long afterward to teach at the high school, the island's handling of John Stenhouse reflected a fundamental sense of proportion and balance that Wichterman believed prevailed at that time on Mercer Island.

The religion to which Stanley Ann was exposed as a teenager was Christian and liberal. Along with the Stenhouses, the Dunhams were among a group of families on Mercer Island that attended East Shore Unitarian Church in Bellevue, known for a while during that period as "the little red church on the hill." It had been started in the late 1940s in an old kindergarten building on Mercer Island and then in a funeral chapel in Bellevue by several families, including Stanley and Madelyn's bridge partners, the Farners. Tired of commuting to a Unitarian church in Seattle, the founding families were interested in religious education and the teaching of moral decision-making for children. The founders were "bright, liberal movers and shakers," as the Farners' eldest daughter, Judy Ware, described them. Her mother, the director of religious education for the church, encouraged Judy to read John Hersey's *Hiroshima* at age twelve. The Reverend Dr. Peter J. Luton, the senior minister when I visited the church in 2009, told me that the original families had emerged from World War II confident in the possibility of building a just, rational, and loving community. They were religious humanists, he said, their faith rooted more in "lived experience" than in supernatural and revealed truth. They had a sense of awe and wonder, an appreciation of what he called nonrational experience—idealism, the mystery of love, the moving power of music—without attributing it to a traditional god. The first minister, Chadbourne A. Spring, delivered sermons with titles like "In Praise of Heretics." At Christmas, children reenacted the birth of Jesus Christ, Confucius, and the Buddha. The church encouraged community service and tolerance, and pushed for social justice. It took up the fight against redlining and in favor of nuclear disarmament, and King County's fair-housing legislation emerged from meetings at the church. Its youth groups, in which Stanley Ann took part, attended services at other churches and synagogues, then would "come back and do comparative religion," said Iona Stenhouse. They would "talk about world religions, good works, what we could do in the world as we got older." Jane Waddell Morris, who attended the youth groups with Stanley Ann, told me that she herself had become, through the East Shore experience, "a lifelong seeker," aware of spirituality around her but not committed to an organized religion (just as Stanley Ann would be described,

I noticed, many years later as an adult). Jane Morris's home in Taos, New Mexico, she said, was filled with religious icons—a Northwest Coast warrior, a Hopi kachina, a Guanyin, various *retablos* and *bultos,* and an old stone Ganesh.

Jim Wichterman, who taught Stanley Ann during her senior year, was a graduate student in philosophy at the University of Washington when he was hired to teach on Mercer Island. The

At seventeen, from the 1960
Mercer Island High School annual

principal of the high school assigned him to teach "contemporary world problems" to seniors, who were barely ten years younger than he was. Since contemporary world problems were philosophical problems, he figured, why not teach philosophy? He did that for seventeen years, thundering through Plato, Aristotle, Saint Augustine, Descartes, Hobbes, Locke, Mill, Marx, Kierkegaard, Sartre, and Camus. After Mercer Island, he taught philosophy at a private school in Seattle for another twenty-two years. He never got his Ph.D., but that had ceased to matter. When I met him in the summer of 2008, he was pushing eighty and still teaching philosophy—this time at the Women's University Club in Seattle and in a night class for adults on Mercer Island. "I had a circus teaching," he said. "I should have paid them." The feeling appears to have been mutual. In high school annuals in the late 1950s, Mercer Island students wrote about Wichterman more often than almost any other teacher. In conversations a half-century later, Stanley Ann's classmates described Wichterman's class as an intellectual coming of age.

His method, modeled on his graduate-school courses, was total immersion. His students read constantly and in enormous quantities. There were research papers every six weeks. In tutorials, students critiqued one another's work. Knowledge is about questions, Wichterman told them. Is the world absurd? Does God exist? What constitutes good? "What do you think that means, Miss Botkin? Miss Dunham?" Susan Botkin Blake recalled Mr. Wichterman asking. How do these ideas relate to the present? Maxine Box remembered typing until three in the morning. "We were the higher-percentile bunch," said Steve McCord. "We thought of ourselves as being brighter than most people at most schools. We were aware of our uniqueness, whether it was real or imagined."

Down the hall, Val Foubert, their humanities teacher, assigned *The Organization Man, The Hidden Persuaders, Atlas Shrugged,* and *Coming of Age in Samoa.* Kathy Powell Sullivan recalled, "We devoured Jack Kerouac. *On the Road* would have been our bible." Conformity was disdained; the very idea of difference was alluring. Foubert, a World War II veteran who some said moonlighted as a drummer in a swing band, is said to have eventually defected to another district in a disagreement over Mercer Island's handling of parents' complaints about his reading list. Parents complained, too, that Wichterman had no business teaching a college course in high school. The course was making trouble at home. "You know how kids are," Wichterman told me. "They see an idea they get in class, they set that up at the dinner table with Dear Old Dad. Dad gets up out of his chair, all exercised. Of course, the kids love that. You don't start out to cause trouble at the dinner table; what you start out to do is get the kid on his tippy toes: 'If you don't like this argument, refute it. Give me reasons you don't like it. You have to *think*.'"

It may have been in Art Sullard's tenth-grade biology class that Stanley Ann fell in with the group of boys who would become her closest friends in her last two years on Mercer Island. Sullard, also young and a musician, would banter with certain students and occasionally make sarcastic asides. Over dissections, students milled around in groups, the humor tending toward black. Stanley Ann's somewhat sarcastic sensibility surfaced. "My seatmate was an old athlete friend, very intelligent," John Hunt recalled. "I remember him making comments about Stanley because he was trying to figure out what was with her. She was so different." The following year, she was assigned to a chemistry table next to one occupied by Hunt, Bill Byers, and Raleigh Roark. They all became friends, fancying themselves as thinkers on the cultural cutting edge. Byers was slightly older than the others, had access to a car, and had glimpsed the wider world—Seattle and Bellevue, anyway. He had friends off the island and, at sixteen, had started dating a girl in Seattle. The son of a liquor-company manager who had abandoned graduate work on Chaucer in order to find paying work during the Depression, Byers was reading Dostoyevsky, listening to Pete Seeger, and borrowing old classical records from the high school librarian. Outside of school, he and a friend would amuse themselves by making gunpowder out of saltpeter, charcoal, and sulfur and creating small explosions in the woods—not to damage anything, just for fun. In the classroom, he was a contrarian on principle. Byers remembered Raleigh Roark as having "a very original type of intelligence. You could count on him saying or doing something that just went crosswise with the accepted norms." Roark had a half sister living in bohemian splendor in the university district of Seattle, from whom Roark's friends got a first glimpse of a counterculture. They discovered foreign films at theaters in Seattle. "Satyajit Ray's Apu Trilogy was one that hit us the hardest," Hunt remembered. "It was totally different from anything we'd seen—Third World poverty, a complete cultural gulf. We had no experience, we hadn't even read about that. We would go and sit and talk and talk. What did it mean? What's it got to do with us? We were trying to acquaint ourselves at second- and thirdhand, and wondering what to do about it." There were coffeehouses in the university district where it was possible to spend hours drinking espresso, eating baba au rhum, sitting on pillows, and listening to classical guitar and jazz. "We'd get in Bill's car, do anything, go for a picnic—anything to get away from the families and to talk," Hunt said. "We all had a very strong need to talk about things we didn't talk about at home." Kerouac's *On the Road* conjured dreams of escape, Roark remembered. San Francisco was Mecca.

Stanley Ann, often the only girl in the group, shared the boys' highbrow pretensions and what Byers described as their us-against-them outlook toward "the dominant culture, the not-very-thoughtful people doing not-very-thoughtful things." He said, "I think it was a big issue for her—these kinds of people that she disliked. My feeling is she did feel ostracized—that she felt that she could never have been one of them even if she had wanted to be one of them, that type of feeling." Unconventional in many ways, she also had a conservative streak. Once, Byers drove her out to Bellevue to meet some friends he had made who were in the process of becoming, in effect, early hippies. Their style of living fascinated Byers. Stanley Ann looked the scene over. "You know, I couldn't live in that place," she told him later. "It's filthy." Which was true, Byers remembered later. "Somewhere, fundamentally, she had a fairly rock-solid, realistic, even conservative outlook," he said. "She knew where the line was, it seemed. She was right about those people. By their lights, they were living free of all these restraints. But of course, that meant free of . . ."

He paused.

". . . hygiene."

By senior year, Stanley Ann's friendship with Kathy Powell had cooled. Kathy had met Jim Sullivan, a fraternity man from the University of Washington, at the Pancake Corral. Because he was five years older than she was, she had lied to him about her age. Now she was wearing his fraternity pin. In Stanley Ann's eyes, Kathy Sullivan told me, she had sold out. Stanley Ann defined herself by her intellect, Sullivan said. If she had any romantic interest in boys, she did not let on. In the spring of 1959, Jim Sullivan suggested to Kathy that he fix up some of his fraternity brothers with her friends. When Kathy suggested including Stanley Ann, Jim dropped her from the list in favor of a girl thought to be the most beautiful in the school. "She wasn't a radiant beauty by any means," Byers said of Stanley Ann. "But, probably more to the point, she was very intellectual, and she could cut people down. She didn't suffer fools gladly." She would have needed some coaching, Kathy felt, not to be supercilious and disdainful to Jim's fraternity friends.

In early 2009, I heard the name Allen Yonge. If Stanley Ann

had ever had a boyfriend in high school, I was told, it could have been Allen. He was a year or two older than she was and lived in Bellevue, though no one seemed to remember how they had met. For a time, friends of theirs said, he developed a crush on Stanley Ann. She seemed willing, sort of, to give it a try. I found an address for Mr. Yonge and sent him a letter asking if he would speak with me. In early March, I received an e-mail from his wife, Penelope Yonge. Her husband was astounded to get my letter, she said: "Allen is enthusiastic about Obama, but he had never connected his Mercer Island friend Stanley with the president, so this came as quite a surprise." However, he was recovering from an accident and not in a condition to talk. He would get back to me, she said, when he was in better shape. Several months later, I wrote to her to say I was still interested whenever her husband felt up to speaking. She e-mailed back two days later to tell me that he had died. "He had been looking forward to talking to you about Stanley," she said. "He remembered her with great affection and admiration— he called her 'brainy' and 'intellectual' and 'adventurous' and 'a whole lot of fun' (descriptions that aren't usually used together, at least not in high school)."

Stanley Ann was, indeed, adventurous. In the summer of 1959, Steve McCord proposed an unusual late-night outing. At a time when homosexuality was kept well hidden, he had developed a crush on a younger boy and had confided in Stanley Ann. He suggested they sneak out late one night, walk to the boy's house at the far end of the island, and watch him through his window while he slept. Stanley Ann was game, McCord recalled when he told me the story; she was a person who was just "up for adventure." (And if she ever felt inner turmoil about a decision, Byers told me, she did not let on: "When she decided to do something, she decided to do it.") So on a warm, breezy night and at the appointed hour, she climbed out her bedroom window onto the moonlit lawn of the Shorewood complex. McCord was waiting, and they set off, heading south. They walked several miles to the house, found the window, executed their mission undetected, then walked several miles home—only to be confronted by Big Stan, stationed in the bedroom window, arms akimbo, awaiting their return. His reaction was stern but not explosive, as McCord recalled it: "It was, 'Young lady, you get in here. And *you*, go home!'" The episode blew over, it seems, without dire consequences for Stanley Ann. But it proved to be a precursor to a far more daring adventure a few months later—a spontaneous breakout that shattered the written and unwritten codes of conduct that kept Mercer Island teenagers on the straight and narrow. It was an act of rebellion that Stanley Ann's father would be unlikely to forget.

Fifty years later, no one seemed to agree on exactly when the escapade went down. Bill Byers thought it took place during the fall, but John Hunt initially remembered the time of year as spring. Either way, it was nighttime and they were driving home to Mercer Island, maybe from a coffeehouse in Seattle, with Stanley Ann. They were in Hunt's parents' car, and Hunt was at the wheel. The conversation turned negative—one of those "This really sucks, school is irrelevant, why bother to go home?" conversations of adolescence, as Hunt described it. Suddenly, someone suggested not going home: They could keep on driving. They could drive to San Francisco. Hunt balked, stunned by the suggestion. He might have expected it of Bill, he said later, but he had no idea that Stanley Ann "had got to the point of just wanting to go chuck it." They began to argue. The argument turned acrimonious and tearful. Hunt tried to talk the others out of it, he told me, visibly anguished by the memory a half-century later. They begged him to join them. But the lark struck him as pointless: They would get in trouble for cutting school; they would be runaways; if the other two went without him, he would have to lie to cover their tracks. "He was certainly torn," Byers remembered. "But he was a sensible person, basically. He would never do a thing like that—which was totally irresponsible and totally crazy and downright dangerous and not even practical." As for Stanley Ann, he said, "She was all for it. Otherwise, it would never have happened. I guarantee it. She would have said, 'No. Take me home.' She didn't." So it was settled. Hunt dropped off the other two at the Byerses' garage, where Byers parked the metallic-green 1949 Cadillac convertible that his father no longer used. The garage was beside the road, uphill from and out of earshot of the house. "Please don't do this," Hunt pleaded. "You're going to ruin things for everybody."

Byers and Stanley Ann headed south in the Cadillac. They had only the money in their pockets and the clothes they were wearing. When Byers and I spoke, his memory of details of the trip was spotty. He said he had forgotten most of what happened, including the route they drove, how long they were away, what they talked about in the car. But, he made clear, it was a road trip. It was neither romantic nor an elopement. He remembered a few episodes in some detail. They picked up a mild-mannered drifter who did them the favor of extracting the car radio from the dashboard to sell it to a gas station attendant when cash ran short. Byers remembered pulling off the road to sleep—the two men in the front seat, Stanley Ann in back—and being awakened in the night by the sound of whimpering. The hitchhiker had swiveled around in his seat and was groping in Stanley Ann's direction, "softly asking her to 'be nice' to him, while she shrank as far away from him as she could," Byers told me. Byers barked at the man, who swung forward and mumbled an apology. "I do not remember feeling frightened. I think I was just angry," Byers told me. "I am most certainly not a brave person. I guess I was naive enough to not consider the possibility of having a rapist or homicidal maniac on our hands." As for Stanley Ann, faced with the unwanted advances of a stranger, she was visibly afraid. It was the only time, Byers told me, that he could remember seeing her in a situation out of her control and feeling frightened.

Later, they unloaded that hitchhiker and picked up another—a homeless boy who regaled Byers with stories about male prostitution and other survival strategies for young people in the city. They rolled into the Bay Area and found their way to the home of Raleigh Roark's half sister, who had left Seattle and was living not far from the campus of the University of California at Berkeley. Byers, Stanley Ann, and the young hitchhiker arrived and settled in.

Meanwhile, back in Seattle, Hunt had barely gone to bed that night—or perhaps woken up in the morning—before the telephone rang. Byers's parents were calling. "My story was, 'Gee, I don't know. I dropped them off at Bill's. I thought Bill was going to take her home,'" he told me. Back in Kansas, too, the telephone rang in the home of Leona and R. C. Payne, Charles Payne remembered. Thinking Stanley Ann and Byers might have headed for Kansas, Madelyn was calling her mother. The two teenagers were reported missing. Hunt, who was not in the habit of lying to his parents about things that mattered, received a visit from a member of the county sheriff's office. Gradually, fragments of the story spilled out. They had all talked about going off on a lark, driving someplace. They had said, "Wouldn't it be fun to drive to San Francisco?" Perhaps Byers's parents remembered Byers having talked about Roark's half sister in the San Francisco Bay Area. Someone called the police in the Berkeley area and in the surrounding county. Officers turned up at the house. The young hitchhiker tried, unsuccessfully, to bolt through an open window. The three runaways were taken into custody and put briefly in juvenile detention, segregated by gender. Stanley Dunham arrived by plane from Seattle and somehow managed to retrieve the car, which had been impounded. Then he drove Byers and Stanley Ann home. As Bill described it, Stanley Dunham seemed to suspect, wrongly, that Bill and Stanley Ann had eloped. Byers told me, "I remember him going off on this strange monologue, saying, 'Sex isn't all it's cracked up to be, you know?'"

There is a temptation to see in the midnight road trip a foreshadowing of events yet to come in Stanley Ann's life. It certainly suggests a willingness to take a risk, an aptitude that flows, like a leitmotif, through the history of the Dunhams and the Paynes. Madelyn, as a teenager, had defied her parents and married in secret. Stanley, at a young age, had struck out for the coast. They may have appeared conventional from the outside, but there was a restlessness about them—the restlessness that had propelled Americans westward and that would eventually take the Dunhams as far west as they could go. Perhaps it is a leap to connect that impulse to a late-night lark in the young life of one high school senior. But the truth is, Stanley Ann would keep traveling for the rest of her life.

When she resurfaced in school, she did not want to talk about what had happened, Hunt remembered. People would not understand, he said, and she could not explain. Such an escapade was unheard of. Kathy Sullivan told me she remembered thinking, "My God, that's worse than getting pregnant." Perhaps Stanley Ann had intended, as Charles Payne put it, "to shake up her father." No one seemed to remember if she was punished. But as senior year wound down, it became apparent that the Dunhams were moving on. Stanley's work selling furniture in Seattle had dried up. Hawaii, in its newness, was courting transplants. The mayor of Honolulu and a delegation of Hawaii businessmen had been at the Seattle Chamber of Commerce in October, talking up business opportunities. Madelyn would have been happy to stay put, her brother Charles remembered. Her career in banking was flourishing. Stanley Ann had no interest in moving, either. Some said she wanted to attend the University of Washington, where many of her closest friends were headed. Or she may have wanted to go east to the University of Chicago. Arlene Payne, who was at the university, getting a Ph.D. in education, remembered Stanley Ann staying with her that year, apparently scouting for schools. In *Dreams from My Father,* Obama writes that his mother was offered early admission to the University of Chicago, but "my grandfather forbade her to go, deciding that she was still too young to be living on her own." Whatever the case, sometime shortly after graduation in 1960, Stanley Ann vanished. "She was upset that she had to move," Maxine Box remembered. "She didn't really have any choice."

Her friends—the first set of close friends she had ever had— moved on, too. Kathy Powell, who had become pregnant in her senior year, had married Jim Sullivan and finished the school year at Edison Technical High School in Seattle. Steve McCord was in San Francisco, studying art. Bill Byers dropped out of the University of Washington and enrolled for a time in a college in Mexico where he had been told that William Burroughs had had a wild time. Later, he returned to Seattle, got a degree in electrical engineering, and went to work for Boeing. Chip Wall joined the Peace Corps after graduating from the University of Washington. He spent two years in India, helping set up chicken-farming cooperatives in a village on the Ganges in Bihar and working in Hyderabad. Upon returning home, he was drafted and sent to Vietnam. Marilyn McMeekin went to Korea with the Peace Corps, Iona

Stenhouse to Sierra Leone. The valedictorian of the class of 1959, the class ahead of theirs, became an anthropologist working in French Polynesia. In the context of Mercer Island, where the idea of conformity was at least in some circles out of fashion, Stanley Ann might almost be seen in retrospect as part of a trend.

Apart from a few fleeting encounters, few of her friends ever saw or heard from her again. "People said she went to Africa and married a black king," Kathy Sullivan remembered. "We all thought that for years and years."

Three

East-West

There are ways in which Hawaii's capital city brings to mind the sun-bleached seediness of Southern California beach towns. But a short drive outside of Honolulu, the fiftieth state feels like another planet. Leaving the city behind, the Pali Highway cuts northeast through the remnants of the Ko'olau volcano, heading toward the windward coast of the island of O'ahu. The road climbs several thousand feet toward Pali Pass, disappears briefly into a tunnel, then plunges toward the beach town of Kailua. Jagged volcanic ridges parade against the sky like dinosaurs' backbones, slopes diving away from the ridgeline in dark, rippling curtains. Smudgy, gray-bottomed clouds congregate upwind of the mountains, sunlight mottling the hillsides in luminous green. In the front yard of a house on a quiet street in Kailua, I met Marilyn McMeekin Bauer, Stanley Ann's high school classmate. Bauer moved to Hawaii in 1968, straight from two years in the Peace Corps in Korea and eight years after Stanley Ann's arrival. Looking back, she said, she could not imagine what it was like for Stanley Ann to be airlifted at age seventeen straight from the monochrome insularity of Mercer Island onto the campus of the University of Hawai'i. It must have been, she said, a shock.

Hawaii in the summer of 1960 bore little resemblance to El Dorado, Ponca City, or any other place the Dunham family had roosted. As a state, it was an infant, admitted to the union on August 21, 1959. The population of the entire archipelago, 2,400 miles out in the Pacific, was fewer than 650,000. Whites made up less than a third of the population and were outnumbered by Japanese-Americans. Nearly one in five people was Hawaiian or part Hawaiian. There were Filipinos, Koreans, Chinese, and nearly 13,000 "other," though less than one-tenth of one percent of the population was classified as Negro. The place prided itself on tolerance. Despite the occasional real estate listing insisting on "no haoles," or white people, or calls for "Americans of Japanese ancestry only," residents saw Hawaii as a laboratory for assimilation and a model of harmonious coexistence. Steeped in its vision of pluralism, the state seemed poised at a moment of infinite possibility.

Hawaii was on the verge of economic liftoff, too. Jet travel had sliced hours off the time required to cross the Pacific. Visitor expenditures had risen fivefold between 1950 and 1960, outstripping the value of sugar and pineapple production for the first time. The total value of mortgages had quadrupled, and bank branches had more than doubled in number. By 1967, Honolulu would rank fifth in the country in the value of building permits issued, trailing only New York, Los Angeles, Houston, and Chicago. *Paradise of the Pacific*—a glossy magazine featuring articles on outrigger canoe racing, the muumuu, and Duke Kahanamoku, the Olympic swimming champion who popularized surfing—was thick with ads for real estate companies, banks, moving and storage services, decorators, flooring. For a footsore furniture salesman with an industrious banker wife and a college-age daughter, Hawaii had promise. With tuition at the University of Hawai'i at eighty-five dollars per semester, enrollment in the fall of 1960 jumped by thirteen percent. For the first time, the number of incoming freshman topped two thousand, Stanley Ann Dunham among them. Arriving on campus in September 1960, she swiftly jettisoned her first name. From then on, Stanley was Ann.

At first glance, the University of Hawai'i in 1960 might have seemed an unlikely fit for a brainy nonconformist with a wry sense of humor and a taste for cool jazz. It was a quiet provincial land-grant college nestled in the tropical lushness of the Mānoa Valley, east of downtown Honolulu and at the base of the Ko'olau Range. The valley was known for its rainbows, produced when the trade winds coming across the windward shore of O'ahu hit the mountains, sprinkling the valley on the far side in showers. The student newspaper, *Ka Leo O Hawai'i,* occupied itself with documenting every beauty contest, sorority pledge week, and race for homecoming queen. Its monthly calendar featured a spread of a comely coed, dressed in something tropical but demure. ("A water sports enthusiast, she likes swimming, surfing and water skiing. Another one of her interests is that of hula dancing.") In the home economics department, the course offerings included "Aesthetics of Clothing and Personal Appearance." The annual, student-sponsored Ka Palapala Beauty Pageant of Nations, with its bathing-suit rally and formal-dress competition, selected seven finalists, one for each of seven ethnic groups. "The University of Hawai'i used to be a good party school," Pake Zane, a Chinese-American born on Maui and an undergraduate in the late 1950s, told me. "We had our share of demonstrations, but it was basically much more conservative. People would say, 'Don't go make trouble.' It's a kind of Oriental attitude—that you don't want to bring shame on your family." There were exceptions to that rule, of course. When James Meredith was barred from entering the University of Mississippi in September 1962 on the basis of his race, five hundred students and faculty members on the Mānoa campus held a rally to protest his treatment, and the political-affairs club fired off a resolution to the University of Mississippi. "We, students in the newest state of the Union—a state dedicated to the principle of racial equality—are distressed by the ungoverned passion and hate that is sweeping Mississippi over the admission of a Negro to its state university," the resolution began.

The campus was changing. At the outset, Ann may well have felt herself to be a fish out of water, but the university was positioning itself in the world in ways that would set the course of her life for the future. In April 1959, a month after Congress voted in favor of statehood, Lyndon B. Johnson, the United States Senate majority leader, who had worked closely with Hawaii's territorial delegate on statehood, called for establishing in Hawaii an international center of cultural and technical interchange between East and West. For too many years, he said, "we have neglected the simple things that would break down the barriers between ourselves and people who should be our friends." The president of the University of Hawai'i went to Washington to help make the case for locating the center on campus. The progress of the proposal became regular front-page news at the school. Professors, politicians, students, and journalists weighed in. "I can see the bright young men from the small towns all over Asia and the bright young men of the United States interested in Asian affairs studying together on the same campus," said William J. Lederer, coauthor of *The Ugly American,* the novel about the parochialism of American officialdom in Southeast Asia, which had become a huge bestseller in 1958. Edward R. Murrow of CBS News, passing through Hawaii, called the proposed center "one of the most exciting educational projects I've heard of in many a long year."

The summer Ann arrived in Hawaii, Congress appropriated $10 million to set up the East-West Center, an institution that more than any would go on, over the next twenty-five years, to influence the direction of her life. An advance team set off for Bangkok, Rangoon, Saigon, Calcutta, Dhaka, Kathmandu, Karachi, Colombo, and points beyond, touring twenty countries that might be encouraged to send students. I. M. Pei, the Chinese-born American architect, agreed to design a complex of five buildings on twenty-one acres at the eastern end of the University of Hawai'i campus. The center's emphasis would be the exchange of ideas, information, and beliefs through cooperative study, training, and research. Theory and practice would be combined, preparing leaders, current and future, to confront real-life problems. Grant recipients, chosen jointly by the center and the participating countries, would receive a full scholarship, covering tuition, housing, textbooks, travel, and field study. In the fall of 1960, the first two students arrived—a professor-poet from Pakistan and a graduate student in soil science from Ceylon. The center's first American student, a graduate student in philosophy, set off in the fall of 1961 on a three-month trip to Japan, Korea, Taiwan, Thailand, Burma, East Pakistan, Ceylon, India, and Hong Kong to research a thesis comparing Buddhism and Western thought. By September 1962, there were 250 grant recipients enrolled at the university. The center's international advisers included Ralph J. Bunche, undersecretary of the United Nations; the vice chancellor of Punjab University; and an undersecretary of state for agriculture in Thailand. At the groundbreaking in the spring of 1961, Johnson, newly elected as vice president of the United States, arrived in a white convertible. "The purpose of this East-West Center is not for West to teach East or East to study the West," he said at the dedication. "The purpose here is to bring together two proud and honorable cultures, and to fuse a new strength—a new strength for freedom that will last through eternity."

Even for students not directly involved, the center quickly became one of the most interesting and exciting things on campus during Ann's undergraduate years. It more than tripled the number of international students enrolled at the university and brought in millions of dollars in federal money. It influenced course offerings in fields ranging from Asian studies and American studies to tropical agriculture and language studies. Hindi, Sanskrit, and Javanese entered the curriculum in 1961. The center attracted speakers like Dick Gregory and Gloria Steinem. There were weekly discussions of topical issues, such as civil rights, internationalism, and the conflict between India and Pakistan, with panels of students and scholars from the countries involved. "Some of the most politically active students the university had were on East-West Center grants," said Jeannette "Benji" Bennington, who worked for the center from 1962 until her retirement in 2004. Its open-air cafeteria, on the ground floor of Pei's Jefferson Hall, became a magnet for students from all over the campus. The grant recipients were strongly encouraged to mix. "We said, 'If we see a whole table of you and you're all Korean, we're going to say something to you,'" said Bennington, whose first job, as a resident assistant in an East-West Center dorm, entailed helping students acclimate. " 'The reason you're here is to learn about other peoples and nations, so you should always be mixing.' And you did! If you were an American, you were usually trying to explain idioms to about six different nationalities. It was a very enriching type of experience to go down there."

In that climate, international students were a source of fascination. They were invited to speak in schools, march in the Aloha Week parade, share Thanksgiving dinner with Duke Kahanamoku. Bill Collier, a veterinarian's son from a family of Indiana farmers, who would later work with Ann in Indonesia, had discovered the University of Hawai'i in the late 1950s in a magazine in a library in Huron, South Dakota. He was in his third year at the South Dakota School of Mines and Technology at the time and had exhausted his interest in surveying and math. *Look* magazine published a photo spread of the multiethnic beauty queens at the University of Hawai'i. "What the hell?" Collier thought. "I'm going." He enrolled as an undergraduate, studied Indonesian, and became vice president of the international students' association and eventually an East-West Center grantee. He spent his study tour in Thailand, Malaysia, and British Borneo, married a Chinese woman, and moved to Indonesia in 1968. "I was fascinated by all kinds of different nationalities," he told me when I met him in Jakarta in January 2009. "I even participated in this beauty-queen contest. They have a big dance afterward, they're all in different costumes. I must have been dressed as a haole and been square-dancing."

Many years later, after Ann's death, her family and friends would choose the Japanese garden at the East-West Center for a memorial service celebrating her life. Laid out in 1963 on a sloping stretch of land behind Jefferson Hall and in the shadow of Wa'ahila Ridge, the garden was intended to provide a window into Japanese culture. Like nearly everything at the center, it was a joint project—conceived by a vice chancellor, paid for by Japanese corporations and individuals, designed by a landscape architect in Tokyo, and constructed by a nursery and landscaping firm in Honolulu. There were lawns, privet hedges, paths, steps, much of it under a canopy of monkeypod trees. A stream, diverted from a Mānoa stream, wound through the garden's three levels. Formosan koa, strawberry guava, mondo, yeddo hawthorn, red bottlebrush, walking iris, juniper, and rose-flowered jatropha graced the garden, along with a coral shower tree planted by the Japanese crown prince. The stream was said to represent a river, a Japanese symbol of life—beginning in turmoil, steadying through adulthood, slowing to "a tranquil and majestic old age." Benji Bennington told me that the crown prince stocked the stream with dozens of koi, which were kept from disappearing downstream by a pair of underwater gates. Dropped into the long, winding stream, most of the fish simply swam in circles, following one another and oblivious to their surroundings, Bennington remembered. But, she added, "every once in a while, one fish would flit off and go look and see what else was in the stream."

When the semester started in late September 1960, it seems reasonable to imagine that Ann was still in a certain amount of emotional turmoil. At an age at which her friends were heading out into the world, she had been steered by her parents, over her objections, to an island several thousand miles out in the Pacific. She was enrolled in a commuter school where students had few options but to live at home. Torn from the first group of close friends she had ever made, she was alone again and an outsider. "Gramps's relationship with my mother was already strained by the time they reached Hawaii," Obama writes, attributing the strain to "his instability and often-violent temper" and her shame at his "hamfisted manners." Charles Payne remembered that Madelyn stayed behind for a time on Mercer Island, to close things out, as he put it. "What was the relationship of Ann and Stanley in that period, without Madelyn to mediate, I don't know," he said.

Shortly after the start of the semester, Ann encountered the first African student to enroll at the University of Hawai'i, Barack Hussein Obama. "We often say that Mom met her husbands at the East-West Center," Maya once said, while conceding that it was not strictly true. Obama was not on an East-West Center grant, and the center had not yet been built. But the family myth contained a kind of truth: Wherever Ann and Obama met, it was in a moment suffused with the spirit in which the center was born. One friend said he remembered Ann saying she had met Obama in the university library. According to the younger Obama, they met in a Russian language class; when they made a plan to meet later in front of the university library, the elder Obama arrived an hour late and found Ann asleep on a bench. Then the man from Kenya awakened the girl from Kansas, literally and figuratively. Renske Heringa, a Dutch anthropologist and friend of Ann's in the early 1980s, said Ann told her that the meeting on the bench was her first encounter with Obama. "She remembered it as a very romantic and beautiful thing," Heringa said. "She was completely not out to 'do the right thing' or behave the way people expected." To Heringa, the story illustrated a quintessential quality of Ann's—a willingness to "just be herself in the world. This whole story about her meeting Barack Senior shows enormous trust—to just leave yourself open to the world when you're sleeping."

Obama, charismatic and sharp, had arrived at the University of Hawai'i one month after the declaration of statehood. He had been flown to the United States with eighty other young Kenyans by Tom Mboya, a Kenyan nationalist who had raised money from Americans to educate a new generation of leaders in anticipation of Kenyan independence. He had attended British schools in Kenya, he told a reporter from the student newspaper shortly after he arrived in Hawaii. Then he had taken British correspondence courses while working for two years as a clerk in Nairobi. He had received "invitations to campus" from the University of Hawai'i,

San Francisco State College in California, and Morgan State College in Baltimore, the article in the student newspaper said. But he had read about Hawaii in *The Saturday Evening Post* and was attracted by the climate, the allure of the islands, and the state's reputation for racial tolerance. He enrolled as an undergraduate in the College of Business Administration and moved into Charles H. Atherton House, a YMCA branch near the campus used to house students. To his surprise, he discovered that Honolulu was not "the skyscraper metropolis of the Pacific" and Hawaiians were not "all dressed in native clothing" and engaged in native dancing. The cost of living was three times as high as he had expected. In an interview in the *Honolulu Star-Bulletin,* he said his money would last only two semesters, after which he would have to find a scholarship or a part-time job. The Americans he encountered evidently had their own misconceptions. Kenya was not a "teeming tropical jungle," Obama informed one reporter. Topographically, it was more like the Great Plains. He delivered a short lecture on the country's natural history, economy, and politics. "Many people have asked me, 'Are the people of Kenya ready for self-government?'" he was quoted as saying. "And to these people I say, 'Nobody is competent enough to judge whether a country is fit to rule itself or not.' If the people cannot rule themselves, let them misrule themselves. They should be provided with the opportunity."

Obama impressed men as well as women. "The tall, well built African," as the student reporter described him, had a powerful presence. Even amid the racial and ethnic diversity of Hawaii, his coloring stood out. Pake Zane, who became a friend of Obama's at the university and later visited him in Kenya, knew Tongans, Fijians, and Samoans whom he thought of as dark, but he had never seen skin as black as Obama's. Charming, sociable, and loquacious, Obama talked politics and drank beer with a group of graduate students and intellectuals of vaguely bohemian leanings, who included Pake Zane; Chet Gorman, later known for his work as an archaeologist at Ban Chiang and Spirit Cave in Thailand; and Neil Abercrombie, who went on to represent Hawaii's First District in Congress for ten terms before being elected governor in November 2010. Obama was ambitious and opinionated, and some said he was brilliant. "He was one of the brightest Kenyans I dealt with," said Richard Hook, who worked with Obama years later in Kenya. "He had a very quick mind—a good numerical mind." He had the kind of personality that commanded attention. When he spoke, people listened. He was one of a few hundred students whose names appeared on the dean's list published in the campus newspaper, and, when he left, he was described as "a straight-A student." Bill Collier, who, like Obama, was studying economics, noticed that their economic-development professor fell uncharacteristically silent and respectful when Obama spoke in class. To Americans, his accent suggested Oxbridge, and his booming baritone brought to mind Paul Robeson. His voice was seductive, almost hypnotic. "He had the most charismatic voice and accent I've ever heard in my life," Pake Zane said. "The most mellow, deep voice with slightly African articulation and maybe a flavor of Oxford. No matter what you were doing in the room, if you heard this voice, you would turn around." It was, Hook said, Obama's "instrument of choice."

Not everyone was charmed. Some found Obama arrogant, egotistical, and overbearing. Mark Wimbush, born and reared in Kenya with a Scottish mother and an English father, arrived at the University of Hawai'i the same month as Ann Dunham, after getting an undergraduate degree from Oxford. He and Obama became acquaintances, if not quite friends. "We were the ugly colonialists," he told me, referring to the attitude of some black Kenyans toward white Kenyans like him. "Part of the tension between Barack and me might have been that fact." They both followed the news from Kenya enthusiastically. Independence was coming, the country was preparing for transition, and Obama kept Wimbush filled in. "I'm sure he envisioned being a big shot in the Kenyan government," Wimbush said. "That's probably why he was studying politics and economics—in preparation for taking a cabinet position." Wimbush found him "almost a domineering man. He was certainly not a wallflower in any way. He was an impressive person, but it wasn't always a favorable impression." In political discussions, they were often on opposite sides. "He would tend to put forward his views and not spend any time listening to anybody else's, because he didn't think they were worth listening to, unless they agreed with his," Wimbush said. Judy Ware, a family friend of the Dunhams who recalled meeting Obama with Ann sometime later in Port Angeles, Washington, said, "I remember that he was very outgoing and friendly, and that he was flirtatious, and that made me uncomfortable. He was just a little bit intimidating to me. He was too close in my personal space." She added, "I thought he was a little bit almost aggressive in his way of meeting and being around women."

Obama was twenty-four years old and Ann was seventeen when they met in the fall of 1960. Though he apparently omitted to mention it initially, Obama was a married man, with a wife and child in Kenya and a second child on the way. Ann had never had a boyfriend, as far as her closest friends knew. She was "a young virgin" when she and Obama met, according to Kadi Warner, a graduate-school friend to whom Ann told the story some years later. "She was totally enthralled by him," Warner said. "Every time she described him, she talked about his brilliance." He was older, more worldly, a well-known figure on campus. He was striking and exotic. Ann, transplanted to a campus where three out of every four students were from Hawaii, was in some ways more of an outsider and more off balance than he. He courted her, and she was attracted to him. Whether she had access to birth control is not known, but it is not likely to have been easy. And as Warner put it, "I doubt he was the sort of man who would have carried a condom in his wallet."

In *Dreams from My Father,* written when the younger Obama was in his early thirties, he pieces together a version of his parents' story from fragments he was told as a child. At the same time, he describes many of the stories he was told about his father as "compact, apocryphal," and allows for the likelihood that important details were intentionally or unintentionally missing. "Even in the abridged version that my mother and grandparents offered, there were many things I didn't understand," he writes. He gives his account of his parents' fleeting coming together and breaking apart in language and cadences reminiscent of those of folktales or myths. His father "worked with unsurpassed concentration," and "his friends were legion," as the younger Obama tells it. In a Russian language course, "he met an awkward, shy American girl, only eighteen, and they fell in love." Her parents were won over "by his charm and intellect." He married the girl, "and she bore them a son, to whom he bequeathed his name." He won a scholarship to do graduate work at Harvard, without money to take his family with him, Obama writes. The couple separated, and "he returned to Africa to fulfill his promise to the continent. The mother and child stayed behind, but the bond of love survived the distances...." Though Obama was writing at a time when his mother and grandmother were alive and well, and available for consultation, he offers little in the way of an alternative version. It appears that parts of the account he was told were wrong.

Whatever happened happened fast. Classes began on September 26, two months before Ann's eighteenth birthday. By early November, she was pregnant. She dropped out of school when the semester ended and married that winter so discreetly, reportedly on the island of Maui, that her son never unearthed a single trace of the event. "There's no record of a real wedding, a cake, a ring, a giving away of the bride," he writes. "No families were in attendance; it's not even clear that people back in Kansas were fully informed. Just a small civil ceremony, a justice of the peace. The whole thing seems so fragile in retrospect, so haphazard. And perhaps that's how my grandparents intended it to be, a trial that would pass, just a matter of time, so long as they maintained a stiff upper lip and didn't do anything drastic."

If so, they got their wish.

On August 4, 1961, at 7:24 p.m., at Kapiʻolani Maternity and Gynecological Hospital in Honolulu, Ann gave birth to Barack Hussein Obama Jr. Eleven months later, the elder Obama was gone. In June 1962, he received his undergraduate degree from the University of Hawaiʻi and left for the East Coast. According to an article in the *Honolulu Star-Bulletin,* he left in late June "for a tour of Mainland universities before entering Harvard in the fall." The article, four paragraphs long, said he had been awarded a graduate faculty fellowship in economics and planned to return later to Africa to work in economic-development and international-trade planning and policy. In *Dreams from My Father,* Obama recalls coming upon that article, along with his birth certificate and vaccination forms, while he was in high school. "No mention is made of my mother or me, and I'm left to wonder whether the omission was intentional on my father's part, in anticipation of his long departure," he writes. "Perhaps the reporter failed to ask personal questions, intimidated by my father's imperious manner; or perhaps it was an editorial decision, not part of the simple story that they were looking for. I wonder, too, whether the omission caused a fight between my parents."

Whatever fight there was may have happened earlier. Ann, it seems, left Hawaii well before Obama. Her friend Maxine Box, from Mercer Island, recalled seeing her in Seattle late in the summer of 1961—happy and proud of her baby, who was with her, but saying nothing about marriage, at least that Box could remember. In the spring quarter of 1962, as Obama was embarking on his final semester in Hawaii, Ann was enrolled at the University of Washington in Seattle, according to Bob Roseth, director of news and information for the university. Her high school friend John Hunt saw her once that spring with her baby, and Bill Byers remembered having dinner with her once in an apartment where she was living. She looked different: She had lost weight and grown her hair long, said Linda Hall Wylie, another high school classmate, who remembered running into her fleetingly on University Way. Her sudden motherhood startled her friends, and not simply because the father of her baby was black. She had had no serious boyfriend in high school that they knew of, and she had never shown any interest in babysitting, a growth industry for teenagers on Mercer Island. Precipitous marriage and maternity seemed to be the fate mostly of girls who had "gotten in trouble." Few would have expected Stanley to hew to the standard female trajectory—from college and sorority life to a short stint in teaching or nursing, followed by departure from the workforce in order to marry and raise children. No one would have imagined this. Sometime after that spring quarter, Ann apparently gave up trying to make a go of it alone in Seattle. She returned to Honolulu, after which she may have seen only one friend from Mercer Island ever again. Her life had taken a hairpin turn, and there was no turning back. A yawning gulf had opened between her and her old friends. "The rest of us were leading the sorority/going on dates/going to the football games/totally different life," Wylie said. "When you go away and your life changes so dramatically, no one else can understand it."

The news of Ann's pregnancy, sudden marriage, and separation was closely held within the extended Dunham and Payne families—not unlike the news of Madelyn and Stanley's elopement twenty years earlier. Ralph Dunham, Ann's uncle, told me that he heard nothing about her pregnancy and marriage until after Barack was born. "They might have been worried about family reaction," he said. "It would have upset my grandmother and my aunt, I think." (He remembered once mentioning to his grandmother, who had raised him and Ann's father, that he had invited an African-American friend, who was a university professor, to his house for dinner. To which, he said, she replied, "You mean to say, you actually sat down and ate a meal with a black person?") Madelyn's brother Charles learned of Ann's marriage before he learned of her pregnancy, which he said he was told of only after she gave birth. When I asked him about his parents' reaction to the news, he said, "They tended to be closed about things. If they were unhappy, I wouldn't expect them to voice anything. Just keep quiet. I heard nothing." Jon Payne, Madelyn's youngest brother, who had spent six months on the Dunhams' living room couch on Mercer Island three years earlier, said he heard the news a full three or four years late. He was back in Kansas on a visit, throwing darts in his parents' garage, when his brother happened to mention "Ann's son."

"What do you mean, 'Ann's son'?" Jon asked.

"Yeah," he remembered Charles saying. "Didn't you know Ann had a baby?"

"No."

"You probably haven't heard it from our parents, have you? He's black."

"Oh, really?"

"Yeah. Somebody she met at the university."

Only Arlene Payne remembered receiving a call from Madelyn. It may have come after the wedding. When I asked her how Madelyn seemed to be feeling about what had happened, Arlene said drily, "A little distraught."

Distraught because Ann was seventeen years old? I asked. Or because she knew that motherhood might derail Ann's education? Or because Ann's new husband was black? Or because he was African, with plans to return home?

"I think that's probably quite enough."

Madelyn and Stanley's views about race were not extreme. In *Dreams from My Father,* Obama says they had given little thought to black people until they were living in Texas when Stanley Ann was eleven or twelve. There, fellow furniture salesmen advised Stanley early on that "the coloreds" should be permitted to inspect the merchandise in the store only after hours and that they would have to arrange for their own delivery. At the bank where Madelyn worked, a white secretary reprimanded her hotly for speaking respectfully to a black janitor she had befriended. Stanley Ann, too, had encountered race hatred for the first time, according to Obama. Madelyn found her and an African-American girl cowering in terror on the ground in the yard of the Dunhams' house, where they had been reading, while a group of white children taunted them. When Stanley reported the incident to the school principal and some of the children's parents, according to Obama's account, he was told, "White girls don't play with coloreds in this town."

Stanley would maintain later that the family left Texas in part because of their discomfort with that kind of racism, Obama writes, though Madelyn said they left because Stanley was not doing well at work and had a better opportunity in Seattle. Obama writes that he cannot dismiss his grandfather's account as "a convenient bit of puffery, another act of white revisionism." After Texas, he says of Stanley, "the condition of the black race, their pain, their wounds, would in his mind become merged with his own: the absent father and the hint of scandal, a mother who had gone away, the cruelty of other children, the realization that he was no fair-haired boy— that he looked like a 'wop.'" In Stanley's mind, racism was mixed in with the attitudes responsible for much of the unhappiness of his early life, "part of convention and respectability and status, the smirks and the whispers and gossip that had kept him on the out-side looking in."

Perhaps for those reasons, the reaction of Stanley and Madelyn to the African man Ann brought home was less hostile than stereo-types about the period and the place they came from might suggest. In his book, the younger Obama only imagines their reaction, pre-ferring constructions like "would have" and "might have." What-ever he knows for a fact, he does not say. "The poor kid's probably lonely, Gramps would have thought, so far from home," Obama writes. "Better take a look at him, Toot would have said to herself." He imagines Stanley being struck by the dinner guest's resem-blance to Nat King Cole, and Madelyn holding her tongue when she glimpses Ann reaching over to squeeze Obama's hand. The younger Obama suggests, too, the conversation his grandparents might have had later, how they would have marveled at the man's intelligence and dignified bearing—"and how about that accent!"

Madelyn and Stanley were, it seems, somewhat awed by Obama. Arlene Payne, who would spend time with the three of them over Christmas in Honolulu some years later, said, "I had the sense then, as I had had earlier, that both Madelyn and Stanley were impressed with him in some way. They were very respectful to him and all this, but they liked to listen to what he had to say." They seemed to have felt that way about him earlier, too. "I was there when he was there, and I felt that they really accepted him," she said. On the other hand, David Mendell, who interviewed Madelyn for his 2007 biography, *Obama: From Promise to Power,* found her at that time skeptical of the elder Obama. "I am a little dubious of the things that people from foreign countries tell me," Mendell quoted her as saying.

It is not known what options other than marriage Ann might have considered once she learned she was pregnant. Abortion was illegal but not impossible, especially for people with connections in the medical community. Had they wanted it, the Dunhams might conceivably have had access to that world. Thomas Farner, whose parents were bridge partners of the Dunhams on Mercer Island, said his parents sent his sister, Jackie, a high school classmate of Stanley Ann's who died in 2007, to Honolulu to stay with the Dunhams not long after she and Stanley Ann graduated from high school. The reason for the trip, Farner said, was to enable his sister to have an abortion. Their father, a physician, must have arranged it, Farner said. The Farners' older sister, Judy Ware, who was not living at home at that time, told me she believed her brother's account was accurate. Ann's graduate-school friend, Kadi Warner, recalling conversations she had with Ann many years later, said Ann married Obama because she was pregnant. "She was a nice, middle-class girl," Warner said. "And she loved him." The decision appears not to have been forced on her by her parents. In *Dreams from My Father,* Obama writes that Ann told him, in his early twenties, that his grandparents "'weren't happy with the idea. But they said okay—they probably couldn't have stopped us anyway, and they eventually came around to the idea that it was the right thing to do.'" When I asked Arlene about the decision, she said, "I think you have to understand that Ann was an independent soul, and she would make her own decisions about this kind of thing. What Madelyn wanted, I don't really know. I think that it was Ann's decision, and I think Madelyn thought she would have to let her do what she wanted."

Madelyn, after all, had done what she wanted at Ann's age.

It was Obama's father in Kenya who vociferously opposed the marriage, according to the younger Obama's telling. He wrote to Stanley Dunham, saying "he didn't want the Obama blood sullied by a white woman," as Obama quotes Ann as having told him. "And then there was a problem with your father's first wife. . . . He had told me they were separated, but it was a village wedding, so there was no legal document that could show a divorce." Nevertheless, they intended to return to Kenya when the elder Obama finished his studies, the younger Obama writes. "But your grandfather Hussein was still writing to your father, threatening to have his student visa revoked," he quotes his mother as saying. "By this time Toot had become hysterical—she had read about the Mau-Mau rebellion in Kenya a few years earlier, which the Western press really played up—and she was sure that I would have my head chopped off and you would be taken away."

Things changed abruptly. Obama, a member of the Luo ethnic group, was from a culture that traditionally allowed for polygamous marriages. He had not only a pregnant wife but a child back home. "The way the story was put to me, she found out he had this family in Africa, so she divorced him because of bigamy," Arlene Payne said. "What all else was involved, I have no idea." According to Warner, Ann "realized very early on that she was in over her head with this guy." Warner said, "His attitude changed when she got married. She became his wife, and he became very critical." One evening, Warner remembered Ann telling her, Ann had cooked dinner for Obama. She put the food on a plate and put the plate in front of him at the table. "You expect me to eat this?" he barked. Then he grabbed the plate of food and hurled it against the wall.

"She said then she knew," Warner said.

By the spring of 1963, Ann had returned to Honolulu from Seattle and had reenrolled as an undergraduate at the University of Hawai'i. She was twenty years old, a single mother of a biracial child, living with her parents. Stanley and Madelyn had bounced through four addresses in their first four years in Honolulu, settling, after Ann's return, in a low-slung bungalow-style house on University Avenue a short walk from campus. Stanley, listed in the Honolulu city directory until 1968 as manager of a business called Pratt Furniture, had acquired an interest in a chain of furniture stores, according to his brother, Ralph. Madelyn, who Arlene Payne said had gone to night school in Washington in order to get ahead in banking, had begun her uphill climb from loan interviewer to vice president at the Bank of Hawaii. Within a decade, she would be one of the bank's first female vice presidents and the formidable "grande dame of escrow," as a younger colleague would remember her when her grandson made her famous decades later. Maxine Box, Ann's friend from Mercer Island whose parents would visit the Dunhams in Honolulu several years later, said, "I pat her mom and dad on the back. The turmoil in that family must have been incredible."

Whatever turmoil there had been, Madelyn and Stanley made their peace with Ann's choices, and they embraced new parental and grandparental roles. "All I know is from at least the day Barack was born, there was total acceptance," Charles Payne said. "He was their baby, and they loved him from day one." Stanley, having seen little of his own father after the age of eight, cannot have forgotten how it felt to be fatherless. He must have also remembered the

Stanley and Barack

haven he and his brother had found in their grandparents' multi-generational home. Madelyn, having been pregnant herself at nine-teen, may have found it easier than some mothers would have to see her daughter as a new mother at roughly the same age. Made-lyn, who was only thirty-eight when her grandson was born, "wasn't particularly grandmotherly, mind you," Maya Soetoro-Ng told me. So she adopted the name Tutu, an affectionate term used in Hawaii for grandmother—more palatable than, say, Granny. Over time, Tutu evolved into Toot. Just as her mother had taken in Madelyn and her infant daughter while Stanley was in the Army, Madelyn and Stanley now took in Ann and her son. And just as Leona Payne had made it possible for Madelyn to work at Boeing, Madelyn and Stanley made it possible for Ann to return to school. Madelyn had no intention of letting Ann's changed circumstances derail her education.

"You have to understand that Ann's mother very much regret-ted her choices," Arlene Payne told me. "She would never have let Ann go that way. She had ambitions. She wanted to get on in the world. She realized what a mistake she had made in not going to college. She expressed that to me a number of times, so I think she would never have allowed Ann to not go to college."

They were opposites in many ways, Madelyn and Ann. In temperament, Ann took after her father, Maya said. They were "people of appetites"—not content with small portions or small vistas, not willing "to walk in the same circle." They were gregari-ous and loquacious. They loved food, words, stories, books, objects, conversation. Madelyn, by contrast, was practical and down to earth. "My mother's favorite color is beige," Ann would joke to colleagues years later. Madelyn was sensible and unsentimental—not a "softie," the term Maya applied to Ann. Maya described her grandmother's dictum as: Buckle down, don't complain, don't air your dirty laundry in public, don't be so restless. "Work hard, care for your family, raise your kids right, and provide for them," Maya added. "Make sure they have better lives than you. And that's about it." Madelyn pushed boundaries in her professional life, but she did it by following the rules. "It wasn't that she was doing it differently, necessarily," Maya said. "She was very much one of the boys in the bank. She wore high heels and women's suits, and she was very ladylike, but she was very aware of bank decorum and the rules of engagement. She just, I think, was incredibly smart and worked really hard. She did whatever was necessary."

By way of illustration of the differences between her mother and her grandmother, Maya imagined the way they might comport themselves on the same hypothetical path. Ann would pause to pick berries and seeds, study them curiously, find another path, veer off, stop, climb a tree, listen to the bamboo whistling in the wind. Madelyn would start at the beginning, march forward, sure-footed, chest up, head up, until she reached the end.

Did Madelyn counsel Ann to be more prudent? I asked.

"Probably with both of her marriages," Maya said.

"Mom said that Tutu worried about her and wished that she could take the easier path," Maya continued. "What was meant by that was obviously that here was someone from a different country, who had different cultural expectations, of a different race—in a country that had miscegenation laws in place. This was not the easy path, this was not the direct path. I think Tutu, according to Mom, expressed some concern. It was given more in a sigh than a scream. It was just sort of like, 'What are we going to do?'" She added, "Tutu wished she would be more sensible and get a house and learn to drive and sit still."

If Ann had a plan, it did not involve sitting still.

She was an unusual figure on campus. Jeanette Chikamoto

Takamura was a sophomore when she met Ann during the 1966 academic year. Ann was working part-time as a student secretary in the office of the student government organization; Takamura, active in student government, hung out in the office between classes. Ann struck Takamura as a "natural intellectual," with an outlook and orientation that was unusually global. She dressed in dashikis, kept African artifacts on her desk, and gravitated in conversation toward international topics. There was something enigmatic about her, Takamura found. She left an impression of detachment, perhaps because she seemed always to be thinking, as though her mind were operating on multiple planes. Takamura met Ann's small, curly-haired son, Barry, whose father, Ann told her, had returned to Africa. The marriage, Ann said simply, had not worked out. On one occasion, Ann stunned Takamura by confiding to her that she wanted to send Barry to Punahou Academy, seen by many as the top prep school in Hawaii. "I'm thinking, 'How in the world is she going to afford this?'" Takamura told me. "I remember thinking, 'Do not say anything discouraging.' So I said, 'You know, Ann? I think you'll find a way.'"

Several years earlier, late in 1963 or early 1964, Ann had shown up at "Indonesian Night" at the East-West Center in a borrowed sarong and *kebaya,* the long-sleeved, often cotton or silk blouse worn by Indonesian women. At her side was a twenty-seven-year-old Javanese graduate student named Lolo Soetoro, who had arrived at the university in 1962 in the second wave of Indonesian students on East-West Center grants. Ann and Lolo may have met at the tennis courts on campus; at least, that is how the story goes. "He was quite a tennis player," Maya said. "She used to comment that she liked the way he looked in his white tennis shorts." He was good-looking, amiable, easygoing, patient, and funny. He liked sports and he liked a good laugh. Benji Bennington, who was in

Lolo's year at the university and went to work at the East-West
Center the month he arrived, said, "He wanted to meet people all
the time. He wasn't shy about using his English. He had a good
sense of humor, and he loved to party. Yeah, he loved to party."

Another Indonesian student, Sylvia Engelen, and a German
student she later married, Gerald Krausse, brought a camera to

*With Lolo and Sylvia Engelen, "Indonesian
Night" at the East-West Center*

"Indonesian Night" that year. In the fall of 2008, the Krausses
opened a well-worn photo album on a coffee table in a living room
in Rhode Island, where they had settled. The album was filled with
fading snapshots taken in Hawaii and at the university in the early
1960s. There was Sylvia, in a green Balinese costume, and Lolo

Soetoro, in a batik shirt and gray trousers. Beside him stood Ann, in her borrowed outfit, her head tilted uncharacteristically and rather demurely downward. "We met her through Lolo," Sylvia Krausse said, sounding amazed even then by the memory. "When he brought her to 'Indonesian Night.'"

Like some Javanese, Lolo had been given one name, Soetoro, at birth. Like the names of his nine siblings—Soegijo, Soegito, Soemitro, Soewarti, Soewardinah, and so on—his began with the *soe-*prefix, meaning "good" or "fortunate," or some combination of

Lolo and Stanley, Hawaii

both. Born in Bandung in 1936 and raised in Yogyakarta, he was the youngest of the ten. "Everybody loved him, maybe because he was the youngest boy," one of his nieces, Kismardhani S-Roni, told me. His childhood nickname, Lolo, came from the Javanese word *mlolo,* a verb meaning "to gaze wide-eyed." All the boys and several of the girls in the family went to college, according to Lolo's nephew, Wisaksono "Sonny" Trisulo. From there, they moved into jobs in fields such as the law, the oil industry, and higher education.

Lolo studied geography at Gadjah Mada University, the most respected university in Yogyakarta. He became a lieutenant in the
Indonesian army, according to Bill Collier, who knew him at the
University of Hawai'i and later in Indonesia. With the support of
the Indonesian government, he became the first member of his
family to study outside of the country. In the fall of 1962, he was
sent to the University of Hawai'i on a two-year East-West Center
grant to get a master's degree in geography. In return for which,
Sonny Trisulo said, Lolo was expected to devote four years to government service on his return.

Lolo was in many ways the opposite of Barack Obama Sr. He
lacked Obama's intimidating intensity, his ambitions, the force of
his intellect. He was kind and considerate. By temperament, and
by culture, he was not inclined to argue. He was calm. All of that
was part of his appeal to Ann, whose gale-force encounter with
Obama had shaken her up. "It was kind of a reaction to her first
husband, who was exciting, but he wasn't exactly a family man,"
said Kay Ikranagara, who would become a close friend of Ann's in
Jakarta in the 1970s. "Lolo was stable, would work, support the
family. She thought that was really appealing." If Lolo had a tendency to open the newspaper straight to the sports pages and stop
there, Ann did not mind that, for a time. He was from a part of the
world that was increasingly interesting to her. He was hoping to
return to Indonesia, which had emerged from three hundred fifty
years of Dutch domination, to teach at the university and become
a part of his country's future. "That was part of what had drawn
her to Lolo after Barack had left," the younger Obama would
write, "the promise of something new and important, helping her
husband rebuild a country in a charged and challenging place beyond her parents' reach."

Whether Ann was looking forward to a lifetime in Indonesia or simply reaching for an escape hatch is difficult to know.

Intermarriage was not unusual among East-West Center students. Gerald Krausse, who had been working as a busboy in Waikiki, had got tired of food service and enrolled as an undergraduate at the university. "I was mesmerized by all these foreign students," he told me. "I wanted to be part of it." He got a job as a grill cook in the East-West Center cafeteria and as a guard in the center's men's dorm, where students would descend from their rooms in pajamas at two a.m. during the Muslim fasting period and start cooking in order to finish eating by dawn. Krausse became interested in Asia. Soon he met Sylvia Engelen, an Indonesian from Manado who had arrived in February 1961 on an East-West Center grant and was studying German and French. When they married in Hawaii in 1966, sixty students turned out for their wedding. There was just one family member—Sylvia's sister, also on an East-West Center grant. The cake, created by Gerald, a trained pastry chef, captured the Hawaii and East-West Center zeitgeist. It was crowned with a globe made of royal icing with two butterflies on top.

From time to time, the East-West Center made an effort to keep track of the marriage patterns of single students on East-West grants. *Impulse,* a magazine published by and for center students, reported in 1975 that students who married after coming to the center had at least a thirty-three percent chance of marrying across national or ethnic lines. "When you put young people in their twenties and thirties together, guess what?" as Sylvia Krausse put it. Were those marriages strong? No, she answered, without hesitation. For years, she and her husband encountered East-West Center alumni at Asian-studies conferences. In some cases, she said, one member of a couple would have had to make his or her career secondary to that of the other—or give it up. In addition, she said, Asian men who had felt free to be "very flamboyant and open" in the United States returned home to cultural expectations, family obligations, and the influence of parents and relatives. "I think the girls didn't understand, when they went back," she said. "Especially the American girls."

On the night of September 30, 1965, six Indonesian army generals and one lieutenant were kidnapped and killed in Jakarta in what the army quickly characterized as an attempted coup planned by the Communist Party. Though immediately quashed, the incident unleashed a bloodbath. Hundreds of thousands of Communist Party members and suspected sympathizers were slaughtered in the following months, often by civilian vigilantes with the support of the army. As Adam Schwarz described the events in *A Nation in Waiting,* people were killed by knife and bayonet, their bodies often "maimed and decapitated and dumped in rivers. At one point officials in Surabaya in East Java complained to Army officials that the rivers running into Surabaya were choked with bodies." The Central Intelligence Agency described the massacres as "one of the worst mass murders of the twentieth century, along with the Soviet purges of the 1930s, the Nazi mass murders during the Second World War, and the Maoist bloodbath of the early 1950s."

On the serene campus of the University of Hawai'i, Indonesian students were summoned to be questioned by people whom Sylvia Krausse remembered as visiting representatives of the Indonesian government. A fellow student warned her to show up "or something will happen to your parents." There were written questions followed by questioning in person. "We were there all day," she said. "They were looking for Chinese and communist connections."

Like many students studying outside the country in that period, Lolo was called back to Indonesia. He and Ann had married on March 5, 1964, shortly after she divorced Obama. Lolo had received his master's degree in geography three months later, but Ann, an anthropology major, would not receive her undergraduate degree until 1967. Andrew P. Vayda, a professor of anthropology and ecology who was visiting the University of Hawai'i in that period, remembered meeting Lolo for the first time at the university in the spring of 1966, then visiting him on a trip to Jakarta late that summer. The two of them traveled together to Bandung, once a Dutch colonial garrison in the northern foothills of the Bandung Plateau, surrounded by volcanic peaks, hot springs, and tea plantations. The inflation rate was seven hundred percent, and the country felt on edge. On one leg of the trip, they encountered tanks rumbling down the main road. "He and all the Indonesians, you could see the fear on their faces—that something was going to happen," Vayda remembered. Throughout the trip, Lolo made a point of trying the spiciest and most exotic foods and the most decrepit toilets. "How do you think Ann would react to that?" Lolo would ask.

"That was the first I had heard of Ann," Vayda remembered. "He said he was going to bring her there."

Four

Initiation in Java

The luncheon invitation was delivered by bicycle one morning in early 1971. Elizabeth Bryant, an American in her early thirties, was living in a converted rice storage facility in the city of Yogyakarta in Central Java. Her husband, Nevin, was doing research in Indonesia on an East-West Center grant. Like pretty much everyone in Indonesia in those years, they had no running water, no plumbing, no telephone service. To brush their teeth, they pumped water from a well, boiled it on a single kerosene burner, and spat it off the front porch. Their three servants, living in what had been the guardhouse, had fenced a five-foot pit in the yard for use as their toilet. Bushes served as a clothesline for the Bryant baby's diapers. Life may not have been easy, but it was good. The Bryants' house was next to the *kraton,* the walled compound surrounding the palace of the sultans of Yogyakarta, the lively center of traditional Javanese arts and culture. In the evening, the aqueous sounds of the gamelan practice drifted out of the compound; neighbors dropped by to lure the Bryants out to an all-night shadow-puppet performance based on tales derived from the Hindu epic the *Mahabharata*. On this particular morning, the invitation to Elizabeth Bryant came by messenger from an older American woman in Yogyakarta whose husband was working for the U.S. Agency for International Development. The Jakarta office had asked her to extend her hospitality to a young American and her nine-year-old son, visiting from their home in Jakarta. Could Mrs. Bryant join them for lunch? the older woman wanted to know. The guest of honor was showing her son around Java before sending him back to Hawaii for school. He was half Kenyan and born in Hawaii, Bryant recalled her hostess telling her in advance. Bryant knew enough about Hawaii to know that a half-African child would have been a rarity. Are you sure? she asked.

It was a memorable lunch—one that Bryant was able to describe in detail when I reached her in Southern California thirty-eight years later. Ann Soetoro arrived at the house with the young Barack Obama. She was dressed in a long skirt made of Indonesian fabric—not the sort of sundress that Mrs. Bryant had noticed that other American women in Indonesia seemed to favor. She instructed Barry to shake hands, then to sit on the sofa and turn his attention to an English-language workbook she had brought along. She was sending him back to Hawaii for an English-language education, Bryant remembered her saying. She was also deciding whether to go back herself. "She said, 'What would you do?'" Bryant told me. "I said, 'I could live here as long as two years, then would go back to Hawaii.' She said, 'Why?' I said it was hard living, it took a toll on your body, there were no doctors, it was not healthy. She didn't agree with me." Ann had left her infant daughter, Maya, in Jakarta with a servant—a choice that startled Bryant, unaccustomed as she was to Indonesian child-rearing. She wondered, too, why Ann, with an Indonesian husband, would consider moving to the United States. Over lunch, Barry sat at the dining table and listened intently but did not speak. When he asked to be excused, Ann directed him to ask the hostess for permission. Permission granted, he got down on the floor and played with Bryant's son, who was thirteen months old. After lunch, the group took a walk near Gadjah Mada University, with Barry running ahead. A flock of Indonesian children began lobbing rocks in his direction, ducking behind a wall and shouting racial epithets. He seemed unfazed, dancing around as though playing dodgeball "with unseen players," Bryant remembered. Ann did not seem visibly to react. Assuming she must not have understood the words, Bryant offered to intervene. "No, he's okay," she remembered Ann saying. "He's used to it."

"I'll tell you what both of us felt," Bryant told me. "We were floored that she'd bring a half-black child to Indonesia, knowing the disrespect they have for blacks. It was unusually bad. I remember thinking, 'Oh, they're more racist than the U.S., by far.'" At the same time, she admired Ann for teaching her boy to be fearless. A child in Indonesia needed to be raised that way—for self-preservation, Bryant decided. Ann also seemed to be teaching Barry respect. He had all the politeness that Indonesian children displayed toward their parents. He seemed to be learning Indonesian ways.

"I think this is one reason he's so *halus*," Bryant said of the president, using the Indonesian adjective that means "polite, refined, or courteous," referring to qualities some see as distinctively Javanese. "It's because of his Indonesian background. I think he's a mixture of cultures, and that makes him more worldly. He has the manners of Asians and the ways of Americans—being *halus,* being patient, calm, a good listener. If you're not a good listener in Indonesia, you'd better leave."

Indonesia was still in a state of shock when Ann arrived in 1967 for the first of three extended periods of residence that would eventually add up to the majority of her adult life. After centuries of domination by the Dutch, followed by Japanese occupation and a four-year revolution, the 17,500 islands that make up what is now Indonesia had become an independent nation in 1949. By the early 1960s, inflation was soaring, foreign investment had stagnated, and poverty was widespread. People waited in long lines to buy basics, such as kerosene and rice. The Communist Party had grown into the third largest in the world. In 1963, Indonesia's first president, Sukarno, suspended elections. The following year, he declared "the year of *vivere pericoloso*," borrowing the Italian phrase for "living dangerously" from a speech by Mussolini. The details of the September 30, 1965, coup and counter-coup remain in dispute, as do the particulars of the slaughter that followed. There is disagreement over who planned the attack on the generals and for what purpose; and estimates of the number of communists, suspected communists, and others killed in the ensuing bloodbath range from 100,000 to more than a million. But it is known that neighbors turned on neighbors. According to Adrian Vickers, the author of *A History of Modern Indonesia*, militias went door-to-door in villages in Bali, abducting suspects, raping women, even targeting children. "The best way to prove you were not a Communist was to join in the killings," Vickers writes. The army became the dominant institution in the country. Soldiers were ubiquitous, armed with machine guns on buses and trains and in public buildings. Major-General Suharto, who took power when Sukarno was sidelined, exercised tight control over internal security and community life. Trials and imprisonments dragged on for years. Many Indonesians chose never to speak about what had happened. Bill Collier, who arrived in Indonesia in 1968 and spent fifteen years doing social and economic surveys in villages, told me that researchers would be told by people living near brackish waterways that they had been unable to eat the fish because of decaying corpses in the water. He recalled how a well-dressed stranger knocked on the door to his house in Bandung in 1968, at a time when many educated people even remotely suspected of communist ties had lost their jobs. The man's children were hungry, and he had no food in the house. Could Collier spare some rice? he wanted to know. Four decades later, slumped in a chair in the extravagantly appointed lobby of a hotel in Jakarta where we met, Collier recalled saying no—an act of such stupidity, he said, that the memory haunted him to that day. "I have wished a thousand times that I had given him all the rice in the house," he said.

The sixteen-million-man megalopolis of glass bank towers, shopping malls, and traffic-choked boulevards where I met Collier was nothing like the city that greeted twenty-five-year-old Ann Soetoro and her six-year-old son. Jakarta was a tapestry of villages—low-rise and sprawling—interwoven with forests, paddy fields, and marshland. Narrow alleys disappeared into warrens of tile-roofed houses in the rambling urban hamlets called *kampung*s. Central Jakarta had just one high-rise hotel—built with war reparations from the Japanese. A few neighborhoods, such as Menteng and Kebayoran Baru, were handsome and leafy, laid out meticulously by the Dutch. But squatter colonies lined the canals, which served as public baths, laundry facilities, and sewers, all in one. During the long rainy season from November through March, canals overflowed, saturating cardboard shanties and flooding much of the city. Cars, buses, and motorcycles were scarce. Denizens of the city traveled mostly on foot or by bicycle or bicycle-propelled rickshaws called *becak*s. Power outages were a fact of life. There were so few working phones that it was said that half the cars on the streets were ferrying messages from one office to the next. "Secretaries spent hours dialing and redialing phone numbers just to get through," said Halimah Brugger, an American hired in 1968 to teach music to the children of foreign oil company executives and missionaries at the Jakarta International School. Westerners were rare, black people even rarer. Western women got a lot of attention. "I remember creating quite a sensation just being pedaled down the street in a *becak,* wearing a short skirt," Brugger said. For adventurous travelers who washed up in Jakarta after hitchhiking across Java, there were no maps or guidebooks. The National Museum, stuffed with antiquities dating back to the ninth century, had languished for a decade. Letters from the United States took weeks to reach their destination. Foreigners endured all manner of gastrointestinal upsets. Deworming was de rigueur. In the open-air markets, where one shopped for food, bargaining was essential. "If you knew how to bargain, you could get a foreigner price down to a Chinese price," said Halimah Bellows, another American who lived in Jakarta in the early 1970s. "But you would never get an Indonesian price." Westerners needed to learn one cardinal virtue: patience.

But like Yogyakarta for Elizabeth Bryant, Jakarta had a magical charm. People who were children in the city in that period, including Obama, reminisce about the sound of the Muslim call to prayer in the days before public address systems, and the signature sounds called or rung out by street vendors wheeling their carts through the *kampung*s. Bureaucrats whiled away their days amid the faded splendor of Dutch colonial buildings. Tea was still served on the portico of the old Hotel des Indes. Ceiling fans turned languidly in the mid-afternoon heat, and kerosene lamps flickered in the houses lining the narrow alleys at night. For anyone of no interest to government security forces, life was simple. "Jakarta was very peaceful in those years," said Samardal Manan, who arrived in 1967 at age twenty-five, a young man from a traditional Muslim family in a village in West Sumatra. The cost of living was low, and the city felt friendly and safe. As an Indonesian with a college degree, he had little trouble finding a job; soon after that, he could afford a house. For a foreigner, it was possible to arrive in Indonesia largely ignorant of the horror of just two years before. "I was quite naive about the whole thing," said Halimah Brugger. "It was all over then. I never felt the slightest bit endangered." Indonesians welcomed Americans, she said. Within a week of arrival, she was paying the equivalent of a few dollars a week, plus rice and soap, for a maid who made her breakfast, ironed her clothes, and worked for her seven days a week. It was in some ways a wonderful place to raise children. Javanese families crave, love, and indulge children. They are a collective responsibility of not just parents but siblings, cousins, aunts, and uncles—the entire community. "It was like the whole world was taking care of the children," said Brugger, who raised three. By 1969, inflation was under control and the economy was improving. The government launched a series of five-year plans aimed at modernizing the country. Foreign investment resumed, and Indonesia was soon accepting more foreign aid than any country other than India. Years later, many would look back on the late 1960s and early 1970s as a honeymoon period, Vickers writes. Restrictions on the press eased, a youth culture flowered, literary and cultural life thrived. For a few years, Indonesia seemed to have emerged from darkness into a time of hope. It was, some later commented, Indonesia's Prague Spring.

The households in which Ann and Lolo lived in Jakarta in the late 1960s and early 1970s were neither grand nor impoverished by Indonesian standards. When Ann arrived in 1967, Lolo was in the army, fulfilling the commitment he had made to the government in return for being sent abroad to study. He had been sent to Irian Barat, the contested area that would later become Papua, Indonesia's twenty-sixth province. He served as a member of a team assigned to map the border. (A photograph taken in Merauke, a former Dutch military post and one of the easternmost towns in Indonesia, dated July 30, 1967, shows Lolo and nine other men in uniform arrayed along a fence line beneath a sign that reads

*Lolo (third from left) with the Indonesian border-survey team
in Merauke, Irian Barat, July 1967*

"Operasi Tjenderawasih II (Team Survey Perbatasan)," or "Operation Cenderawasih, Border Survey Team.") As long as he was in the military, Lolo's salary was low. On her first night in Indonesia, Ann complained later to a colleague, Lolo served her white rice and *dendeng celeng*—dried, jerked wild boar, which Indonesians hunted in the forests when food was scarce. ("I said, 'That's delicious! I love it, Ann,'" the colleague, Felina Pramono, remembered. "She said,

'It was moldy, Felina.'") Lolo's pay was so paltry, Ann later joked, it would not have covered the cost of cigarettes (which she did not smoke). But Lolo had a brother-in-law, Trisulo, who was a vice president for exploration and production at the Indonesian oil company Pertamina. When Lolo completed his military service, Trisulo, who was married to Lolo's sister, Soewardinah, used his contacts with foreign oil companies doing business in Indonesia, he told me, to help Lolo get a job in the Jakarta office of the Union Oil Company of California. By the early 1970s, Lolo and Ann had moved into a rented house in Matraman, a middle-class area of Central Jakarta near Menteng. The house was a *pavilyun,* an annex on the grounds of a bigger main house, according to a former houseboy named Saman who worked in those years for Lolo and Ann. It extended straight back from the street, perpendicular to the roadway, into a garden. It had three bedrooms, a kitchen, a bathroom, a library, and a terrace. Like the households of other Indonesians who could afford it, and of foreigners living in Indonesia, it had a sizable domestic staff. Two female servants shared a bedroom; two men—a cook and the houseboy—slept mostly on the floor of the house or outside in the garden, according to Saman. The staff freed Ann from domestic obligations to a degree that would have been almost impossible in the United States. There were people to clean the house, prepare meals, buy groceries, and look after her children—enabling her to work, pursue her interests, and come and go as she wanted. The domestic staff made it possible, too, for Ann and Lolo to cultivate their own professional and social circles, which did not necessarily overlap.

On August 15, 1970, shortly after Barry's ninth birthday and during what would turn out to be Madelyn Dunham's only visit to Indonesia, Ann gave birth to Maya at Saint Carolus Hospital, a Catholic hospital thought by Westerners at that time to be the best

Lolo and Maya, about 1971

in Jakarta. When Halimah Brugger gave birth in the same hospital two years later, she told me, the doctor delivered her baby without the luxury of a stethoscope, gloves, or gown. The doctor, a woman, was wearing a pink suit. "When the baby was born, the doctor asked my husband for his handkerchief," Brugger remembered. "Then she stuffed it in my mouth and gave me eleven stitches without any anesthesia."

Ann tried out three different names for her new daughter, all of them Sanskrit, before settling on Maya Kassandra. The name was important to Ann, Maya told me; she wanted "beautiful names." Stanley, it seems, was not on the list.

Ann had wasted no time finding a job—both to help support the family and to begin to figure out what she was going to do with her life. By January 1968, she had gone to work as assistant to the American director of Lembaga Indonesia-Amerika, a binational organization funded by the United States Information Service and housed at the U.S. Agency for International Development. Its mission, it said, was promoting cross-cultural friendship. Ann supervised a small group of Indonesians who taught English classes for Indonesian government employees and businessmen being sent by USAID to the United States for graduate studies, said Trusti Jarwadi, one of the teachers Ann supervised. Ann built a small library, stocked largely with textbooks on English grammar and writing, for use by the teachers and students. It would be an understatement to say she disliked the job. "I worked at the U.S. Embassy in Djakarta for 2 horrible years," she wrote bluntly, with no further details, in a letter in 1973 to her friend from Mercer Island, Bill Byers. As Obama describes the job in his memoir, "The Indonesian businessmen weren't much interested in the niceties of the English language, and several made passes at her. The Americans were mostly older men, careerists in the State Department, the occasional economist or journalist who would mysteriously disappear for months at a time, their affiliation or function in the embassy never quite clear. Some of them were caricatures of the ugly American, prone to making jokes about Indonesians until they found out she was married to one." Occasionally, she brought Barry to work. Joseph Sigit, an Indonesian who worked as office manager at the time, told me, "Our staff here sometimes made a joke of him because he looked different—the color of his skin."

Joked with him—or about him? I asked.

"With and about him," Sigit said, with no evident embarrassment.

Ann soon moved on. At age twenty-seven, she was hired to start an English-language, business-communications department in one of the few private nonprofit management-training schools in the country. The Suharto government was embarking on a five-year plan, but Indonesia had few managers with the training to put the new economic policies into practice. The school, called the Institute for Management Education and Development, or Lembaga Pendidikan den Pembinaan Manajemen, had been started several years earlier by a Dutch Jesuit priest, Father A. M. Kadarman, with the intention of helping build an Indonesian elite. It was small, and its courses were oversubscribed. In 1970, the Ford Foundation made the first in a series of grants to the institute to expand the faculty and send teachers abroad for training. At about the same time, Father Kadarman hired Ann, who had found a group of young Americans and Britons enrolled in an intensive course in Bahasa Indonesia, the national language, at the University of Indonesia. "I think she found out about us because she had some connection to the University of Indonesia," recalled Irwan Holmes, a member of the original group. "She was looking for teachers." A half-dozen of them accepted her invitation, many of them members of an in-

ternational spiritual organization, Subud, with a residential compound in a suburb of Jakarta. Ann's new business-communications
department offered intensive courses in business English for executives and government ministers. Ann, who may have begun to
pick up Bahasa Indonesia from Lolo while she was still in Hawaii
and acquired it rapidly once she was in Jakarta, trained the teachers, developed the curriculum, wrote course materials, and taught
top executives. In return, she received not a simple paycheck but a
share of the revenue from the program. Few Indonesians understood the department's potential, said Felina Pramono, an English
teacher from central Java whom Father Kadarman hired as Ann's
assistant and soon promoted to teaching. But the program took off.
"She was a very clever woman," Pramono told me. "Young as she
was, she was quite mature intellectually."

Ann became a popular teacher. For many of the students, the
classes were at least as much a social activity as they were about
serious learning, said Leonard Kibble, who taught part-time at the
institute in the early 1970s. They took place in the late afternoon
and evening, after the students got off work. Because there was just
one miserable state television channel at that time, Kibble said,
there was little else to do at that hour. "In such a situation, Indonesians can laugh and joke," Kibble told me. "They love acting. The
teachers had something called 'role simulation'—which the students called 'role stimulation.' Some students did very occasionally
feel guilty about laughing so much at their fellow students, but that
didn't stop them." Ann's classes in particular "could be a riot of
laughter from beginning to end. She had a great sense of humor,"
Kibble said. "The laughter in class came not only from Indonesian
students making all sorts of funny mistakes trying to speak English
but also Ann making all sorts of funny mistakes trying to speak
Indonesian." In one classroom slip that Kibble said Ann delighted

in recounting, she tried to tell a student that he would "get a promotion" if he learned English. Instead of using the phrase *naik pangkat*, she said *"naik pantat."* The word *naik* means to "go up, rise, or mount"; *pangkat* means "rank" or "position." *Pantat* means "buttocks."

Among the perks of working in the business-English department were the snacks, served in a crowded teachers' lounge during the half-hour break between afternoon and evening classes. In Indonesian, the term *jajan pasar* is used for the ubiquitous home-made snacks sold at food stands and markets. *Pasar* means "market"; *jajan* means "snack." They include seafood chips, peanut chips, fried chips from the *mlinjo* tree, chips made from ground cowhide mixed with garlic, sweet-potato snacks, mashed cassava snacks, sweet flour dumplings made with sesame seeds, sticky rice flavored with pandanus leaves, sticky black rice sprinkled with grated coconut, and rice cakes wrapped in coconut leaves or banana leaves, to name a few. Some come wrapped in a banana-leaf envelope, ingeniously pinned shut with a wooden toothpick that doubles as a disposable (and biodegradable) utensil. Ann loved Indonesian snacks—at first perhaps simply for the undeniable pleasure of eating them, compounded later by admiration for the enterprising people who made them. At the school, there were sticky rice croquettes, *lemper,* with meat in the middle; rice-flour cookies called *klepon,* with sesame seeds on the outside and palm sugar in the center; *nagasari,* made with bananas, flour, and sugar steamed in a banana leaf; and Dutch cream cakes. The snacks in Ann's department were the envy of other departments. "I think most of us worked there for the really good snacks," said Kay Ikranagara, an American who met Ann at the school in the early 1970s and became a close friend. Food accompanied every graduation. Felina Pramono and Ann would collaborate on the menu. On one occasion, Pramono ordered a personal favorite, fried brain. Ann instructed her never to order it again.

Ann was a striking figure who did not go unnoticed. "Maybe just her presence—the way she carried herself," said Halimah Bellows, whom Ann hired in the spring of 1971. She dressed simply, with little or no makeup, and wore her hair long, held back by a headband. By Javanese standards, she was, as Pramono put it, "a bit sturdy for a woman." She had strong opinions—and rarely softened them to please others. When she discovered that Irwan Holmes had organized a club in which students would pay to meet at a café and put their English to use in an informal setting, she fired him with no advance warning, he said. "She was obviously very concerned about her business being successful and didn't want anybody moving in on her," he said. Pramono, a Catholic in a country in which one is asked to identify one's religion in the course of ordinary transactions, such as applying for jobs, felt she detected a mocking quality in Ann's attitude to her religion. "She would just smile and laugh, you know? And a sneer. I could feel it," Pramono told me. She chose not to be offended, because she liked Ann and believed she would never intentionally hurt anyone. But Pramono made a practice of avoiding the topic of religion. When Kay Ikranagara complained that her students were not working hard enough, Ann told her to stop taking the lessons so seriously and let the students enjoy themselves. They would learn better that way. "She was absolutely right," Ikranagara said. "But she was not sympathetic: 'This is your problem. . . .'"

"She used to tear me apart," Ikranagara remembered in a tone that sounded almost fond. Ann told her she needed to be bolder and stronger. She made fun of her inadequacy in the kitchen. She told her she should give her housekeeper explicit instructions, not simply let her do whatever she wanted. "With everybody she was like that: She would tell them what was wrong with them," said Ikranagara, who was far from incompetent. (After receiving her Ph.D. in 1975, she went on to a career designing and implementing academic degree and training programs for developing countries.) "I don't think anyone ever found her annoying, because it was done in a very loving way," Ikranagara said. "You knew that she was a very outgoing, outspoken person." Family members were not spared. Some years later, while Ikranagara worried about the influence of Indonesian machismo on her two sons, Ann worried about the pressure for Indonesian girls to be passive and accommodating. "She was very scathing about the traditional Indonesian wife role," Ikranagara remembered. "She would tell Maya not to be such a wimp. She didn't like this passive Indonesian female caricature. She would tell me not to fall into that."

Ann's forthrightness was in sharp contrast to the preferred Javanese style. The Javanese place great value on keeping the surface of social relations smooth, I was told repeatedly by Indonesians and non-Indonesians alike. Keeping the surface placid is often more important than getting one's message across. Meaning emerges indirectly, as much from what is unsaid as from what is said. "Here, it's all on the unspoken level," said Stephen des Tombes, who moved to Indonesia in 1971. "Showing your anger is considered childish. They simply don't do it."

Fortunately, Indonesians do not expect foreigners to be like them. "Indonesians are very generous and very kind as long as you're not too arrogant," des Tombes said. "They're willing to put up with all our Western foibles. We are rather rough and abrasive, as far as they are concerned. We are less able to pick up on the subtext." After all, Indonesians are accustomed to living in a diverse society in which cultural differences are common. "They're already used to dealing with Bataks," Ikranagara told me, referring to the

Stanley Ann Dunham

Stanley, Stanley Ann, and Madelyn, Yellowstone National Park, summer 1947

During her first year in Hawaii, late 1960 or early 1961

ABOVE: *Barack Obama Sr.*

LEFT: *Lolo Soetoro at the University of Hawaiʻi in 1963 or 1964*

With Barack

At Borobudur, early 1970s

*During her fieldwork in Kajar,
1977 or 1978*

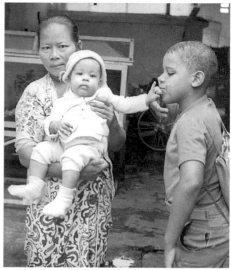

TOP: *Barack (right) with Maya and her nanny, 1970*

LEFT: *Barack (right) with Lolo (left), Lolo's mother (center), and members of Lolo's family*

Holding Maya, with Lolo's mother (left) and Madelyn Dunham (right) in Jakarta, August 1970

With Barack at the Punahou School commencement, 1979

With Barack and friends, Manhattan, summer 1987

ABOVE: *In the field, late 1980s or early 1990s*

LEFT: *On the island of Lombok, early 1990s*

BELOW: *In the field*

At Barack and Michelle's wedding, October 1992

ethnic group from the mountains of North Sumatra known for, among many other things, straightforwardness. "So they're willing to accept Ann as a sort of Batak."

Ann had little trouble making close friends, including Indonesian and expatriate men. By the standards of Indonesian society, as well as expatriate society, that may have been unusual for a married woman. But Ann did not seem to care. There was Anton Hillman, an affable Indonesian of Chinese descent, who went on to host an English-language show on Indonesian television and work as an interpreter for the first lady, Ibu Tien Suharto. He is said to have met Ann at USAID and to have encouraged her to move on from her first job to the management school, where he worked part-time. Mohammad Mansur Medeiros, a reclusive and scholarly Subud member from Fall River, Massachusetts, and Harvard, whom Ann hired as a teacher, had immersed himself so deeply in Javanese culture, language, and religion that friends nicknamed him Mansur Java. When he died in 2007, friends recalled his preference for the company of ordinary Indonesians—street vendors and *becak* drivers—over that of other Subud members and expatriates. Samardal Manan, an anxious young teacher who went on to a career as a translator for Exxon Mobil, used to listen, awestruck and in silence, to Ann's freewheeling conversations with Medeiros. "You would think they were in love, but they were not," Manan said. "Ann was a person who got so close, happy, and cheerful when talking with a person who was equally fluent. They would move from one subject to another—students, corruption, politics, anthropology. She didn't really worry about the impression it would have on others."

Manan was new to Jakarta when he met Ann at the binational organization where she was working in 1968. He was a nervous, dark-skinned young man from a traditional Muslim family, trying to be somebody in the big city. He lacked confidence in dealing with people whom he considered to be of higher status. He had studied English at a teachers' college in Bukittinggi, funded by the Ford Foundation, where he had first encountered Peace Corps volunteers. "We Indonesians admired Americans, especially women," Manan recalled. "We knew that Americans were very, very civilized people, very educated, very intelligent. There were a lot of things we could learn." Ann was a magnet for people, including him, he said. Decades later, he remembered her, and conversations they had, in vivid detail. She encouraged him to be more confident, expressive, and outgoing. She told him that he worried too much. She staged a mock television interview show and interviewed him in front of their colleagues. They often talked about Indonesia. She told him she admired Indonesia's Bataks for their frankness, pragmatism, and willingness to assume responsibility. She also made it clear that she hated corruption. "She said the only way to solve this problem was through education and making people aware that corruption was bad," Manan said. "I believe she taught her students that, because she spoke her mind very freely."

Kay Ikranagara, one of Ann's closest friends, was the daughter of a development economist from the University of California who had taught at the University of Indonesia in the late 1950s. She had lived in Jakarta as a teenager; studied anthropology and linguistics at Berkeley in the 1960s, where she had been jailed for political activism; then returned to Jakarta, where she met her husband, Ikranagara, then a freelance journalist and actor. She met Ann while teaching part-time at the management school and writing her dissertation in linguistics. They had a lot in common: Indonesian husbands, degrees in anthropology, babies born in the same month, opinions shaped by the 1960s. They were less conscious than others of the boundaries between cultures, Kay Ikranagara

told me, and they rejected what they saw as the previous generation's hypocrisy on the subject of race. "We had all the same attitudes," she remembered. "When we met people who worked for
the oil companies or the embassy, they belonged to a different culture than Ann and I. We felt they didn't mix with Indonesians, they
were part of an insular American culture." Servants seemed to be
the only Indonesians those Americans knew.

But by the early 1970s, Lolo's new job had plunged him deeply
into that oil company culture. Foreign firms doing business in Indonesia were required to hire and train Indonesian partners. In
many cases, the exercise struck some people as a sham: Companies
would hire an Indonesian director, pay him well, and give him
little or nothing to do. Trisulo, Lolo's brother-in-law, told me he
did not recall the exact nature of Lolo's job with Union Oil. It may
have been "government relations," his son, Sonny Trisulo, said.
Whatever it was, Lolo's job included socializing with oil company
executives and their wives. He joined the Indonesian Petroleum
Club, a private watering hole in Central Jakarta for oil company
people and their families, which offered swimming, tennis, dining,
and rooms for receptions. Ann, as Lolo's wife, was expected to socialize, too. Any failure to do so reflected badly on him. "It's the
society that asks it," Kay Ikranagara said. "Your husband is supposed to show up at social functions with you at his side, dressed in
a *kain* and *kebaya*," a costume consisting of the traditional, tightly
fitted, long-sleeved blouse and a length of unstitched cloth wound
around the lower part of the body. "You're supposed to sit with the
women and talk about your children and your servants."

Ann begged off.

"She didn't understand these folks—the idea of living an expatriate life that was so completely divorced from the world around
you, that involves hiding yourself away in these protective cells of

existence," Maya said. "That was peculiar to her, and she was bored by it." Ann complained to her friend Bill Collier that all those middle-aged white Americans talked about inane things. Lolo, she told Collier, "was becoming more American all the time." Occasionally, the young Obama would overhear Lolo and Ann arguing in their bedroom about Ann's refusal to attend his oil company dinners, at which, he writes in *Dreams from My Father*, "American businessmen from Texas and Louisiana would slap Lolo's back and boast about the palms they had greased to obtain the new offshore drilling rights, while their wives complained to my mother about the quality of Indonesian help. He would ask her how it would look for him to go alone, and remind her that these were her own people, and my mother's voice would rise to almost a shout.

"They are *not* my people."

The relationship between Ann and Lolo appears to have begun deteriorating even before Lolo took the oil company job. As Obama describes it, something had happened between them in the year they had been apart. Lolo had been full of life in Hawaii, regaling Ann with stories from his childhood and the struggle for independence, confiding his plans to return to his country and teach at the university. Now he barely spoke to her at all. Some nights, he would sleep with a pistol under his pillow; other nights, she would hear him "wandering through the house with a bottle of imported whiskey, nursing his secrets." Ann's loneliness was a constant, Obama writes, "like a shortness of breath."

Ann's colleagues noticed. At times, she seemed downright unhappy. When one fellow teacher asked about her husband, she told him grimly, "I'm never asked. I'm told." Trusti Jarwadi, one of the teachers Ann met in her first job, could see that something was wrong but feared violating Ann's privacy by asking her questions. Reflecting on her marriage some years later, Ann told her Indonesian friend, Yang Suwan, somewhat bitterly, "Don't you know that you don't argue and you don't discuss with a Javanese person? Because problems don't exist with Javanese people. Time will solve problems."

Ann could not have known what she was getting into, said another close friend in the 1980s, Renske Heringa, a Dutch anthropologist who herself had married a man who was half Indonesian. "She didn't know, as little I knew, how Indonesian men change when suddenly their family is around," she said. "And how Indonesian men like women to be easy and open abroad, but when you get to Indonesia, the parents are there, you have to behave. You have to be the little wife. . . . As a wife, you were not supposed to make yourself visible besides being beautiful. By the time I knew Ann, she was a hefty woman. She didn't care about getting dressed, wearing jewelry, the way Indonesian women do. That was not her style. He expected her to do it. That is one reason she didn't stick it out. She absolutely refused to. I understand why he couldn't accept it."

Ann had also pieced together some of what had happened in Indonesia in 1965 and afterward from fragmentary information that people let slip. Men employed at the embassy told her stories that would never have appeared in Indonesian newspapers, according to Obama's account in *Dreams from My Father*. Her new Indonesian friends talked to her about corruption in government agencies, police and military shakedowns, the power of the president's entourage. When she asked Lolo about it, he would not talk. According to Obama, a cousin of Lolo's finally explained to Ann the circumstances of Lolo's unplanned return from Hawaii. He had arrived in Jakarta with no idea what fate awaited him. He was taken away for questioning and told he had been conscripted and would be sent to the jungles of New Guinea for a year. Students returning from Soviet bloc countries had been jailed or even van-ished. According to Obama, Ann concluded that "power had taken Lolo and yanked him back into line just when he thought he'd escaped, making him feel its weight, letting him know that his life wasn't his own." In response, Lolo had made his peace with power, "learned the wisdom of forgetting; just as his brother-in-law had done, making millions as a high official in the national oil company."

Lolo had disappointed Ann—just as Stanley had disappointed Madelyn. If Lolo worked in "government relations" for the oil company, what did that entail? Where was the line between curry-ing favor and corruption? Perhaps the nature of Lolo's professional activities was ambiguous. But as long as there was any suggestion of anything questionable to Ann, it would be impossible for her to take a positive interest in his work. "She was upset," Suwan re-called. "'How could a bright person take such a position?' She said, 'Suwan, after he did that, my whole respect for him was gone.'" Carol Colfer, another anthropologist friend, said Ann came to the conclusion that Lolo would never understand her motivations and her values. In Indonesia, Colfer said, "to do business, there's a lot of corruption. Even if he went in wholeheartedly not wanting to be corrupt, in that context I don't think you could have kept a job like that if you weren't willing to be corrupt."

There were other tensions, too.

One morning in January 2009, I met Felina Pramono, Ann's former assistant, in a conference room at the offices of the manage-ment school for which Ann had worked. A tiny, brisk woman, attired in a tailored turquoise jacket with black piping, she spoke impeccable English with a very proper British accent. A few min-utes into the interview, a man in his late fifties entered the room and was introduced as Saman, a longtime employee of the school.

Speaking in Bahasa Indonesia, with Pramono translating, he told me that he had worked as a houseboy for Lolo and Ann in the early 1970s, after which Ann had helped him get a job as a custodian at the school. One of seven children from a family of farmers, Saman had moved to Jakarta as a teenager to find work. When he worked for Ann and Lolo, his duties included gardening; taking care of a pet turtle, dog, rabbit, and bird; and taking Barry to school by bicycle or *becak*. Ann and Lolo paid Saman well and treated all four members of the household staff equally. Saman remembered Lolo as stern and Ann as kindhearted. When he accidentally knocked over an aquarium that Lolo used for freshwater fish, Lolo insisted that Saman pay the four-thousand-rupiah cost, or two months' pay, to replace it. If Ann had known, Saman thought, she might have objected to the punishment. "She wouldn't have the heart," Pramono explained, translating for Saman. "Her social sense, her sense of helping others, was so high, she would never have allowed that."

At times, Ann's lack of concern for appearances added to the trouble between her and Lolo. She would finish teaching at nine in the evening and sometimes not return home until midnight, Saman said. ("After four hours of teaching, Ann still had an appetite for more social interaction," Leonard Kibble, a fellow teacher, told me.) As far as Saman could tell, she seemed barely to sleep. She would stay up, typing and correcting Barry's homework, then be up before dawn. On one occasion, Saman said, "She got home late with a student, but the student didn't see her home properly. So he dropped her near the house, and Soetoro got very mad because of that." An argument ensued, which Saman overheard. "He said, 'I've warned you many times. Why are you still doing this?'" Saman recalled. Lolo summoned a witness from the neighborhood. Whether Lolo's worry was infidelity or simply what others might think is unclear from Saman's story. After the argument, he said,

Ann appeared in the house with a towel pressed to her face and blood running from her nose. It is difficult to know what to make of the nearly forty-year-old recollection. The confrontation occurred within earshot, Saman said, but out of his sight. No one else I interviewed suggested there was ever violence between Ann and Lolo, a man many people described as patient and sweet-tempered. But Saman's story suggests, if nothing else, the rising tension in the marriage.

With her children, Ann made a point of being more physically affectionate than her mother had been with her, she told one friend. She was cuddly and would say "I love you," according to Maya, a hundred times a day. "She loved to take children—any child—and sit them in her lap and tickle them or play games with them and examine their hands, tracing out the miracle of bone and tendon and skin and delighting at the truths to be found there," her son would write many years later. She was playful—making pottery, weaving decorations, doing art projects that stretched across the room. "I think that we benefited a great deal from her focus when we were with her, when she was beside us," Maya told me. "So that made the absences hurt a little less." She was not firm about bedtimes, said Kadi Warner, who, with her then husband, John Raintree, lived with Ann for several months when Maya was nine, but she insisted that her children get up in the morning. She preferred humor to harping. Where her children were involved, she was easily moved to tears, even occasionally when speaking about them to friends. She took her role seriously, while acknowledging, sometimes jokingly, the limits of her influence. As she told an Indonesian friend, Julia Suryakusuma, "One of the areas where I failed as a mother was that I couldn't get my children to floss their teeth." At the same time, Ann was exacting about the things she believed mattered most. Those included such things as honesty, hard work, and fulfilling one's duty to others. Richard Hook, who worked with Ann in Jakarta in the late 1980s and early 1990s, said she told him that she had worked to instill ideas about public service in her son. Because of his intelligence and education, she wanted Barry to have a sense of obligation to give something back. She wanted him to start off, Hook said, with the attitudes and values she had taken years to learn.

"If you want to grow into a human being," Obama remembers her saying, "you're going to need some values."

> Honesty—Lolo should not have hidden the refrigerator in the storage room when the tax officials came, even if everyone else, including the tax officials, expected such things. Fairness—the parents of wealthier students should not give television sets to the teachers during Ramadan, and their children could take no pride in the higher marks they might have received. Straight talk—if you didn't like the shirt I bought you for your birthday, you should have just said so instead of keeping it wadded up at the bottom of your closet. Independent judgment—just because the other children tease the poor boy about his haircut doesn't mean you have to do it too.

If some of Ann's values sound midwestern, as Obama suggests, some were also Javanese. In a detailed survey of scholarly studies of Javanese society and culture, an anthropologist at the University of Indonesia, named Koentjaraningrat, included, in a list of ideal human virtues, "keeping good relations with others, helping as much as possible, sharing with neighbors, trying to understand others, and placing oneself in the situation of others."

When necessary, Ann was, according to two accounts, not unwilling to reinforce her message. Don Johnston, who worked with her in the early 1990s, sometimes traveling with her in Indonesia and living in the same house, suggested to me that President Obama's work ethic reflected Ann's standards. "She talked about disciplining Barry, including spanking him for things where he richly deserved a spanking, according to her," Johnston recalled. Saman, speaking in Indonesian with Felina Pramono interpreting, said that when Barry failed to finish homework sent from Hawaii by his grandmother, Ann "would call him into his room and would spank him with his father's military belt." But when I later asked President Obama, through a spokeswoman, whether his mother ever resorted to physical discipline to reinforce a point, he said she never did.

One evening in the house in Matraman, Saman said, he and Barry were preparing to go to sleep. They often slept in the same place—sometimes in the bunk bed in Barry's room, sometimes on the dining room floor or in the garden. On this occasion, Barry, who was eight or nine at the time, had asked Saman to turn out the light. When Saman did not do it, he said, Barry hit him in the chest. When he did not react, Barry hit him harder, and Saman struck him back. Barry began to cry loudly, attracting Ann's attention. According to Saman, Ann did not respond. She seemed to realize that Barry had been in the wrong. Otherwise, Saman would not have struck him.

"We were not permitted to be rude, we were not permitted to be mean, we were not permitted to be arrogant," Maya told me. "We had to have a certain humility and broad-mindedness. We had to study. If we said something unkind about someone, she would try to talk about their point of view. Or, 'How would you feel?' Barack has famously mentioned that she said to him, always, 'Well, how would you feel if X, Y, and Z? How would that make you feel?' Sort of compelling us ever towards empathy and those kinds of things, and not allowing us to be selfish. That was constant, steady, daily."

It was clear to many that Ann believed Barry, in particular, was unusually gifted. She would boast about his brains, his achievements, how brave and bold he was. Felina Pramono sensed that Ann had plans for his future. Benji Bennington, from the East-West Center, told me, "Sometimes when she talked about Barack, she'd say, 'Well, my son is so bright, he can do anything he ever wants in the world, even be president of the United States.' I remember her saying that." Samardal Manan remembered Ann saying something similar—that Barry could be, or perhaps wanted to be, the first black president.

"What do you want to be when you grow up?" Lolo asked Barry one evening, according to Saman, the houseboy.

"Oh, prime minister," Barry answered.

What mattered as much as anything to Ann, as a parent, was her children's education—just as it had mattered to generations of her Kansas forebears. But that was not simple. Because they were living in Indonesia, she wanted her children to know the country, have Indonesian friends, and not grow up in an expatriate bubble. At the same time, she wanted them to have the opportunities she had, including the opportunity to attend a great university. For that, they needed to be academically prepared. Indonesian schools in the late 1960s and early 1970s were inadequate. There were not enough of them, the government controlled the curriculum, teachers were poorly trained. They were paid so little that many also worked second jobs, dividing their time, energy, and attention. Westerners sent their children to the Jakarta International School, which offered what many say was an excellent education. But the school was expensive and difficult to get into. At its founding, money had been raised by selling bonds to institutions such as the Ford Foundation. Slots went to the children of diplomats, executives of foreign firms, and employees of international organizations including Ford. Without a job in one of those institutions, few people could get a child in or afford the tuition. Furthermore, there were few if any Indonesian students in the school. There were not many educational options in Jakarta that would have provided what Ann was looking for. When Maya was about five, Ann enrolled her in a multinational bilingual playgroup run by the wife of an American minister in a large house in Kebayoran Baru. Kay Ikranagara enrolled her son, Inno, too. The teachers were Western as well as Indonesian. Maya and Inno were native speakers in both languages, speaking Indonesian with their fathers, English with their mothers, and both with their teachers. But that sort of school in Jakarta was hard to find.

For Barry, Ann tried two Indonesian schools, one Catholic and one Muslim. Though she eventually sent him back to Hawaii, the experience of an Indonesian education cannot have failed to have left a mark. Michael Dove, who got to know Ann when they were both anthropologists working in Java in the 1980s, told me he discovered, as an American with allergies teaching in Java, that to sneeze was to exhibit an untoward lack of self-control. The Javanese, especially the Central Javanese, place an enormous emphasis on self-control, Dove said: "You demonstrate an inner strength by not betraying emotion, not speaking loudly, not moving jerkily." Self-control is inculcated in part in Indonesian schools, Kay Ikranagara and her husband told me. And it is done through a culture of teasing. "People tease about skin color all the time," Kay Ikranagara said. Having dark skin is a negative—as would have been plumpness and curly hair. If a child allows the teasing to bother him, he is teased more. If he ignores it, it stops. Kay Ikranagara's husband, Ikranagara, who grew up in Bali, said he was teased mercilessly about being skinny. He learned to compensate by being clever. "Our ambassador said this was where Barack learned to be cool," Kay Ikranagara told me. "If you get mad and react, you lose. If you learn to laugh and take it without any reaction, you win."

As Obama tells it, Ann's attitude toward his future gradually shifted.

> She had always encouraged my rapid acculturation in Indonesia: It had made me relatively self-sufficient, undemanding on a tight budget, and extremely well mannered when compared with other American children. She had taught me to disdain the blend of ignorance and arrogance that too often characterized Americans abroad. But she now had learned, just as Lolo had learned, the chasm that separated the life chances of an American from those of an Indonesian. She knew which side of the divide she wanted her child to be on. I was an American, she decided, and my true life lay elsewhere.

Ann's efforts to prepare Barry for his return to school in Hawaii are the subject of an oft repeated story told in *Dreams from My Father* and recounted occasionally in President Obama's speeches. The story concerns what Obama describes as a common practice in the Jakarta household (a practice which Saman, the houseboy, said he did not remember). Five days a week, Obama writes, Ann would enter his bedroom in Jakarta at four a.m., force-feed him breakfast, and teach him English lessons for three hours before he left for school. When he resisted, Ann would tell him: "This is no picnic for me either, buster."

In early 1971, Ann told Barry, then age nine, that he would be returning to Hawaii. He would live with his grandparents in Honolulu and attend Punahou Academy, a respected prep school within walking distance of the Dunhams' apartment. His application had been considered, Obama says, only through the intervention of an alumnus who was Stanley's boss. "It was time for me to attend an American school, she had said," he writes. "I'd run through all the lessons of my correspondence course. She said that she and Maya would be joining me in Hawaii very soon—a year, tops—and that she'd try to make it there for Christmas." Madelyn's brother Charles Payne told me he suspected that Madelyn played a part in the decision. "Madelyn always had a great concern about Barack getting a good education," he said. "I think that was her defense against his racial mixture—that education was the solution to whatever problems that would bring."

Ann, too, may have doubted the wisdom of her decision to take Barry to Indonesia at the moment she did. Yang Suwan, her Indonesian friend, remembered Ann once saying as much: "She said if she had known before, she wouldn't have come and brought Barack." And in *The Audacity of Hope*, Obama writes, "In later years my mother would insist that had she known what had transpired in the preceding months, we never would have made the trip."

Now she was dispatching him, alone, on a trip halfway around the globe. As he later described his send-off in *Dreams from My Father*, an Indonesian copilot who was a friend of Ann's escorted him to the plane "as she and Lolo and my new sister, Maya, stood by at the gate."

Ann's decision to marry Lolo had required that she uproot Barry, at age six, and transplant him to Jakarta. Now she was uprooting him again, at barely ten, and sending him back. She would follow him to Hawaii only to leave him again, less than three years later. When we spoke, Obama recalled those serial displacements.

He was less aware at that time, he said, of the toll they took than he would become many years later.

"I think that was harder on a ten-year-old boy than he'd care to admit at the time," Obama said, folded into a chair in the Oval Office and speaking about his mother with a mix of affection and critical distance. "When we were separated again during high school, at that point I was old enough to say, 'This is my choice, my

With Lolo, Maya, and Barack, 1970

decision.' But being a parent now and looking back at that, I could see—you know what?—that would be hard on a kid."

The years in Jakarta had marked them all. For Ann, who would return repeatedly as an anthropologist and as a development consultant over the next twenty-five years, the experience had given her powerful insight into the lives of ordinary Indonesians that few Western advisers would ever be in a position to acquire. She would never adopt what Yang Suwan thought of as typical expatriate attitudes—acquisitiveness, arrogance, and an insistence on having the last word. She would never become one of those infatuated "Java junkies" or "Java freaks." She had lived through a dark period in the country's history. She had lived like an Indonesian woman, worrying at times about how to feed, protect, and educate her children. As Yang put it, "She knew how to solve problems that other expatriates don't know exist."

Barry, too, had been shaped in ways that would remain with

In Indonesia, June 1972

him, for better or for worse. One colleague of Ann's in Indonesia in the late 1970s, John Raintree, who raised his two children abroad, said Ann, by the choices she made, gave Barry not one but two important experiences: First, she gave him an extraordinary adventure and the chance to be broadened and strengthened by living overseas; then, by enabling him to return to the United States and live out his teenage years there, she allowed him to begin to develop his identity as an American.

A few weeks before the presidential election in 2008, I traveled to New Haven, Connecticut, to meet Michael Dove, a professor of anthropology at Yale and a longtime friend of Ann's. Dove had spent his mid-twenties in Kalimantan, his thirties in Java and Pakistan, his forties in Hawaii—and had known Ann in almost all of those places. Expatriate life has its advantages, he told me: It's exciting, there is boundless hope, you leave things behind. You are in limbo overseas. "I didn't know how many family problems I had until I came back from Asia," he said. Your American values are thrown into relief, he suggested. You think about them in new ways. Dove had been thinking about the suggestion that Lolo had become more American and Ann more Javanese. "I think it's more complicated than that," he said. "By becoming more Javanese, she was getting more insights into what it meant to be an American, both the good and the bad. Because, of course, we never become Javanese. That lies beyond us."

Five

Trespassers Will Be Eaten

In the summer of 1973, Ann touched down on the U.S. mainland for the first time in eleven years. She was thirty years old, finishing her first year as a graduate student at the University of Hawai'i, divorced from one husband, separated from another, a single parent of two on a five-week cross-country road trip with her children and her mother. "Pretty exhausting," she wrote to a friend, "especially since we travelled by bus most of the way." Stopping first in Seattle, Ann visited Jackie Farner, the only high school classmate with whom she had stayed in contact. Like Ann, Jackie had made some unorthodox life choices—moving to rural Alaska to teach, living in a log cabin, marrying an Aleut. On a day trip into the Cascades, Barry and Maya saw snow for the first time. Then they headed down the West Coast through California, across the desert into Arizona, and over to the Grand Canyon, then east to Kansas City and Chicago, doubling back finally through Yellowstone National Park and San Francisco en route home to Honolulu. "Actually, I was surprised how little change we saw," Ann wrote. "More bluejeans, campers and mustaches, but the countryside around Seattle looks about the same." In Kansas City, they bunked in the basement recreation room of Arlene Payne, Madelyn's sister, who was teaching at the University of Missouri. Jon Payne arrived from Colorado, not having seen Ann since his months on the Dunhams' couch on Mercer Island sixteen years earlier. They all spent a few days talking and playing darts, Jon venturing out into the sweltering heat to take Barry and Maya to a baseball game. Jon was struck by Ann's evident happiness, her pride in her children, the confidence she had acquired. She was, in some ways, a different person than the one he remembered. Having weathered the turbulence of the intervening years—pregnancy at seventeen, raising biracial children, her years in Jakarta—she seemed to have come into her own.

Back in Honolulu in early August, Ann wrote a long letter to Bill Byers, the wheelman on the fateful, Cadillac-convertible flight to the San Francisco Bay Area. She had telephoned him during the bus trip but had found him at the end of a marriage, facing the death of his father and in no mood for conversation. Her letter was humorous, unself-conscious, earthy, self-mocking, mordant, gently teasing, and emotionally direct. "If you could find it in your CRABBY heart to scrawl me a note I would be overjoyed!" she wrote. "Surely, out of the last twelve years, you could sift a couple of tarnished badges to flash at me. I am not such a harsh critic after all, having screwed up royally a few times myself." She enclosed two photographs, one of her children and one of herself, dressed in a black dashiki with bright orange trim and a pair of oversized sunglasses, her brown hair thick and loose, swept over one shoulder. "Would like one of you if you have a spare," she scribbled in a

In Hawaii, 1973

postscript, soliciting a photo in return. "Doesn't matter if you're bald and fat or skinny and hairy. I've gained about 15 pounds in the rear since coming back from Asia too."

She recounted the bus-tour itinerary, then described, with caustic amusement, a chance encounter in downtown Honolulu with a certain "rather dull, round-faced boy," a mutual acquaintance who had gone on to some success in retail. "Fingers aglitter with diamonds and rubies, he offered me a ride in his limousine and gave me an invitation to a fashion show he was staging that afternoon," she wrote in fluid, loopy script. "I didn't especially appreciate it since I was dressed in the baggiest most non-descript dress I own, pigtail and rubber slippers and looking very scroungy that day (I believe his exact words when he saw me were: 'Well, well, just look at you!') I could have clobbered him, but it wasn't worth it (is anything?)" Recapitulating the recent events of her rather eventful life, she brushed past her second marriage. "I remarried, to an Indonesian geographer," she wrote, then dropped the subject abruptly. She ventured a guess at her future: "Just recently I got an East-West Center grant which will carry me, albeit meagerly, through my Ph.D. plus field work, that is till the end of '75. After that, I shall be most content to spend the rest of my life, I suppose, exploring obscure topics and obscure corners of the world. Probably a useless sort of life and not very socially relevant, especially since I hate applied anthropology (neo-colonialism in bad disguise—I had a lot of bad experiences with it in Asia). I do hope to spend most of my time for the next few years in the islands, since my son Barry is doing very well in school here and I hate to take him abroad again till he graduates, which won't be for another 6 years."

She had kept her earlier commitment. The year Barry returned to Honolulu and entered fifth grade at Punahou, Ann traveled nearly seven thousand miles to spend Christmas with him and her parents, leaving Lolo and Maya in Indonesia. Before she arrived, Barry was told by his grandmother that his mother had lined up an unexpected gift: Seven years after his parents had divorced, his father was coming to visit. Obama Sr. was living in Kenya, where he had moved with his third wife, an American he had met while he was at Harvard and with whom he had produced two more children. When Ann arrived, she plied Barry with information about Kenyan history—none of which he retained, according to his account. She assured him that his father knew all about him from her letters. "'You two will become great friends,' she decided," Obama writes in his memoir, leaving the verb dangling dubiously off the end of the sentence. Ann had worked to keep alive the connection between Obama and his son. Her friend Kadi Warner told me, "She really was committed for him to have some presence in Barry's life. She knew it was up to her to maintain it."

Obama's account of his father's Christmas visit is poignant. He notices the effect of his father's presence on his mother and grandparents—his grandfather "more vigorous and thoughtful," his mother "more bashful." As the weeks lurch along, tension builds— "my mother's mouth pinched, her eyes avoiding her parents, as we ate dinner." After his father scolds him for wasting his time watching a cartoon special of *How the Grinch Stole Christmas!* an argument breaks out between his parents and grandparents. Ann seems to mediate at first, then sides with Obama against her parents. "I listened to my mother tell her parents that nothing ever changed with them," the younger Obama writes. Dispatched by his grandmother the next day to collect any dirty laundry from the apartment where his father is staying, he finds his father shirtless and his mother ironing. She appears to have been crying. He delivers his message and declines an invitation to stay. Back upstairs at his grandparents' apartment, Ann appears in his room. "You shouldn't be mad at your father, Bar," she tells him. "He loves you very much. He's just a little stubborn sometimes."

When he refuses to look up, she adds, "I know all this stuff is confusing for you. For me, too."

With Barack Obama Sr., Christmas 1971

Ann returned to Indonesia in early 1972, after the Christmas visit, and negotiated a leave of absence from her job in Jakarta in order to enter graduate school at the University of Hawai'i. She even managed to line up some financial support through a foundation grant to the management school where she had been working. Taking Maya with her—and for a time, Lolo—she returned to Hawaii and found her way that fall into the master's-degree program in anthropology, the field that had been her undergraduate major. In an application to the East-West Center in December 1972, she described her academic specialization as economic anthropology and culture change. "But I'm more interested in the human and psychological factors that accompany change than purely technological factors," she wrote. She said she was planning

Barack Obama Sr. and the young Barack, Christmas 1971

"a possible joint project" with Lolo, who was involved in a population-studies program under the department of geography. But Lolo did not stay long. He remained enrolled only for the spring semester of 1973, according to university records. By the time of the cross-country bus trip in July, he was gone.

By that summer, Ann had landed a grant from the East-West Center to cover her university tuition and field research. Married students with children were exempt from the East-West Center requirement that students live together as a community in the center's dorms, but the housing allowance was too low to permit students to live above the poverty level in Hawaii, said Benji Bennington, who had become an administrator at the center. So Ann found an apartment in a low-slung, cinder-block building reminiscent of a budget motel, with hot water heaters on the balconies and utility meters bolted to the outside wall. The apartment, on Poki Street, was a mile and a half from the university and a short walk from both the Dunhams' apartment and Barry's school. She furnished it with the help of a furniture pool run by the off-campus housing specialist for the East-West Center, who also helped many of the students qualify for food stamps. When Ann overheard Barry's school friends commenting on the limited refrigerator inventory and his mother's unimpressive housekeeping, he says, she would take him aside and let him know that as a single mother back in school, baking cookies was not at the top of her priority list. She was not, she made it clear, putting up with "any snotty attitudes" from him or anyone else.

The status of Ann's marriage was ambiguous, it seems. According to Obama's account, Ann had separated from Lolo. But that was less clear to her friends. "She certainly considered herself married," said Kadi Warner, who was also a graduate student in anthropology on an East-West Center grant when she met Ann in the early 1970s. "But she had a different sense, perhaps than he did, of what that meant." Lolo, calling from Jakarta to speak with Maya, would be in tears. "Ann thought it was cute and amusing but nothing like, 'I have to pick her up and go back,'" Warner said. "Her thing was, 'You just have to do this to finish school, that's how it is. This is what we have to do.'" Her attitude seemed to be that she and Lolo were married, they would see each other occasionally, and that was what adults did when they had other obligations. She intended to work, to make a living, and to at least contribute to, if not fully underwrite, the education of her children. She had returned to Hawaii because she knew she would need an advanced degree, her friend Kay Ikranagara told me. That required that she live apart from Lolo, at least for a time. "Clearly, Ann put her children's education above all," Ikranagara said.

Ann was unlike the other graduate students in her department. She was older than most and, in effect, a single mother. It was unusual for women to go back to school, especially with young children, or to start a family while preparing to do fieldwork. "When I showed up wearing maternity clothes, my professor came up to me and said, 'You're kidding, right?'" said Warner, who became pregnant several years later. (She promised her professor, she told me, that she would not give birth in class.) Ann was not simply a mother, she was raising two biracial children with different fathers. "It struck me that she was doing something unusual and dangerous and difficult, raising multicultural children on her own," said Jean Kennedy, another graduate student. Kennedy, who had grown up in what she described as a racially stratified university town in New Zealand, had become intrigued with Southeast Asia after a group of Indonesian, Malaysian, and Thai students arrived on the campus where she was an undergraduate. She had gotten interested in how people would "sort themselves," as she put it, in the future. "Somebody like Ann, who was cutting across all of this with such strong-minded determination to cut the bullshit and get on with what needed to be done—I admired her," Kennedy said. "I could barely make it as a graduate student, and could not even think about getting myself into these sorts of conflicts and responsibilities."

There was something almost matronly about her. By the time she reached her early thirties, Ann had been an adult for a long time. Other students went out drinking, lay on the beach, flirted, gossiped, threw parties, shied away from commitments, toyed with trendy academic ideas. They lived in what Kennedy called "capsules of theoretical, highfalutin nonsense, very far from the real world." Ann kept her distance from the chitchat, both theoretical and social. She seemed to be looking for a way to pursue her interests—in anthropology, in Indonesia—while also making a living. Ben Finney, a professor who had grown up in Southern California and had written an ethno-history of surfing, was put off initially by what he took to be Ann's well-bred manner. Her fastidious diction reminded him of WASPs he had encountered as a graduate student at Harvard. "We did things much more informally than she seemed to," he said. "After I got to know her, I said, 'Well, Ann is just this upright person. That's her, no problem.'" She had an inquiring mind, and she was endlessly curious. She was absorbed by handicrafts, a topic that was not trendy but that interested Finney, too. He had done fieldwork in Tahiti, where, he said, traditional craft industries had all but disappeared, supplanted by the production of whatever tourists would buy. He had seen the strength of the handicraft sector of the Indonesian economy, where craftspeople still made textiles, tools, ceramics, and other items for everyday life. It was one of the reasons, he said, why anthropologists loved Indonesia: the persistence of a recognizably Indonesian way of life. But some had ruled out working there because of the difficulties inherent in getting the government's permission. Ann, however, had already lived there and was going back. Between the fall of 1972 and the fall of 1974, she completed sixty-three credits and all the coursework required for her Ph.D. When I asked Alice Dewey, the chairman of Ann's dissertation committee, what Ann was like as a student, she answered, "Ah! All business."

Ann's application had caught the attention of Dewey, a professor of anthropology who had gone to Java herself in the early 1950s as a twenty-three-year-old graduate student on a field team from Harvard. Settling in a town in east Central Java that they called Modjokuto, the members of the team did pioneering work on subjects ranging from the Javanese family to the rural economy. Their work became the basis of a series of seminal books, the best known of which was *The Religion of Java* by Clifford Geertz, who went on to become the most celebrated anthropologist of his generation. Dewey studied peasant markets, which are run by women in Java. She lived for more than a year in a rural village north of Modjokuto, bicycling every morning into the main Modjokuto market, spending afternoons visiting the homes of the market people, and passing the evenings on visits to her neighbors. Her most important market informants were two middle-aged half sisters, one of whom sold coffee and hot snacks "and provided me not only with information about her own business affairs but also with the current gossip of the marketplace, of which she had extensive knowledge because coffee stands are important social centers," Dewey wrote later. "Her half sister, who dealt first in dried corn and later in onions, was the most important informant for my study of wholesaling. She, her husband, a married daughter, and a son, married while I was there, were all experienced traders; between them, with great patience, they managed to teach me the workings of the market." Dewey's 1962 book *Peasant Marketing in Java* covered, among other things, bargaining, the division of labor, trade discounts, loans and interest rates, moneylenders, pooled savings plans, traders' rights and privileges, interpersonal relationships in the marketplace, small-scale cash crops, mountain crops, prepared-food vendors, and door-to-door peddlers. It also touched on the role of craftsmen, including metalworkers, leatherworkers, tailors, and bicycle repairmen. The book was, Jean Kennedy told me, not fashionable but brilliant—"a piece of pioneering work that seemed to have been bypassed." Koentjaraningrat, an Indonesian anthropologist and the author of *Javanese Culture,* a sweeping survey of scholarly work on the subject, called Dewey's book "the best and most comprehensive study on the Javanese market system."

Dewey, hired by the University of Hawai'i in 1962, had arrived on campus shortly after the elder Obama graduated and headed for Harvard. Over the years, she would become a mentor and friend to generations of graduate students, serving on countless doctoral committees and dispatching dozens of young anthropologists into the field, armed with what she considered to be four essentials: a flashlight, a penknife, heavy string, and a few mystery stories. (Dewey, who received *The Complete Sherlock Holmes* for her thirteenth birthday, once explained to me in some detail the uses of the first three. Then she added, "The reason for the mystery stories is self-evident.") The year Ann applied to the anthropology department to do graduate work, Dewey was on the committee that reviewed applications. "She obviously knew her way around Indonesia," Dewey told me. Ann spoke Indonesian fluently, she was knowledgeable about all things Indonesian, and her interest in handicrafts intersected with Dewey's interest in markets.

"I said, 'I want this one,'" Dewey recalled.

Dewey was charmingly unconventional herself. A granddaughter of John Dewey, the American philosopher and educator, and a descendant of Horace Greeley, the crusading newspaper editor, Alice Greeley Dewey had grown up in Huntington, Long Island, with a certain amount of parental license to be fearless. In games of cowboys and Indians, her sympathies did not incline toward the cowboys. As a high school student, she worked in what is now the Cold Spring Harbor Laboratory, where James D. Watson would deliver his first public lecture on his discovery, with

Francis Crick, of the double-helix structure of DNA. At Radcliffe College, she was lured into cultural anthropology by the enticing prospect of field research. Fieldwork, she once told me, comes as close as any experience to being somebody else: "Because they don't know who you are." She wanted to go to China, where her grandfather had lived, but Mao Zedong had proclaimed the People's Republic of China two years earlier, and the United States and China were fighting on opposite sides in the Korean War. So when her professor suggested Java, Dewey jumped at the chance. Arriving in Indonesia in 1952, she and the other members of the field team were introduced to a cousin of the sultan of Yogyakarta, and his wife, who was affiliated with the junior court. The couple took the students under their wing, getting them in to performances of shadow-puppet theater, gamelan music, and Javanese dance at the palace. Men in batik and turbans wandered barefoot through the lantern-lit halls, speaking high Javanese. "If I had walked into the court of King Arthur, I couldn't have been in more of a fairyland," Dewey remembered. She became captivated by Java, returning again and again over many decades. In 1989, at the investiture of Sultan Hamengku Buwono X in Yogyakarta, Dewey was in attendance.

Generous and tolerant, Dewey had a reputation for accepting the world on its own terms. "She felt that things work the way they do because they make sense that way, and that people are ultimately rational," said John Raintree, a former student of Dewey's. "If you don't understand why somebody is saying or doing something the way they are, then you don't understand their point of view. This is the article of faith for those of us who've worked in development— trying to explain that. Alice communicated that to her students."

In 1970, two years before Ann resurfaced on the University of Hawai'i campus, Dewey acquired a handsome old house in Mānoa, a short bicycle commute away from the campus. One of the attractions, as she told me, was a tree in the garden that produced avocados the size of footballs. The house also had four bedrooms, solving Dewey's dilemma, being a globetrotting anthropologist with a fondness for big dogs. Dewey recruited graduate students as housemates, along with, at various times, two German shepherd mixes, a Newfoundland, a gray cat, a Great Dane that matched the cat, and a kitten that matched the Newfoundland. There were also zebra finches, Java ricebirds, a waxbill, and other birds. By the time I saw the place in 2008, the house had settled into a state of advanced dilapidation. A botanical census of the garden would have included jacaranda, breadfruit, miniature mangosteen, lychee, Surinam cherry, rose apple, macadamia nut, cashew nut, yellow shower, tangerine, lemon, banana. Avocado pits, lobbed out a side door, had given birth to an avocado grove. An abandoned car had been reborn as a planter. "Trespassers will be eaten," read one of several plaques by the door. Jean Kennedy recalled arriving at the house for the first time in 1970 and finding every door wide open. Making her way to the kitchen, she called out and waited for a response.

"This highly distinctive voice yelled back, 'Put the kettle on and make tea.'" Kennedy told me. "There was a profusion of tea, I made the right one, I think it was lapsang souchong. That day, Alice said, 'Why don't you move in?' The basis for her household was very clear: She liked to live with people, she didn't want to be a landlady, she didn't charge us rent. She liked to be fed, she liked to have company, she liked to have a household that ticked over. There was always going to be someone who was there, so she could have dogs and not be worrying about traveling. It seemed to me on the one hand quite eccentric and on the other hand utterly sensible."

Ann became a regular visitor and occasional short-term denizen of Dewey's house in Mānoa. At any time, there were five or six people in residence and others dropping by to talk to Dewey or stay for dinner. An anthropologist in transit might be camped on a mattress on the floor. In several periods during the 1970s, Ann and Maya—and even, on one occasion, Lolo—occupied a second-floor bedroom overlooking a breadfruit tree at the northwest corner of the house. Kadi Warner recalled long discussions between Dewey and Ann on, say, the impact on Java of the introduction of Bahasa Indonesia, the national language, gradually supplanting the more status-attuned language, Javanese. For a book of anecdotes put together on the occasion of Dewey's retirement in October 2007, Maya reminisced in writing about "the wonderful labyrinth" of the house, with the secret staircases and "oversized flora" she knew as a child. She remembered being awakened by the cat, Kretek (the Indonesian word for clove cigarettes), sitting on her chest. Dewey introduced her, Maya wrote, to Alfred Hitchcock and good British mysteries. There were long meals followed by Javanese coffee, clove cigarettes, and fine storytelling.

"I remember feeling quite proud when one day Alice said that I was the most tolerable child she knew," Maya wrote.

Ann loved to talk. If she got interested in a topic, she seemed able to remember everything she had ever heard about it. "She could remember conversations almost verbatim," said Benji Bennington, who shared Ann's interest in Indonesia and the arts. "If you were reading, say, about a particular textile technique and talking to Ann, she seemed almost to be playing back a mental tape recording of some conversation she'd had with the source of the information." Garrett Solyom, who met her when they were graduate students, found that once he started talking with Ann, everything else seemed to disappear. "There was a certain amount of fencing," he said "She was smart. We have all these stupid words in English that don't say anything. Well, she would stick you. She would say, 'I wouldn't put it that way.' Or, 'No, I don't think so. Wouldn't it be this?' There would be a flash of the eye; and then you realized it was a flash of the brain." In a box of Ann's papers, I happened on a comment in her handwriting in the margin of an unpublished article by Solyom and his wife, Bronwen, that they had given her to read. "I guess we'll avoid our usual argument on what is iron versus low-grade steel carburized by forging in the presence of charcoal," she wrote. "It's really a continuum."

The Solyoms had lived in Indonesia in the late 1960s and had returned to the United States, as Bronwen Solyom put it in a talk at the University of Hawai'i in 2008, "fired up for one reason or another about Indonesia." Like Ann, they had arrived at the university as graduate students in the early 1970s, a time when, in the waning days of the Vietnam War, programs in Southeast Asian studies were blossoming. They were captivated by traditional Javanese art, ancient patterns on textiles, the origins of rituals they had witnessed. They were especially interested in "the making of things," Bronwen Solyom said—batik, shadow puppets, and the asymmetrical, often wavy-bladed, ceremonial dagger known as the kris, or *keris*, seen as both magical and sacred. Over the course of a twenty-year friendship, their interests and Ann's intersected and overlapped. The Solyoms focused on the object, its aesthetics and iconography, and its meaning in a ceremonial context; they studied the kris as a high art form, a court art, in its most refined form. Ann came to focus on the lives of craftspeople in the present day. When she studied blacksmiths, she immersed herself in everything from the making to the marketing of everyday agricultural tools. Her interest was function.

I once asked Maya if she could identify the source of her mother's interest in handicrafts. Using a phrase that stuck with me, she said her mother had always been "fascinated with life's gorgeous minutiae." When Ann was young, she had owned a loom and had woven wall hangings as a hobby. After moving to Indonesia, she began collecting batik and other textiles, handcrafted silver jewelry, rice-paddy hats, and woven baskets. In a foreword to the version of Ann's dissertation that was published in 2009 by Duke University Press, Maya wrote that her mother "was interested in the place where vision meets execution, and where the poetic and the prosaic share space. She loved the way something beautiful could speak about the spirit of both the maker and the owner; the skill and soul of the blacksmith are revealed in the *keris,* but so too is the desire and perspective of the buyer."

Ann had landed in Indonesia when the country was on the cusp of a renaissance in the traditional arts—a rebirth that resulted from scarcity. "Artistically, the 1960s were the best time for traditional arts, because people were so poor," Garrett Solyom told me. Renske Heringa, who lived in Indonesia in the same period, said, "We didn't have books, we couldn't buy clothes, we all went around in batik because that was all there was. There was nothing—but suddenly people became aware that they had something that nobody else had." Indonesians who traveled abroad noticed that Indonesian handicrafts were treasured elsewhere. With the growth of tourism in Indonesia in the 1970s, the market for handicrafts grew. At the same time, opportunities for women to earn a living in agriculture were shrinking. With the introduction of mechanical rice hullers, for example, fewer women could expect to make a living by hand-pounding rice. Many turned to small industries, including handicrafts, and petty trade. The government even adopted policies intended to encourage rural craft industries as a source of income for the poor. Ann had lived through that period.

In 1968, on her first visit to Taman Sari, the ruins of an

eighteenth-century pleasure park built for the sultan in Yogya-karta, she learned that there were four or five factories in the area making traditional *batik jarik,* an ankle-length wraparound skirt. "I did not visit these but I did see a number of older women sitting in groups in front of their houses doing *tulis* work on *jariks,*" she recalled in a field notebook some years later, referring to the tradi-tional method of hand-painting patterns in wax onto fabric before dyeing. There were no younger people involved in batik-making at that time, she noticed. But she wrote, "During a second visit in the early 70's a handful of galleries had sprung up; many of the cheaper paintings were being done by quite young children (8-12-ish) who were knocking them out at a very fast rate." By the time she returned, in July 1977, she found "about 40 establishments" on the west end of the ruins. As an anthropologist, Ann recognized that this was the last moment to witness the richness of Javanese culture still being produced by ancient technologies and traditions, Garrett Solyom told me. The opportunities, he said, were extraor-dinary.

In late 1974, Ann passed the oral exams for her master's degree, moved on to the Ph.D. program, and received approval to study the role of cottage industry "as a subsistence alternative" for peasant families on Java. Ann's choice of subject was unusual, Dewey told me, in its focus on the production of handicrafts and on their eco-nomic dimension. "People have been so overawed by their beauty that they talked about them as art—but not the market, not the busi-ness," Dewey said. Under the terms of her grant from the East-West Center, Ann had been required to take a course in entrepreneurship. The institute of which she was a part—the technology-and-development institute within the East-West Center—also had a particular focus on entrepreneurship. "She, I think, knew that these guys were smart businessmen," Dewey said. "But I don't think she knew the background literature." Dewey pointed her to the work of two of the most influential names in Javanese development—the Dutch economist J. H. Boeke and the American anthropologist Clifford Geertz, Dewey's colleague from the Modjokuto project. In Dewey's view, both had left a powerful but incorrect impression, picked up by Indonesian government officials, that the traditional handicraft industries were dying out, taking the cottage-industry villages with them. "The best scholars said it was crap, but the middle-level bureaucrats took it as the bible," Dewey told me. So she suggested to Ann: Bounce your data off the work of Boeke and Geertz.

In early 1975, Ann set off for Indonesia to begin her fieldwork. Maya went with her. Barry, who at that point had spent twelve of his thirteen years with his mother, remained behind. As Obama tells it in his book, the choice was his. "But when my mother was ready to return to Indonesia to do her fieldwork, and suggested that I go back with her and Maya to attend the international school there, I immediately said no," he writes. "I doubted what Indonesia now had to offer and wearied of being new all over again." Furthermore, there were advantages to living with his grandparents: They would leave him alone, he says, as long as he kept what he calls his "trouble" out of sight. The arrangement suited him, he says, because he was engaged in a solitary project of his own. He was learning to be a black man in America—in a place where there were few people to turn to for guidance.

Ann's decision to leave Barry, at thirteen, with her parents in Hawaii offends the sensibilities of many Americans who know almost nothing else about her. When people learned that I was working on a book on the president's mother, the question I encountered most often was: "Do you like her?" Sometimes people asked, "Was she nice?" The line of questioning puzzled me: Why were those the first things people wanted to know? Gradually, it became apparent that those questions were a way of approaching the subject of Ann's decision to live apart from her child. They were followed by ruminations on how a mother could do such a thing. As many Americans see it, a mother belongs with her child, and no extenuating circumstances can explain the perversity of choosing to be elsewhere. Ann's decision was a transgression that people thirty-five years later could neither understand nor forgive.

For Ann, leaving Barry behind was the single hardest thing she had ever done, Maya told me. But Ann felt she had no choice. Barry, who would enter high school the following fall, was flourishing at Punahou, which dispatched its graduates to some of the best universities in the country. If he had returned to Jakarta, Ann might not have had the money or connections to send him to the international school. If she had stayed in Hawaii, it is not clear what she would have done for employment. Perhaps she could have worked as a university lecturer, for relatively little money, or as a development consultant, traveling for months at a time. But she needed to do her fieldwork in order to get her Ph.D. She needed a Ph.D. to be considered for many jobs in her field. She had a second child to support, with a father in Indonesia, to whom she was still married. Other expatriate families might have sent a child in Barry's position to boarding school. But there was no boarding school tradition in Ann's family.

"It was terrible for her to leave Barry in Hawaii," recalled her friend Kadi Warner, who knew Ann during that period and lived with her and Maya several years later in Java. "But I think she agreed with his decision. It would have appealed to her intellect: Of course, this is the thing to do if you're in a great school. That's easy to say on one level, but it means you're leaving a child behind. She did trust her parents. There was no question in her mind that he would be well taken care of and nurtured. Looking back, with her first marriage, when everything fell apart there, they were extremely supportive and helpful. They enabled her to go back to school; there were no recriminations. So she knew Barry was in a situation where he was well taken care of. But nonetheless, to leave him—she adored him, she loved him terribly. She wanted to be his mother."

Ann, however, was not inclined to regret.

"Might she have tried to do things differently?" Maya said. "Perhaps, yeah. But at that time, I don't think she thought that there was any real alternative. That's how I think she thought about everything—the dissolution of her marriages to Barack Obama Sr. and my father. She was sad about that, just like she was sad about leaving her son in his high school years without her. It was one of those things where she felt like, 'Well, life is what it is.' She gained a great deal—not only the experiences in the world shared by her husband, but also her children. I think that's how she felt about Indonesia: 'The transition may have been difficult, but look . . .'"

Did Maya ever question Ann's judgment, in retrospect? I wondered.

"I think she did the very best that she could," Maya said. "And that she wanted only the best. And that she made some good choices, given what was available to her."

Ann returned with Maya to Jakarta and resumed teaching English at the management school in the late afternoons and evenings, banking her East-West Center grant money until she was ready to go into the field. She spent much of 1975 laying the groundwork required before she could begin her research. She needed a formal proposal and letters of reference certifying that she was a student and that she had funding. She needed the approval of the Indonesian Institute of Sciences, which often took months. She needed permission from every level of government, each of which levied its own fee. She set about clearing the twenty-two research permits needed to enable her to do intensive survey work in cottage-industry villages. She lined up an Indonesian government sponsor. She interviewed government officials, buyers, exporters, and aid-agency representatives. In the end, said Terence Hull, an American-born demographer who was working in Indonesia at the time, "You'd wander around with this great file of letters of permission so you could talk to an illiterate farmer about what the harvest was like."

By January 1976, Ann had moved to Yogyakarta, a short distance from the villages she intended to study. She settled temporarily in her mother-in-law's house in the heart of the city. The house stood inside the compound that encompassed the sultan's palace, or *kraton,* and its surrounding neighborhood, traditionally reserved for royal relatives and retainers. If Yogyakarta was the soul of Java, the compound within the crumbling, cream-colored walls was the soul of the city—the center of classical dance and drama, gamelan, batik, and puppet theater. There was a school for *dalang*s, the master puppeteers of *wayang kulit,* the shadow-puppet theater. Dancing masters instructed students in classical court dancing. Batik workshops produced by hand the classic brown-and-cream designs originally conceived for the sultan's family. Because foreigners were barred traditionally from living inside the compound, Ann told Dewey, she received special dispensation from the palace on the grounds that she was taking care of Lolo's mother. "She is 76 and strong as a horse but manages to look nice and frail," Ann wrote to Dewey. Her mother-in-law's house stood on a corner of Taman Sari, the ruins of the sultan's "water castle," a network of pools and waterways, like an early and more exclusive version of the water parks of today. The house was also adjacent to the bird market, where stalls stacked high with tubs of cracked corn and boxes of crickets lined narrow alleys; cages of roosters, parakeets, mynah birds, golden orioles, and turtledoves dangled from above. (In addition to a wife and a house, the markers of a man's success in Java include a singing bird.) "I am very happy to be staying now in Jogja," Ann wrote to Dewey, using the nickname and older spelling for Yogyakarta. "What an enjoyable city it is, especially as compared with Jakarta. I am getting a little tired of people saying 'Hello Mister' to me everywhere I go, but otherwise love it."

Like any anthropologist contemplating fieldwork in Java, Ann found her way to the Population Studies Center at Gadjah Mada University, a research institute established several years earlier by an Indonesian anthropologist named Masri Singarimbun, whose pioneering research on rural poverty had challenged official claims about the progress of poverty eradication. The center, which has now trained generations of Indonesian social scientists, was a lively gathering place for scholars. It also contained a mother lode of data of interest to international development institutions. There were ongoing research projects on everything from marriage, fertility, and family planning to infant mortality, poverty, and divorce. There were workshops on how to conduct village research. International visitors, such as Ivan Illich and E. F. Schumacher, would drop by. "Ann and hundreds of others came to Masri for advice," said Terence Hull, who, with his wife, Valerie, had done a village study under Singarimbun's supervision in the early 1970s and worked with him from 1975 to 1979. During the hot, dry season, he told me, development consultants descended like locusts, ravening information and data. They would drink tea and eat snacks on the porch, skimming off the impressions of scholars who had been immersed for months or years in village life.

"When you're in that crowd, there are a lot of discussions about what people are doing in development—the World Bank, et cetera," Hull said. "There's a lot of cynical humor. Ann was not a cynical person, but she did appreciate the ironies that you would encounter all the time. The fact that the World Bank teams would always come between June and September with their vacuum cleaners, taking up reports every which way in any Indonesian institution, sometimes sitting down, taking their tea, telling people to go and photocopy hundreds of documents. Ann would appreciate the total inappropriateness of that sort of behavior, the irony of these people blowing in from Johns Hopkins or Michigan State or Iowa State or wherever, on what must be really, really high salaries or consultants' fees, and coming into a research institute where people are being paid a pittance to do really hard work with 24/7 kind of responsibilities. They just showed no sensitivity to the vast gaps. Ann was totally attuned to the enormous gaps between Westerners' lives and people who were really living tough lives in Indonesia."

Ann found other kindred spirits in Yogyakarta. Nancy Peluso, the daughter of a Fuller Brush salesman from Bridgeport, Connecticut, had arrived in the city in 1975 as an undergraduate from Friends World College in the United States, doing independent research. She learned Indonesian, moved to a village, and decided to study the economic roles of women. "This was a big topic at that time," she told me thirty-three years later in her office at the University of California at Berkeley, where she was a professor in the department of environmental science, policy, and management, specializing in forest politics and agrarian change in Southeast Asia. Women were breaking into academic fields in which they had once been scarce; research on women and development was in vogue. When Peluso applied to the Ford Foundation for a grant, she landed $2,000, which seemed to her an extravagant sum. "They asked me what I wanted to live on and I said, 'Fifty dollars a month,'" she remembered. "They said, 'How about a hundred?'" She began studying market traders—women who bought household items, such as ceramic pots, from craftspeople and sold them in markets. At two or three in the morning, Peluso would set off with a trader on a four-hour hike into the mountains, the woman maneuvering a cart piled high with pots up the slopes of a volcano in darkness, to arrive at the market as dawn was breaking. "These people had nothing," she recalled. "It was often women—women in a family where there wasn't a lot of agricultural land would go into these other kinds of businesses. They would either do small-scale trade or they would do crafts, like in the villages that Ann worked in."

Ann and Peluso would meet in Yogyakarta and wander over to the marketplace for snacks, fried noodles, or durian in season. (The fruit of the durian tree is a local delicacy, but its smell disgusts many foreigners. At the Phoenix Hotel in Yogyakarta, it gets special mention in the directory of services. Coming after "duty manager" and before "extra bed," the durian entry states, "By respect to others, it is strictly forbidden to bring durian into the hotel.") At other times, Ann and Peluso would take Maya to dance performances at the palace or to shadow-puppet performances in the *alun-alun,* the grassy square with its two sacred banyan trees. "To this day, I nearly faint with pleasure when I smell hot wax, because I grew up roaming around the batik makers," Maya told me. She remembered running in the ruins of the sultan's "water castle," gazing at the animals in the marketplace, watching the court dancers performing stories from the Hindu epics. She and Ann lived on a budget, she remembered her mother telling her, of about seventy-five dollars a month. Ann would take her to a bakery on Jalan Malioboro, the main commercial street in Yogyakarta, and pretend to look around while the owners plied her captivating child with chocolate and coconut breads. On one occasion, Peluso recalled, the three of them spent a night on a mountain. A professor had told Peluso of the practice of spending the night on certain mountains in pursuit of good fortune. People would climb to the top, burn incense, eat, talk, sleep, or stay awake. There would be people selling food. "It's supposed to bring you good luck or you're supposed to get a wish

With Nancy Peluso, Yogyakarta, 1977 or 1978

or get money," Peluso remembered. "Well, we didn't get money. We just did it to do it. Maya went with us. We took public transport to get out to this mountain. I remember getting there and starting to walk up the hill with Ann. You did things like this. You were single—and she was effectively single."

Not long before moving to Yogyakarta, Ann had appeared in the office of a young assistant curator at the National Museum in Jakarta named Wahyono Martowikrido, an archaeologist specializing in material culture, particularly gold objects and textiles. A museum guard brought her to his office, Martowikrido told me, after Ann had asked to speak with an anthropologist, who turned out not to be in the building at the time. She seemed to be looking for someone to explain certain objects in the collection. According to Martowikrido, they talked and Ann invited him to join her for a meal. When he arrived later at the designated restaurant, he found her talking and laughing with a friend. They were celebrating Ann's birthday, it seemed. After that encounter, Martowikrido told me, he and Ann became friends. They would talk about Javanese culture and the meaning of certain handcrafted objects—how the design on a piece of fabric indicated that the wearer was a widow, or the significance of a certain crescent-shaped comb. After Martowikrido moved to Yogyakarta to study, and Ann moved there to begin her research, she would stop by the room he rented, where students often came by to study and talk. "She is very openhearted," he told me. "Nothing to hide." She did not reveal, however, where she was living, Martowikrido said. He introduced her to *lurik,* the handwoven striped cotton from Yogyakarta, which he collected. He explained its history, the meaning of its design, and the varieties of stripes. Because Yogyakarta was famous for its silversmiths and goldsmiths, he took her to workshops in Kota Gede, a section of the city, so she could see how silver jewelry was made. "I told her that I am not interested in the objects but in the making of them," he said. After a while, he said, "I think she is now looking at the object differently. At the beginning, she looks at the object as it's written by the scholars. But she saw objects made by Javanese in society, then you see it a little bit differently."

Their friendship created talk, according to Renske Heringa, a close friend of Ann's in the early 1980s. "He exposed her to all kinds of things that, without him, she might not so easily have gotten access to," said Heringa, known as Rens. "He knew all kinds of villages that would not have been easy for her to go to. And he liked to be with her in the field." He knew where to buy fabric and objects for little money. "She went all over Yogyakarta, as far as I know, with him on this motorbike," Heringa said. "Why not? She was free, and he was free. Most of all, it was just the fact that they went around so much. For Indonesians, that would immediately mean that there was an affair. For Westerners, not so. Ann was there by herself. Why wouldn't she be able to do what she wanted?"

With friends at Nancy Peluso's, Yogyakarta

Martowikrido told me, when I asked, that he did not know how Ann felt about him. Perhaps she liked him, he said, because she would come by to visit. When I asked him about his feelings for her, he turned away, as though embarrassed by the question, and said he could not answer.

Ann's return to Indonesia had done little to shrink the distances that had opened up in her marriage to Lolo. According to Maya, the day she and Ann arrived in Jakarta, they found a young woman, who was quite beautiful, in Lolo's house—the woman he would marry five years later, after he and Ann divorced. Maya, who was four at the time, told me she remembered little about the encounter. She did remember, however, her father's nervousness and a lingering impression that her parents had argued about the woman's presence.

Ann and Maya lived in Lolo's house in Menteng Dalam that year, but it seems that much of the time he did not. "I think he had another place that he lived," Kay Ikranagara told me, but she said Lolo was often there when she and her son would visit. On the van ride to and from the business school, Samardal Manan, who had known Ann well during her first couple of years in Jakarta, said he was struck now by how free she seemed, as though "relieved from something." After Ann and Maya moved to Yogyakarta in early 1976, Lolo would fly in to visit, staying in the house with his mother. Ikranagara recalled Ann telling her, on a visit to Yogyakarta, that Lolo was involved with another woman. "At that point, they were separated," Ikranagara said. "I didn't feel that they were husband and wife anymore, whether or not they were divorced formally." To Maya, Ann said Lolo's job with the oil company kept them apart. "They were still, though, supposedly trying to make the marriage work," Maya recalled. Years later, Ann suggested to Maya that Lolo, whose health was poor, had been feeling mortal and contemplating the possibility that his name might not carry on. "He must have been lonely, though, on some level," Maya told me. "I mean, there was a lot of back-and-forth: She was in Hawaii; he was in Indonesia. I'm not sure that you can really build a satisfying marriage with so much movement. So that's understandable—a pretty, lively thing who's present when your wife is not. I'm not saying that I forgive him, because I was upset that he hurt my mother. But I can't see that, even in advance of that, there was a marriage in the sense that I would expect a marriage to be—a sort of daily negotiation and conversation and affection and that sort of thing."

Sometime in the late 1970s, Lolo became seriously ill. Returning home from a game of tennis at the Petroleum Club late one afternoon, Kadi Warner remembered Ann telling her, Lolo collapsed. The diagnosis was liver disease. Maya referred to it as cirrhosis; others told me that the damage to his liver was the result of a childhood illness acquired during the Japanese occupation. After at least one hospitalization in Jakarta in June 1977, it became apparent that Lolo needed a level of medical care that was not available in Indonesia. "They couldn't treat him in Indonesia," Warner said. "But because he was a local hire, he didn't have the benefits to go outside. What Ann said was that she shamed the oil company into sending him out." She appealed to his boss at Union Oil to allow Lolo to be treated in the United States. "She went in and wept on his boss's desk, begging him to pay for Lolo to go to the United States," Kay Ikranagara remembered. "She said, 'You must send him to the United States, he will die without care.' She cried on the desk till he agreed." When I asked how Ann felt about having done that, Ikranagara said, "She was proud she'd done it. But she didn't want to have to go through that again."

Lolo was flown to Los Angeles, hospitalized, and treated there. His nephew, Sonny Trisulo, a student at the University of California at Los Angeles in the late 1970s, recalled visiting him in the hospital on several occasions. Before returning to Jakarta, Ann and Maya took Lolo to Honolulu to recuperate in the second-floor bedroom at Dewey's house, overlooking the breadfruit tree.

Once, I asked Maya how her parents' marriage had ceased to be a functioning marriage. She said she did not know. For a long time, she said, she was too "young and foolish and self-centered" to ask that sort of question. Later, she said, her mother may have shielded her from the truth. "She probably wanted to be very careful that my memories of him weren't blemished in any way," she said. "I mean, she was a great mom and really wanted to make sure that I wasn't too hurt by things. It was not just that she didn't want to speak ill of the dead; she didn't want to speak ill of my father."

Maya had written a short story, she said, in which a child keeps asking her mother, "Did you love him?" The mother keeps batting away the question. "I never really asked those questions," Maya said. "It's just a short story because I wondered later why I didn't ask those questions about how much they loved each other. It was sort of like I felt, maybe in my youthful arrogance, that I knew. What I surmised, I guess, ultimately, was that they did love each other, but sometimes love isn't quite enough. That it was a gentle love that followed a very passionate love that she had with Barack's father. That my mother thought of my father as being a very sweet man but could be frustrated by his lack of communication about certain things. And ultimately, I think that she was disappointed that the marriage didn't work. I felt so certain in that assessment of her feelings for him and her perception of him that I don't think I ever asked."

Six

In the Field

It is not difficult to understand why people become entranced by Java. The landscape is breathtaking—shimmering paddy fields, terraced hillsides, luminous green plains carved by rivers and studded with volcanoes. The people are, as Francis Drake wrote after sailing there in 1580, "sociable, full of vivacity and beyond description happy." The culture is the product of centuries of cross-fertilization—Hindu, Buddhist, and Islamic influences mixed with elements of animism, ancestor worship, and Javanese legend. The past lives on in the patterns in textiles, in the performing arts, in thousand-year-old temples. Before dawn, visitors clamber up the sides of the twelve-centuries-old Buddhist monument of Borobudur to watch Gunung Merapi, Indonesia's most active volcano, materialize out of the darkness, swathed in mists, the silence broken only by roosters and the whine of a motorcycle in the distance. At first glance, Javanese life seems to unspool in the open, as though on a vast and meticulously painted canvas: The dusty village streets shaded by mango and *mlinjo* trees where children skitter barefoot, the man bending in the flooded paddy field with his pants rolled, the women selling peanut fritters and *gado-gado* in the market. But the fact is, Java reveals itself, layer by layer, only over time, challenging Western assumptions about what it means to understand or know. "It's not that they *do* it differently," a British friend of Ann's, Clare Blenkinsop, told me. "You have to *be* in a different way." After returning to Java and Morocco several decades after doing fieldwork there as a young anthropologist in the 1950s and 1960s, Clifford Geertz confessed to having had, as he put it, a rather shaking experience—"the reawakening of an imperfectly suppressed conviction that I have never understood and never will understand a damn thing about either of these peculiar places, or, for that matter, myself." Java rewards patience, Garrett Solyom told me one afternoon in Honolulu. His observation struck me as cautionary, not just about Java but about trying to understand his friend Ann. Java rewards patience, he said: diligence, patience, and long study.

When Ann began her fieldwork in Central Java in the mid-seventies, sixty percent of all Indonesians lived on the island of Java, though it makes up just seven percent of Indonesia's total land area. It was, and remains, among the most densely populated agricultural areas in the world. Most Javanese were peasants living in rural villages, working on small farms, raising crops by hand. But aspects of that life were changing. The "Green Revolution" of the 1970s had increased rice production, but it also had less immediately visible effects. The introduction of pesticides, sickles, and mechanical rice hullers took away much of the work of weeding, harvesting, and hand-pounding, traditionally done by women. Meanwhile, circuit traders driving trucks, mostly men, were taking the place of female traders who traditionally traveled on foot. Wage labor had been rare in rural areas before 1965. Now handicraft industries—including weaving, batik, and ceramics—faced competition from imported goods and products made in new factories set up with foreign capital. Hand-loom weavers, predominantly women, were being squeezed out of production. Many Western-style factories favored men in hiring, training, promotion, and pay. By the end of the 1970s, hundreds of thousands of women had moved out of agriculture and into rural manufacturing, many of them as part-time unpaid cottage-industry workers, Ann estimated in an apparently unpublished paper in the early 1980s. Some had difficulty finding stable employment as hired workers. With credit hard to come by and interest rates high, they also lacked the capital needed to become successful small-scale entrepreneurs.

The subject of Ann's fieldwork was cottage industries and their role as a subsistence alternative for peasant families on Java. "In many areas of the developing world the native handicraft industries have either died out completely in this century, or have managed to hang on only in a very weakened state, catering to a much-reduced market of curio-seekers and tourists," she wrote in an early proposal to the East-West Center. Time once spent making handicrafts now went to "more profitable pursuits," such as wage labor in foreign-owned operations. "Java offers the startling contrast of a case where cottage industry has not only survived, but rapidly expanded in the last fifteen years," she continued. As many as six and a half million people on Java worked in cottage industry production—up from as little as half that number in 1961. Many Javanese villages specialized in a single product—bamboo birdcages, clay roof tiles, leather puppets, to name a few. In some villages, almost every adult took part. "Instead of being merely a quaint and minor survival of days gone by, cottage industry is the major mode of manufacturing many types of light consumer goods, including such items as roof tiles, bricks, ceramics, textiles, furniture, shoes, umbrellas, wall matting, baskets and containers, cigarettes, silver and brassware, herb medicines, snack foods, etc.," Ann wrote. "The central problem of my research is to explain this expansion of cottage industry on Java."

Her hypothesis arose out of a harsh fact of Javanese life: As the population grew and the amount of agricultural land remained constant, more and more laborers worked the same finite plots of land. As a result, each laborer's share of the yield decreased, requiring that he or she work longer just to keep up. The rural economy, however, was based not only on agriculture but also on petty commerce and cottage industry. Rather than work unnaturally long hours with diminishing returns, peasants found it more profitable to spend more time on other ways of making a living. "This tendency to turn to subsidiary occupations in the face of declining agricultural returns lies, I suggest, behind the expansion of cottage industry activities on Java in recent years," Ann wrote.

Ann was challenging what she believed was a common misconception. In the literature on peasant societies, she argued, peasant industries got short shrift. "Typically an ethnography of a peasant group will devote a hundred pages or more to describing the agricultural sector in great detail, and then dismiss peasant industries in a few throwaway lines," she wrote. "Peasant industries are frequently characterized as 'spare time' activities, low in productivity and profitability, which are carried out mainly by poor women and children, and then only when they can find no agricultural work to do." Ann started from a different premise—one rooted in her years of experience on Java, and in an appreciation for the economic decision-making of Javanese peasants. Peasant society, she said, "produces rural generalists rather than specialists. By this I mean that nearly every peasant has a repertoire of various skills which can be utilized for productive or income-generating purposes. A Javanese man, for example, may have skills in plowing and land preparation which are related to rice agriculture, but he may also know how to repair bicycles, make bricks, drive a pedicab (*becak*), raise fish or eels in ponds, make noodle soup and hawk it around the streets of a nearby town, etc. Similarly, a Javanese woman may have agricultural skills in transplanting, weeding and harvesting rice, but she may also know how to make batik cloth, operate a roadside stall or coffee shop (*warung*), collect teak leaves from a nearby forest for sale as food wrappers, trade vegetables or spices in a nearby marketplace, deliver babies for her neighbors, make palm sugar or cassava chips, etc." Some researchers had remarked on this pattern. But Ann intended to expand the concept to encompass not simply an "observable pattern of activity" but a conscious strategy.

She began her fieldwork with short visits to several dozen cottage-industry villages near Yogyakarta. For a time, a nationwide ban on village research in the six months leading up to the May 1977 general elections forced her back to Jakarta (where she taught a course for development planners at the University of Indonesia until she could return to the field). But by late June, she was back in the villages. In a long entry in her field notebook about a visit on June 25, 1977, to a basketry village called Malangan, her recorded observations included such things as the percentage of the village population active in making basketry products (fifty percent), an accounting of the products made (rice steamers, lampshades, nesting boxes, et cetera), the age at which children are considered fully productive (ten years old), a description of the photos in the industry leader's living room, a list of raw materials and their sources, a list of sources of credit, and a detailed accounting of "prosperity indicators," which included school attendance, livestock, crops grown in house yards, bicycles and motorcycles, a television, and sweet tea and snacks offered to visitors. "Twice asked whether women did modern work (no) and why not," Ann wrote. "Answer that they are too 'busy' and too 'lazy' to study the new techniques." Over the next few weeks, she could be found noting the benefits of burning coconut husks in the fire pit in a candy factory in Bantul, counting the twenty-eight sizes and types of chisels on the work-table of an elderly maker of masks and wooden puppets, and examining the buffalo hides used by a leather puppetmaker in Gendeng ("Cow hides having a tendency to roll up and curl," she noted). From there, she moved on to bamboo villages, batik villages, and weaving villages, as well as to factories producing fruit wine, coconut-fiber matting, and dolls.

On August 3, Ann left Yogyakarta, heading southeast on the road to Wonosari, a market town in the dry, hilly district of Gunung Kidul, which lies between Yogyakarta and the Indian Ocean. About a half-hour outside of Yogyakarta, the road to Wonosari climbs into the hills in a series of loops overlooking the Central Java plains. From Wonosari, a smaller road heads northeast toward Kajar, a cluster of hamlets where, in 1977, hundreds of village men worked as blacksmiths at backyard forges, hammering agricultural tools out of old railroad rails and scrap iron. By eight a.m., Ann would later write, the sounds of forging could be heard coming from every corner of the village—the three-beat rhythm of the hammer swingers striking metal on metal, the "light counterpoint" of the master smith tapping instructions on the anvil, "the muffled plops of the bellows," the scraping sound of the filing and polishing of tools. Peak-roofed houses with woven bamboo walls and earthen floors lined a loose grid of narrow dirt and gravel roads. Bamboo, coconut palms, and fruit trees grew in the house yards, alongside a few cattle and goats. Women and children operated roadside stands selling snacks, kerosene, cooked food. There was no plumbing in

Kajar; only one household had electricity, supplied by a diesel en-
gine. Ann had first heard of Kajar one week earlier in an interview
with a consultant on a World Bank team looking into possible development projects in the area. "There is a cooperative in the village, which has been controlled since 1962 by the same three men
(elections are open, not by secret ballot) which purchases and farms
out 30 million rupiahs worth of scrap iron per year!" she had written in her notes on the interview. The following week, having attached herself to a ten-day press tour organized by the Indonesian
Department of Industry in connection with the anniversary of its
ladies' auxiliary, she was there. The smiths made more than tools,
she learned that day; they also hammered gamelan gongs for village orchestras, using the ends of kerosene and diesel-fuel drums.
They used a double-piston bellows made of two hollowed-out tree
trunks—a style of bellows so old it can be found in a scene of a
smithy in the reliefs at Candi Sukuh, a fifteenth-century temple on
the slopes of Gunung Lawu, seen as one of the holiest mountains
on Java. "The work is backbreaking and earsplitting, but no protective equipment is used," Ann wrote after that first day in Kajar.
The hammer swingers, positioned around the forge, stood up to
their knees in a pit—a position, she learned later, designed to prevent their calf muscles from atrophying from constant squatting.

Farming was a tough way to make a living in Kajar, Ann was
to discover. Flanked to the east by barren karst limestone hills, the
village was situated in an ecological transition zone. The rocky soil
was fertile enough for cassava, corn, and dry rice as staples, and
peanuts and other legumes for sale to traders. But rainfall was un-
predictable. Drought had wiped out crops, and famine had killed
off most of the livestock and some villagers, as recently as the early
1960s. Not long afterward, there had been a plague of rats. Over
several decades, blacksmithing had edged out farming as the dom-

inant occupation. The industry was said to date back to the arrival in Kajar in the 1920s of two migrant smiths, who then married local women and brought their sons and sons-in-law into the business. During the Japanese occupation, Japanese military officers brought broken weapons and confiscated scrap metal to the village; they ordered the original smiths to teach other villagers how to turn scrap into tools. Forced to copy new items, village smiths learned to custom-make whatever a buyer might want. They also discovered that tools could be made more economically from scrap iron than from imported bar iron. After the famine and the rat plague of the 1960s, more smithies opened. The market for agricultural tools grew during the Green Revolution and under the Suharto government's policy of transmigration, in which impoverished Indonesians were being induced to move from crowded Java to less populous corners of Sumatra, Kalimantan, and East Timor. In the late seventies, thirty more smithies opened in Kajar, bringing the total to ninety-eight, employing a total of six hundred men. Because of the demand for workers, the ancient taboo that had kept women from working in the forge began to crumble. "Kajar men consider themselves craftsmen first and agriculture a *sambilan*," Ann wrote after her first full day of surveying in Kajar, using the Indonesian word for a sideline or second job. Kajar would prove a fascinating case study of the phenomenon she had set out to explain, the expansion of cottage industry.

Ann returned repeatedly to Kajar over the next year, sometimes for many weeks at a time. John Raintree, an anthropologist who worked with Ann several years later, told me that "the predominant anthropological method is to put yourself in the village context. You are the outsider, the childlike neophyte. You let them socialize you into their worldview." Ann had hired two research assistants—a jovial, strapping young economics student named

Djaka Waluja and his wife, Sumarni, a graduate student and an assistant at the Population Studies Center at Gadjah Mada. In January 2009, I met them in an office at Dr. Sardjito Hospital in Yogyakarta, where Sumarni, a lecturer in medicine at Gadjah Mada, was working. Djaka told me that he and Ann spent four months in the district of Gunung Kidul, living at least part of the time in the house of an Indonesian government fieldworker assigned to Kajar. Ann and Djaka would set out for the field every morning at five a.m. Dressed in a long skirt and loaded down with a shoulder bag stuffed with notebooks, books, and a camera, Ann would ride behind Djaka on the back of Sumarni's small, not entirely reliable Yamaha motorcycle. When I asked why Djaka Waluja, rather than Sumarni, accompanied Ann to Kajar, he said, "Gunung Kidul was far away, Ann was a big woman. To get to Gunung Kidul, uphill, you can imagine." His greater weight, he suggested, was needed for balance and control. Ann took to calling the motorcycle Poniyem, making a bilingual pun out of a name that sounds like the English word "pony" but also happens to be given to Javanese girls born on the third day (Pon) of the five-day Javanese week. "Ayo, Poniyem!" she would cry out as the motorcycle lumbered toward a hill, while she pretended to swat its imaginary rump. (The meaning of that expression falls somewhere between "C'mon, Poniyem!" and "Hi-Yo, Silver!") She and Waluja would conduct interviews from dawn until seven p.m., then stay up until midnight, transcribing their data into English in one of the hard-backed, pale green composition books Ann used as field notebooks. "Kajar is certainly an interesting village from several points of view, not the least of which is political," she wrote to Dewey. "I can envision a little article someday with a model of the balance of power there and the shifts affected by various styles of tinkering from outside." According to Waluja, he and Ann slept four hours a night, on average. He returned to Yogyakarta on weekends, he said; she returned less often. When I asked him if he found the schedule demanding, he told me he made a habit of drinking a liquid multivitamin supplement "to keep my strength up and my eyes open."

Ann was ambitious. That was how Waluja and Sumarni put it, at least when they expressed the idea in English. "She would often tell us, 'I want this, that, this. I have to get that,'" Waluja told me. She liked to put her plans in writing, often in the form of a diagram with multiple steps, as though it were proof that she intended to deliver. The working conditions were rough, but she never complained, even walking long distances in heat or rain. "She just exhaled loudly," said Waluja, whom Ann took to calling Joko. Then she would say, "It's nothing compared to hell, Joko." In the village of Pocung, the river that ran through the bottomland would overflow, preventing her from reaching the home of a craftsman she was observing. She would overhaul the day's schedule on the spot. She adapted easily to the customs of her informants. In a culture in which tea and snacks materialize at almost every encounter, Ann accepted whatever was offered rather than risk appearing rude by declining. "Speaking of cash crops, we arrived in Kajar just at the time of the peanut harvest," she wrote to Dewey in July 1978. "This meant that at every house we surveyed we were given large glasses of sticky sweet tea, refilled at least 3 times despite all of my '*sampuns,*' and big plates of peanuts in the shell to consume. Considering some days we visited 5 or 6 households, I don't think either Joko or I will be able to look a peanut in the face again (yes, peanuts <u>do</u> have faces—smirky, nasty little faces, in fact). At any rate you can be sure that before moving on to the next village we are checking out very carefully what <u>they</u> have just harvested." (*Sampun* is a Javanese expression, roughly equivalent in this context to the American expression "I'm full.")

On one occasion, in a village called Jambangan in Ngawi, a town in East Java on the Central Java border, Ann was invited to watch a *tayub,* a dance performed by young women at which men in the audience may join in. It was rare for an outsider to be present, Sumarni told me, and men in the audience turned out to be drunk. When the men began shoving money down the dancers' strapless tops, Sumarni said, she watched Ann closely. "She laughed," Sumarni said. "Uncomfortably."

With her interview subjects, she could be tender. "She was always touching," Sumarni said. Before beginning an interview, she might put her arm around a farmer's shoulders and ask if he had eaten recently. If the answer was no, she sometimes would say sorrowfully, almost to herself, as though trying to come to grips with the fact, "He said he didn't have anything to eat." Occasionally, Waluja and Sumarni noticed her turn away and wipe tears from her face. Once, she was visibly upset by the sight of an elderly woman in the village of Kasongan who, despite her age, was forced by her circumstances to work. "I wondered if she was too sensitive," Waluja told me.

Ann was nothing if not methodical. She accumulated lists—of raw materials, of people to contact, of nineteen steps in making agricultural tools. "Steps in Surveying New Village," she wrote in pencil inside the back cover of one notebook; twelve instructions followed, covering everything from how to secure government clearances to the need to summarize all data in charts. "Photos needed from Kajar," she once wrote, going on to list forty-three. To say the questionnaires she administered to villagers and village officials were comprehensive would be an understatement. Geography, demography, technology, labor investment, purchasing, output, distribution, capital, returns, cash expenditure patterns, assistance from outside agencies, history, land tenure, agricultural yields, trading: Those were a few of her areas of interest. Her notes from a single day of fieldwork in Kajar might include the price and sources of scrap iron; rates of pay for bellows workers, hammerers, and the smith; an accounting of one smith's expenditures and revenues; types of charcoal used; an inventory of fifteen blacksmithing tools; discussions of marketing practices, the function of the cooperative, cooperative dues, the availability of credit, seasonal shifts in labor supply; and observations on child labor, women's roles, diet, and land use. "Difficult person to interview," she reported in her notebook after a routine interview in Pocung. "Interview cut after 3 or 4 hours with poor results." Her six pages of notes on a conversation with Garrett Solyom about field photography covered shutter speeds, film speeds, filters, lens paper, liquid lens cleaner, processing, storage of negatives, and a lot more. "The smaller the F stop, the wider the aperture," Ann noted. "Need a fast lens." Solyom, who had bought his photographic equipment with a gift of one thousand dollars from Dewey, had learned his technique from his father, a game biologist. "Look with your entire being," his father had told him. "Sit still. Things will begin to happen because you're not there." The advice that Ann chose to write down had a practical cast. "Ask yourself before each photo: What am I trying to show in this photo?" she wrote. "Don't decapitate people."

Yes, don't decapitate. Ann's descriptions of her informants were precise, affectionate, and not without humor. "Pak Atmo is a small, shrewd, comical man, fond of a good joke," she wrote in her notes, describing the head of the biggest hamlet in Kajar. One man was "shy, vague, pleasant"—and utterly without business sense. Another struck her as "open, good-hearted, modest and sexy." After interviewing one man, she scribbled parenthetically, "Wife a bit of twit." After a visit from a team of German engineers: "Much nonsense talked." She regaled Dewey with details of one Pak Harjo

Bodong: "Roughly translated, 'Father Harjo with the Long Belly Button,' though I never had the courage to really ask why," Ann wrote in a letter. "Pak Harjo Bodong used to be the most famous *dalang* in the Wonosari area. He also used to be a famous thief and was in jail four times when he was young. Now he is . . . a pillar of the community and lives there with his twelfth wife (he is her tenth husband). They are both in their seventies and quite a sketch. We enjoyed many evenings at their house hearing stories about the old days, and I got a free course in the *wayang* to boot!"

Pak Sastrosuyono, the head of the blacksmithing cooperative and Kajar's leading entrepreneur, became one of her most important informants—a man of average build with "an intelligent-looking face and a habitual expression that could be described as slightly worried or puzzled-looking," she wrote in her dissertation. "Although one hears many stories about Pak Sastro from other villagers, some of them bordering on the fantastic, he seldom talks about himself or his accomplishments. When he does, he tends to downplay those accomplishments. If asked to discuss the extent of his property, his wealth, his financial contributions to village ceremonies or improvement projects, etc., he always gives underestimates. In part, this can be attributed to Javanese culture, which places a high value on personal modesty and abhors bragging. In part, however, it is probably due to a realistic assessment of his situation in the village. He is both highly respected, and resented to a considerable degree."

She went on to describe what struck her as a particularly telling moment.

One scene of Pak Sastro and his wife stands out in the author's memory and expresses the poignancy of his relations with the other villagers. While returning from household interviews one evening in 1978, the author passed by Pak Sastro's house.

He had just purchased the first television set in the village, and was able to pick up programs broadcast from Jogjakarta. Since the village electrification program had not yet begun, the first sets used in rural areas were battery-operated. Pak Sastro and Bu Sastro had tried to watch the set in their own home, but hundreds of other villagers crowded uninvited into their house in order to get a glimpse of this strange new phenomena. Finally, in exasperation, Pak Sastro was forced to place the set in the window of his house, facing outward toward the house-yard. As a sign of their superior status, and the fact that the set did in fact belong to them, Pak Sastro and Bu Sastro were allowed to sit on two chairs placed in the yard in front of the set. The rest of the village stood up to watch, crowded around behind them in the yard.

Kajar's charms and mysteries, natural and supernatural, fascinated Ann. There were three sacred springs in the village. One, shaded by a large and sacred banyan tree, was to be avoided at night because the Javanese believe that ghosts and spirits live in banyan trees. At the base of another was a flat stone on which one could see coloration in the shape of the wavy-bladed Javanese dagger, the kris, or *keris,* in Indonesian. "Villagers consider this image of a *keris* as proof that the men of Kajar are fated to be smiths, and that men from neighboring villages do not share this fate," Ann wrote in her dissertation. Blacksmithing was considered sacred; so were the forge, the hearth, and the nail-shaped anvil, which resembled a lingam, the stylized phallus worshipped in Hinduism as a symbol of the god Shiva. Smiths were revered, and old smiths were believed to have special powers. Before opening a new forge, a smith would prepare an offering of molded rice, fruit, and flowers to be burned along with incense in the smithy. There were offerings to the anvils on the first day of the Javanese week. Every year, on the first day of the first Javanese month, all the smiths would dress formally in sarongs, high-necked jackets, and small folded batik turbans. Walking in single file and each carrying a tray laden with food offerings, they would circle the village and climb one of the limestone hills behind it to the graves of the two original smiths. There, they would make their offerings and meditate or pray. "Whenever villagers have a problem such as illness or sterility, or when they are looking to improve their luck, they bring offerings of rice, flowers, etc. to those graves," Ann wrote. When she developed an eye infection on one occasion, she was advised to rinse her eyes in the waters of the sacred spring. When the infection persisted, villagers suggested a pilgrimage to the top of the limestone hill and offerings to the smiths' graves.

In June 1978, Ann learned of an elderly kris smith living in Kajar. In Javanese tradition, the kris is an object of extraordinary importance and power—a weapon, an heirloom, a mark of rank, a male symbol, an item of male ceremonial dress, an art form, a sacred object with protective powers and a life of its own. "There are numerous stories of kerises rattling about in their cases, wanting to get out, or of kerises flashing about in mid-air, independently attacking their owner's enemies," Ann wrote in the early 1980s. According to the Solyoms, who have written extensively on the kris, a man might go so far as to trade his car or his house for a kris that he senses is right for him—one that makes him feel spiritually complete and personally content. The makers of krises were believed to be descended from the gods. Like wizards or magicians in Western cultures, master kris smiths possessed special knowledge. Their craft was passed on only within families, and was seen as dangerous; it demanded, as the Solyoms put it, "the release and control of threatening powers that could go astray if not treated properly." By the late 1970s, there were said to be no master smiths left in Java, just a few village smiths carrying on the tradition of their fathers. On June 19, 1978, Ann wrote in her notes that she had learned that there was one kris smith left in Kajar. (She later learned there were two.) "He still has the magical power to make pamor kerises," she wrote, referring to the light-on-dark dama-scened patterns on a kris blade, made of layers upon layers of iron and meteoritic nickel sandwiched together. "He has not been able, however, to pass the tradition on to anyone and he is old now."

In early July, she and Waluja interviewed the kris smith, Pak Martodinomo, one of two surviving sons-in-law of Kasan Ikhsan, one of the two original smiths in Kajar. He was about eighty years old, Ann estimated. In his prime, he had received seven or eight commissions a year. Now he rarely received one. "People don't at-tach importance to kerises any more," Ann wrote in her notes. "A change in the times." Martodinomo's father-in-law had been an expert in a type of Javanese mysticism known as *ilmu kebatinan,* which Ann described later as a set of practices, Hindu and Bud-dhist in origin, intended to increase a person's spiritual power and insight into the meaning of life. Ann listed the steps required be-fore starting a kris: Fast for three days; hold a private *selamatan* with barbecued chicken, coconut rice, and boiled rice to protect the kris during forging; hold a personal *selamatan* to protect the smith from bad spirits. Work on a kris was to commence at the beginning of the Javanese month called Suro, continue intermittently through-out the year, and end the following Suro. A smith could kill no animals during Suro and was required to fast Mondays and Thurs-days. "Get acquainted with the spirit of the iron to be used," Ann wrote. "If you don't get acquainted, can have an accident while working e.g. be blinded, paralyzed, very sick, insane or even die suddenly."

Ann appears to have had little difficulty convincing her subjects to talk. In small script at the bottom of one page of field notes, she noted, "None of the people interviewed so far are comfortable in Indonesian." For that reason, Djaka told me, he and Ann conducted all of the interviews together. She would discuss with him, in Bahasa Indonesia, the questions she wanted to ask; he would then ask them in Javanese and record the responses in his book. In the evenings, he would translate the answers into Indonesian for Ann, who in turn would translate them into English in her notes. When I asked why he thought the villagers were as forthcoming as they were, he first said, "Because I asked them in Javanese." In addition, he said, "If a foreigner asks questions, they want to answer. They're happy to be asked, and they're delighted to answer." Furthermore, he added, they came to think of Ann as a good woman.

During a visit to Kajar in July 2009, I met two women, Suparmi and Mintartini, who, like many Indonesians, did not use surnames. They identified themselves as daughters of Pak Sastrosuyono, head of the blacksmiths' cooperative when Ann first arrived in the village. They told me that they remembered seeing Ann in Kajar when they were children, and they recalled the pleasure she seemed to take in talking with villagers. "People would shout, 'There's a *londo* here!'" one of the women told me, using a Javanese word for Dutchman that is often used for any European, Westerner, or Caucasian. "Everybody came. She was like a celebrity here. They really liked it. Some people couldn't answer the questions, but they were happy that she was here." In the acknowledgments in her dissertation, Ann described the Indonesian villagers she encountered as "invariably friendly, pleasant and willing to patiently answer many questions concerning their enterprises and personal finances, even when dozens of neighbors and village children are crowded in the doorway or looking in the windows. I do not recall ever being treated rudely by an Indonesian villager, or ever having had an unpleasant fieldwork experience while in Indonesia." On one occasion, the headman of the largest hamlet in Kajar announced at a village meeting that he had "adopted" Ann and Djaka Waluja as his children. He renamed Ann, Sri Lestari. "I gather it means 'Forever Beautiful,' and wasn't that gallant of him," Ann wrote to Dewey. "Thank God for nice comfortable middle-aged men who don't give you any complexes. *Amien!*"

Everything about blacksmithing captivated this native Kansan. If she could be reincarnated, she told a colleague, Don Johnston, years later, she would come back as a blacksmith. "I still dream of the day I can visit you and go upriver to see those big blacksmithing villages you told me about," she wrote to another acquaintance in Kalimantan in 1981. She was not simply interested in the technical aspects of the craft; she could see that, in the hands of a skilled smith, utilitarian objects emerged as something closer to art. She became almost proprietary about her village. "She was very possessive of Kajar," said Garrett Solyom, who was doing research on the kris, working closely with a smith in another village in Java. "It was very clear that she knew she'd stumbled on something special. She made it clear, in indirect ways, that she didn't want me poking around there."

Kajar was just one of a half-dozen villages, each with its own handicrafts industry, on which Ann had chosen to focus. There was Kasongan, a center of crockery production seven kilometers south of Yogyakarta, where competition from factory-made pottery was cutting into the market for traditional earthenware products. There, tourism was creating a new market for animal banks, toys, and terra-cotta souvenirs. Malangan, fifteen kilometers northwest of Yogyakarta, had been a center of hand-loom weaving, specializing in striped sarongs and solid-colored waistcloths. When shortages of yarn and competition from mechanized textile mills put most of the weavers out of business, villagers turned to converting bamboo and palm leaves into items such as baskets, winnowing trays, and rice steamers. That industry, too, was encountering competition from factory-made housewares. Pocung, like Malangan, had once been a thriving hand-loom weaving village specializing in *lurik*. When that industry faltered, villagers switched to trading or to making perforated leather shadow puppets out of animal hide. With the rise of tourism had come increased demand for leather *"wayang-style"* souvenirs, including bookmarks, lampshades, miniature puppets, and key rings. "Problem with marketing through stores because stores only want cheap wayangs and don't care about quality while Sagiyo doesn't want to make cheap wayangs," Ann observed in her notes from a long interview with a puppetmaker named Sagiyo from the village of Gendeng. (Her notes from that day included a sketch of a birthday cake with four candles. "Joko's birthday," she wrote.)

Patterns and themes began to emerge. It became increasingly apparent, for example, that women were not necessarily benefiting from industrialization. When female-dominated industries adapted to competition by producing new products for new markets, the best paid jobs often went to men. The most profitable industries—the ones requiring expensive raw materials and access to working capital—were almost exclusively male. In one village, Ann found that nearly every household made bamboo basketry, but only forty of those had the capital to work with more lucrative rattan. In all forty, the entrepreneurs were men. Another pattern that captured Ann's attention involved the industriousness of Indonesians. "We found almost every family to have an incredible array of subsidiary activities which they juggle around to make sure that they are always occupied and always have something coming in," Ann wrote to Dewey from Kajar. That ingenuity seemed to defy the assumptions of scholars, such as J. H. Boeke, the early-twentieth-century Dutch economist whom Dewey had mentioned. Boeke had described the economy of the Indies as "dualistic," with a gap between Western-style, capital-intensive enterprises and the more labor-intensive peasant enterprises. He attributed the gap largely to cultural differences—an Indonesian inclination toward cooperation rather than competition, a lack of interest in capital accumulation, and a tendency to engage in wage labor only until one met one's limited needs. But Ann found village industry producers intensely interested in profits and keenly aware of fluctuations in the prices of fuel, labor, and raw materials. Instead of cultural differences, Ann thought, a lack of information and lack of certain technologies might help explain economic "dualism." But what about access to capital? Even the relatively large investment in equipment of a successful entrepreneur such as Pak Sastro in Kajar paled by comparison with the money required to set up a Western-style factory.

The main cause of the gap in the Indonesian economy was not cultural, Ann came to believe. It was differences in access to capital.

In March 1978, Ann found herself face-to-face with the problem to which she would end up devoting much of her professional attention in the coming years. She was attending a meeting of the Indonesian government agency that had sponsored her research, a unit within the Department of Industry that worked with small enterprises. According to her field notes, the subject of the meeting was income distribution and employment. The question arose: Why was the government's development aid not reaching the lowest levels of the landless? The answer given was that credit was going to farmers—not to village industries, including handicrafts.

Under the government's five-year plan, special banking units had been set up to make loans to small farmers. But there was no similar program for rural craftspeople. Banks were interested in efficiency and profit, not in employment and income distribution. When craftsmen filled out loan forms and took them to the bank, even with the help of Department of Industry officials, the banks turned them down. Employment would increase and income distribution would improve, someone pointed out, only if small entrepreneurs got help.

"Ask Subroto where the credit is," someone said, referring to a Department of Industry official. "We never see any credit."

When Ann was not in the field, she was in Yogyakarta, sometimes with Maya, sometimes not. Lolo Soetoro's niece Kismardhani S-Roni, who was a teenager when Ann moved to Yogyakarta, remembered Ann and Maya living for a time with Lolo's mother in the house near the bird market and Ann homeschooling Maya in a room hung with Maya's drawings. "Tante Ann" was an exacting teacher, Lolo's niece and her brother, Haryo Soetendro, recalled. Maya got no favored treatment just because she was the only student, Soetendro remembered. "You had to work hard to get a good mark from your 'teacher,'" he wrote in an e-mail to Maya in 2008. At other times, while Ann was in the field, Maya sometimes stayed with her cousins and their parents in a big house on the edge of the campus of Gadjah Mada University, where Lolo's sister and brother-in-law taught. "I wandered around a lot," Maya recalled. "Mom was working sometimes, and I would be taken care of by a collection of people—possibly some were employed by the family, possibly some were family, some were neighbors. There was a complex across the way. I remember old Dutch gates and wrought iron and running around there. Sort of like 'it takes a village' kind of thing. A lot of the women who took care of me had other kids. . . . But I also remember her being very present in the afternoons and teaching me."

For several months, apparently in mid-1978, Ann stayed with an Indonesian family in their house next to the Pakualaman Kraton, a smaller compound not far from the main compound of the sultan. Maggie Norobangun, who was teaching English at the time, had met Dewey in 1976. Dewey had become a close friend of the family's and a regular guest. With Dewey's help, Ann stayed for several months in what Norobangun called "Alice's room." She would leave early every morning on the back of the motorcycle of yet another graduate student who was working as her research assistant in the field. She would return late in the day, saying, "Oh, Maggie, I'm dead beat." She was friendly, easygoing, and happy to be living in Yogyakarta, but she never spoke about her family, Norobangun told me. On one occasion, to Norobangun's surprise, Maya, then age eight, came to visit for several days. Norobangun had not understood that Ann had a daughter. On another occasion, Lolo stopped by with Barry and Maya on a trip to Borobudur. "I didn't even know about Mr. Soetoro," Norobangun told me.

By the fall of 1978, Barry was seventeen and a senior at Punahou in his last year at home in Hawaii. Ann had never found the distance separating them easy, commuting between continents and trying to remain engaged in his life. Now his childhood was coming to a close. Nancy Peluso, Ann's friend from Yogyakarta, told me she remembered meeting Ann earlier that year in a small hotel in the southern part of Yogyakarta. They made a practice of getting together when they were both in town—to eat dinner, catch up, get a massage. On this occasion, Peluso recalled, Ann broke into tears. "She just started crying," Peluso said. "And she said, 'You know, I've got to go back to the U.S. for the last year that Barry is in high school. I really want to do that. After that, he's gone and I won't have any chance to experience that. I just want to be back there.'"

So she returned to Honolulu for several months that fall. In a haunting scene from *Dreams from My Father*, Obama describes a confrontation between mother and son during that visit. A friend of his has been arrested for drug possession. Ann confronts Obama, with the intensity of a parent fearing that the opportunity to influence her nearly adult child is running out. His grades are dropping, she says; he has yet to start his college applications. Isn't he being a bit cavalier about his future? In a manner at first patronizing, then hostile, he brushes Ann off. He tries an old gambit—a smile, a few reassuring words, the verbal equivalent of a pat on the head. When Ann is not appeased, he informs her that he is thinking of not going away for college, just staying in Hawaii, taking a few classes, working part-time. She cuts him off: He could get into any college he wanted, she tells him, if he would make a little effort. He cannot just sit around like a good-time Charlie, counting on luck. "I looked at her sitting there, so earnest, so certain of her son's destiny . . ." Obama writes. "I suddenly felt like puncturing that certainty of hers, letting her know that her experiment with me had failed."

Instead of shouting, he laughs.

"A good-time Charlie, huh? Well, why not? Maybe that's what I want out of life. I mean, look at Gramps. He didn't even go to college."

Obama realizes, from Ann's expression, that he has stumbled upon her worst fear.

"'Is that what you're worried about?' I asked. 'That I'll end up like Gramps?'" Then, having done his best to sabotage her faith in him, Obama walks out of the room.

One can only imagine how Ann took that exchange. She came from a family of teachers, though neither of her parents had received a college degree. Her mother, regretting her own decisions, had gone to extraordinary lengths to ensure that Ann, then Barry, would have the education and the opportunities that she had missed. The University of Hawai'i had thrown wide Ann's horizons—emotionally, intellectually, and professionally. For Barry to have the same chances, she had accepted their living half a world apart. She could not have helped worrying about the toll of that aching separation on the connection between them. Ann had the highest expectations for her son; she had emphasized from his earliest years the value of education and hard work. Now, to spite her, he was professing to reject both.

What was Ann's "experiment"—as Obama referred to it in the book?

When I asked President Obama that question, he explained that he had written the scene in the voice of his cynical, sarcastic, teenage self. His mother thought he was special, he believed at the time; she imagined that the values she had inculcated would make him the person she wanted him to be. But he was angry, full of self-doubt, and unconvinced that her efforts were worthwhile.

Who was the person she wanted him to be? I asked him.

"You know, sort of a cross between Einstein, Gandhi, and Belafonte, right?" he said, laughing. "I think she wanted me to be the man that she probably would have liked my grandfather to be, that she would have liked my father to have turned out to be."

Then he added, "You know, somebody who was strong and honest and doing worthwhile things for the world."

Seven

Community Organizing

The village of Ungaran was a speck in the mountains above the port of Semarang on the north coast of Central Java. A two-lane road between Semarang and Yogyakarta wound steeply through terraced rice fields and past the village. Trucks broke down or crashed so often that the road was said to be inhabited by spirits. There was a village square, some food stalls, a market, and a movie house that screened second-rate Hollywood movies. Ann Hawkins, a young American, was living outside Ungaran, working with an Indonesian organization, training village people in organic farming. To reach the training center from the road, one walked a mile along a footpath through paddy fields. One day in late 1979 or early 1980, Hawkins looked up from the ditch in which she was mixing compost and dirt, and was startled to see a Western man and woman watching. The woman, porcelain-skinned and smiling, sunglasses parked on the top of her head, was Ann Soetoro. The man was an official of an international development organization. "What are you doing?" one of them asked Hawkins. She was wondering the same thing. White people never came to Ungaran, she was thinking. Especially white women.

In early 1979, Ann had moved from Yogyakarta to Semarang, the ancient trading port that is the capital of Central Java. She had completed her fieldwork, for the time being, and had drained the last of her East-West Center grant. Barry, in his final year at Punahou, would be applying to colleges; Maya, still being educated at home, would soon need to be enrolled in a school. Even with Madelyn Dunham's bank salary subsidizing Barry's education, Ann needed money. "Please don't forget to put me down for assistanting spring term," she wrote to Alice Dewey from Java in the summer of 1978, announcing her intention to return to Honolulu in time for her favorite holiday, Halloween. "I'm going to be really broke when I get back." But rather than settle down as a teaching assistant at the university, she returned to Java in January. "Although I finished fieldwork at the end of 1978, family finances and the exhaustion of my EWC grant prevented me from returning immediately to Honolulu for write-up and comprehensives," she explained later in a progress report to the anthropology department. Instead, she accepted a job as a consultant in international development on a project in Central Java funded by the U.S. Agency for International Development. The job came with a salary, a house in Semarang, a car and driver, and home leave. She persuaded the University of Hawai'i to grant her an initial nine-month leave of absence. "Well, now that I'm working I'm hoping to clear all debts soon," Ann wrote to Dewey several months into the job.

Her reasons for taking it were not exclusively financial. The project, the first of its kind in Indonesia, was designed to build the capacity of provincial planning offices to do development planning in direct response to the needs of poor communities. "It was perfect for her," Ann's friend Nancy Peluso told me. "To be able to find something where she could directly apply the knowledge that she had been collecting in a very good way, and at the same time get enough of an income to maybe start paying for some of these things and saving up for college." The prospect of solving problems, not just describing them, appealed to Ann. After a fellow anthropologist wrote to her jokingly that she had heard that Ann had "sold your soul to the large international organizations," Ann apparently mounted a persuasive defense. The friend wrote back, "I must say that your job with AID sounds fascinating and challenging. . . . I can well understand the excitement of doing something practical rather than theoretical and actually working in the field of development rather than theorizing it and criticizing it from the safety of a U.S. university. In addition, I know what you mean when you describe the people you work with (or at least some of the people in your team) as being dynamic, progressive, social minded and involved."

The project in Java represented a new approach. Development agencies had tended to operate by lending governments money for large-scale infrastructure, such as water systems and roads. When the work was completed and the agency moved on, the new facilities were often not maintained. By the late 1970s, the U.S. Agency for International Development was moving toward a different approach. Projects would be multifaceted—say, a little infrastructure, some skills training, some rural electrification, some microcredit— and decisions would emanate less from the top down than from the bottom up. "The idea was that we should embark upon programs that involved local communities, and we should be responsive to their needs," Carl A. Dutto, the rural development officer for the agency in Jakarta at that time, told me. "The theory behind it was if you're working that way, it's sustainable, because people want it." There was increasing attention, too, to addressing the problems of the rural poor. After the upheaval of the 1960s, the Suharto government had set about tackling rural poverty, which was seen as a cause of social and political unrest. The government enlisted the banking system to diversify the economy and encourage rural development. It would begin setting up credit programs to channel money to rural entrepreneurs, promoting small industries and reducing dependence on farming. To understand poor communities better, some development agencies began hiring anthropologists like Dutto, who joined the Agency for International Development in 1976 from a teaching job at the University of Nairobi. Their job became articulating the community's perspective.

The project for which Ann was hired was an experiment in what was called bottom-up development. Decisions would not be made by the central government in Jakarta; instead, the development agency and its contractor, a firm based in Bethesda, Maryland, that did economic development projects around the world, would work with the planning offices in the two provinces where the project was based. The aim was to cultivate the provincial offices' capacity to come up with and carry out small-scale projects in response to local demand. Dutto, who oversaw the project from 1978 to 1983, said it began with the preparation of detailed profiles of each province and district, based on social and economic data, sometimes gathered for that purpose by local universities. There were meetings with village residents to determine what their communities needed—for example, rural roads, a market for selling their vegetables, higher-yielding varieties of rice. Initial meetings in Kudus, a center of the clove-flavored *kretek* cigarette industry, and Jepara, a wood-carving center, revealed a need for access to credit, especially for women. As a result, Dutto said, credit for small industries became one component of the development project. Jerry Silverman, whom the contracting firm Development Alternatives Inc. hired straight from a similar project in Ethiopia to head the one in Sema-rang, told me, "The project was built on the premises that DAI had been advocating and which I believed in. This was, 'We're really going to show the world what can be done with a bottom-up, demand-responsive process.' It was the new model."

That model embodied a particular attitude toward the poor.

"You know the old adage 'You give a man a fish . . .'?" Silver-man asked me. Here is the adage: Give a man a fish and you feed him for a day; teach him how to fish and you feed him for a life-time. The project in Central Java, Silverman said, was about nei-ther. Here is how he explained it. According to one view, the poor are charity cases and we need to give them stuff. (That would be the fish.) According to another view, the poor are not as technically sophisticated as we are, so we need to teach them stuff. (That would be how to fish.) But there is a third possibility. That is, the poor know what they are doing, but circumstances prevent them from escaping poverty. "How do we go in and help them remove an obstacle, reduce a constraint, make a technical connection they didn't understand?" Silverman said. "It's not like, 'We're smart, they're dumb. We can tell them how to do it.' It's beyond the teach-him-how-to-fish. It's 'Understand that he knows how to fish, but maybe what he needs is somebody who will allow him access to fish, or a stronger line so it won't break.' That's a step further."

When Ann arrived on the north coast of Java in early 1979 at the age of thirty-six, she was one of relatively few Westerners in Semarang. The city, a centuries-old trading port and commercial hub, bore traces of its colorful, cosmopolitan past. There were Chi-nese temples and shop houses, an Arab quarter, one of the oldest remaining Christian churches in Java. There was a Dutch colonial administration building, which had served as a refuge for Javanese independence fighters during the Japanese occupation. Dilapidated and hot, Old Semarang spilled across the flatlands of the coastal plain. In the hills rising behind the city, expatriates lived in neighborhoods such as Candi Baru, where grander houses and gardens laid out by the Dutch enjoyed panoramic views of the coastline. "They lived in their own expatriate ghetto," said Clare Blenkinsop, who moved to Semarang with Richard Holloway, her husband and the country director for Oxfam, the international relief and development organization, in 1979. It was possible very quickly to sort "the sheep from the goats, the serious versus the less serious development people," Holloway told me. You knew by whether or not they learned to speak Indonesian and by whether they felt any empathy toward village people or simply saw them as grist for their projects. There was an active chapter of an expatriate running and beer-drinking club founded in Kuala Lumpur called the Hash House Harriers. "I must say, we had a philosophical objection to wealthy expatriates pouring beer over each other's heads in the presence of villagers who don't have threepence ha'penny," Blenkinsop said.

Ann lived on the Indonesian end of the expatriate spectrum. She spoke the language, ate the food, sat with her legs folded under her on the floor. She accumulated Indonesian friends and ran her household in an informal, open Indonesian style. Blenkinsop was amazed by the sheer numbers of people there often seemed to be in the house. "She had quite a staff because she was such a softie with people who said they had relatives who needed a job," recalled John Raintree, who lived in the house for a time with his wife, Kadi Warner, and their two-year-old daughter. There were long-term houseguests, friends of Maya's, the friends' mothers, young volunteers such as Ann Hawkins, colleagues dropping by. In a letter to Dewey in May 1979, Ann put out the word: "By the way, if anyone should need a stopover in Semarang while I'm gone, feel free to use my house. We have a good old dog named Spot (we inherited him from another family), two rabbits and two absolutely hilarious baby goats born on Easter evening."

Hawkins rode the bus down from Ungaran on weekends to visit. No matter how early in the morning she got up, she would find Ann seated at a small table with a large cup of coffee, reading or writing in the relative cool before the sun rose and the heat set in. "She had such a wealth of background, information, contact with Indonesia, perspective—books, colonial history, things I hadn't yet grappled with," remembered Hawkins, who, because of her work, had on-the-ground information that was useful to Ann. "In an interesting way, we traded things with each other." Don Flickinger, another volunteer, could hardly believe that a person like Ann existed in Semarang. When Hawkins introduced him to Ann, Flickinger quickly realized she knew everything he knew and a lot more. She knew the villages in Gunung Kidul where he was working, trying to develop prototypes for fuel-efficient stoves. She had all sorts of connections. Because she was married to an Indonesian, she had standing and was not easy for Indonesian officials to dismiss. "I remember her saying, 'You're dealing in the mountains of Central Java, I can help you with this,'" he told me. "'Let me see if I can let somebody know that this is a project that should be supported.'"

To Flickinger, her house felt like a haven. It was possible to talk openly there about politics, about the relentless control exercised by the Suharto regime. Ann seemed almost maternal. Flickinger would want her to say something encouraging about the country's future, but she was simply realistic, always looking for ways to make the situation better. "Because she was living the life she was, I guess I would have to say she was optimistic," he remembered. "But with her eyes wide open." Richard Holloway described her sitting on a settee, clutching a cushion to her chest "and sort of, I suppose, 'tut-tutting' is the way I would put it. Not a spinsterish tut-tutting, but she would tone down some of the outrageous statements people were making." On Thanksgiving, she held a "Ducksgiving" feast. Colleagues, friends, and younger volunteers living on stipends all turned up. In the absence of turkey, they plucked and cooked several ducks. "Ann was extremely gregarious and, of course, entertaining and fun," Blenkinsop said. "She was generous-spirited."

Ann did not, as has been said, suffer fools gladly. Semarang, like any place, had its share of fools. Ann found it incredible that one American family ate only imported food, said Glen Williams, Holloway's predecessor at Oxfam, who was also friendly with Ann. She could not see the point. She found it bizarre that many expatriates made little effort to learn the language. There were hilarious malapropisms to savor: In a speech to an audience of Indonesians, a colleague of Blenkinsop's intended to use the expression *masuk angin,* which means a draft of wind has entered the body, and which is used to refer to a slight cold with flu-like symptoms. Instead, he said *masuk anjing,* which would mean a dog had entered the body. "She was not like most of the other expatriates there, who would never, ever have dreamed of going to a *wayang* performance," said Williams, who went once, determined to sit through the performance, but drifted off. "It was out of their comfort zone, but she didn't respect expatriate comfort zones." She and Blenkinsop were not above laughing about other expatriates.

If Ann found their behavior curious, however, the feeling was mutual.

"In Semarang, Ann was—I wouldn't say eccentric, but she was an unusual woman," Blenkinsop said. "Living in Central Java as a single white American woman with her own household setup—I can't think of another one." Ann's decision to educate Maya at home may also have struck some as questionable: "Running tiny schools in your garage may not have been what they thought was mainstream," Blenkinsop said. Ann's friendliness with Indonesians "was thought to be strange and perhaps a little inappropriate." Ann "must have represented something that was a bit of an eyebrow raiser, frankly," Blenkinsop said. Remarks were made. "The gossip in those sorts of communities was absolutely fantastic," she said.

There were advantages and disadvantages to being a Western woman working in Indonesia. Blenkinsop, who had academic degrees in sociology and business and was working for both an Indonesian organization and the United Nations Food and Agricultural Organization, was often asked in villages why her husband was not with her. But she had access to women that men in the field did not. In fishing villages on the east coast of Sumatra, where the infant mortality rate was astronomical, women flocked to speak to her— especially when they had seen her before and after giving birth to her own child. Ann Hawkins, on trips to villages, found herself invariably seated, during welcoming ceremonies, up front with the men. The other women would be off to the side, passing out fried bananas and tea. Jerry Silverman, Ann's colleague, worried initially that having a woman in Ann's job might be a problem in a Muslim country with what he described as a largely patriarchal family structure and male power structure. But he found he need not have worried. She had an entrée with women that Western men in her position did not have, Silverman came to realize; and because she was a foreigner, Indonesian men saw her as gender-neutral. If Ann had "gone native," that would not have been the case, Silverman told me. "There are people who think the way you work effectively in other cultures is to try to deny your own and become them," he said. "Ann never did that. She understood the differences, she was

respectful, she was knowledgeable, but she was 'us' and not 'them.'
I think that's a point that a lot of people looking at her miss: It
wasn't that she got inside so well, it was that she was outside but
appreciative." Silverman, who went on to live half of his life outside
the United States, said that was a lesson he learned from Ann. It
made him more comfortable in his own skin.

Being a foreigner could be liberating. "It kind of doesn't matter
what I do, because I'm from Mars," Ann used to say to John Raintree. The impossibility of fitting in, in any conventional sense,
seemed to make it possible to find a place of a different sort. Ann
Hawkins had been shy, bookish, and tongue-tied as a child. After
graduating from college, an organization called Volunteers in Asia
sent her to teach English in South Sulawesi. "If one has grown up
and always thought to oneself, 'I don't know quite what it is, I don't
seem to fit, people don't quite seem to get me,'" she told me, "then
you go to someplace like Indonesia and you think, 'It's true, they
don't get me, and it doesn't matter, it's a given.' Just walking off the
plane and having that sheer wall of heat and humidity in your face,
your body, your bones—you're not sure you will survive. Then you
realize, 'That's right. I'm a foot taller than everybody else, I'm
white, I have blue eyes, I totally stand out, and I can barely say
hello. I am back to essentials.' In a very funny way, through having
to learn another language, I became verbal and social in a completely different way."

Javanese manners and behavior were so appealing that some
Westerners found themselves dressing differently, pointing with
their thumb instead of their index finger and being careful how
they crossed their legs. The Javanese temperament seemed well
suited to Ann. Her personality, Richard Holloway told me, was
"ameliorative." From time to time, she would be called on to take
visiting representatives from the aid agencies into the field. They

might not speak the language, know the country, or know how to behave. They would insist on visiting villages, eyeballing projects, and seeing results, whether it was convenient or not. Some were aggressive or arrogant or unaware, say, that it was rude to plant your hands on your hips. In her now flawless Indonesian, Ann would soothe any hard feelings. "All he was trying to do was cool his armpits down," Holloway remembered her once explaining to some Indonesians. Several years later, when she was living in Jakarta, Holloway recalled a rash of kidnappings of dogs from expatriate-dense neighborhoods, to be sold for eating. Because Ann owned a dog, her driver became alarmed at the sight of a stranger in her garden, grabbed a cable, and began beating the interloper to a pulp. "Ann stopped him with real difficulty, calmed him down, uttered the palliative Javanese phrases," Holloway remembered. "She generally tried to lower the tone of the tension, which is a very Javanese thing to do, but I had the impression that it was also her. She lived Indonesia without playacting. It was her."

Ann also had a certain Javanese sense of propriety, which Holloway went so far as to describe as prudery. It surprised him, because most of the Americans he knew were the opposite. Indonesian women in villages kept their arms and legs covered and wore nothing open at the neck. Ann followed the same rules: She wore dark skirts down to the mid-calf and loose shirts made of hand-loomed textiles or batik. She bought fabric and took it to a tailor, who would copy other pieces. "Her wardrobe was primarily blue and black and some tan," Kadi Warner told me. "That was all the batiking colors. Rusty browns and blacks." She wore sturdy utilitarian sandals without a heel. She kept her hair long, she told Warner, to cover her ears, which left her head at an uncommonly wide angle. "She wasn't flash," Holloway said. "She was dumpy." She would express displeasure with behavior that violated Indonesian standards. In the countryside, where it was common to encounter people attending to bodily functions, anyone approaching would stop, turn his back, and wait for a cough or some other signal to proceed. On one occasion, Holloway said, he and Ann happened on some women gathered beside a spring. As he and Ann approached, it became clear that the women were naked. Ann stopped abruptly, turned on her heel, and walked briskly back down the hill they had just climbed. "As a man, I would probably have called out that I was coming and asked them if it was okay if I came on— which threw the ball in their court," Holloway said. "She would just defer." She was deeply attuned to the way the Javanese lived.

In Bali with the Solyoms some years later, she passed up the opportunity for an outdoor shower. In a tone of humorous self-mockery, she explained, "A girl from Kansas never bathes outdoors."

Ann's title on the development project was adviser on small-scale industries and rural credit, an area of expertise that had arisen naturally out of her fieldwork for her dissertation. The firm that hired her felt lucky to have an anthropologist who also happened to be married to an Indonesian, fluent in the language, and writing a thesis on small-scale industries. The job entailed supporting the ability of the provincial planning agency to oversee small-scale development projects in twenty-two villages in five of the poorest districts in Central Java. That included helping set up a credit program for poor people in those villages. Ann served as an adviser to the planning office and was charged with cultivating closer ties between the planning office and local civic organizations. She oversaw the work of a team from a local university that had been enlisted to collect data, and she monitored the participation of village women in the projects. The work was not unlike the work that her son, who was entering college in California, would take up in

Chicago four or five years later. Like a community organizer, Ann understood the need to foster trust, build credibility, and be sensitive to the way other people did things.

"For me, Ann is not the anthropologist doing research," Silverman said. "For me, Ann is the community organizer in Central Java."

Ann's style was nonconfrontational but direct. Silverman said he could not remember a single conversation in which Ann came to him, told him he was off track and needed to do something her way. They lived two blocks apart and shared a small office a half-mile away. They did not have meetings, he said, they just talked. The fact was, Ann knew more about what she was doing than he did, he said. His job, he came to believe, was to keep the bureaucracy off her back. "Initially, we're just a bunch of stupid foreigners," he said. "Over time, I think we emerged as something other than that. Ann was an important part of that. It had to do with demonstrating to them that we saw them as our client, rather than USAID or the central government in Jakarta—i.e., that they could trust us."

In the summer of 1979, Ann wrote to Dewey asking her to pass along a job offer to a former student and housemate of Dewey's, John Raintree. A newly minted anthropologist, Raintree had intended to become a physicist, majored in psychology, then spent two years in the Peace Corps in Sierra Leone with his wife, Kadi Warner, before they both enrolled in graduate school at the University of Hawai'i. He was fascinated by technology. The late 1970s were the heyday of so-called appropriate technology—often simple gadgets especially suited to the social and economic conditions of a developing community. "At that time, appropriate technology was on everybody's to-do list," Raintree told me. Development Alternatives Inc. needed an expert in the subject to work in Central

Java with Ann. Raintree moved to Semarang with Kadi, their daughter, and a small library of appropriate-technology resources. Over the next six months, he developed half a dozen prototypes designed to relieve production bottlenecks in small industries. For blacksmiths, who used files to sharpen the tools they were making, he came up with a grinder powered by a person pedaling a kind of stationary bicycle. He found a simple method of pressing roof tiles that cost a fraction of the cost of the machine it would replace. "You have to get up very early in the morning to suggest anything of any real relevance to these people," Raintree told me. "Occasionally, you can. What was nice about working with Ann was she understood the villages and the rural industry situation so well that she could prime me, so that I could find a lot of things that really seemed to make sense. Ann had it all figured out long before I got there."

Using her dissertation field notes as a guide, Ann took Raintree on an orientation tour, giving him the deepest and most insightful anthropological perspective on rural industry he told me he had ever encountered. With Semarang as their base, they would drive up to four hours out of the city to villages all over Central Java. They paid countless courtesy calls on provincial officials, district heads, and village headmen—formal meetings in which Ann would introduce Raintree and their project. The government official would preside from a chair on a dais, looking down on his visitors, seated below. Raintree, who had done fieldwork in the Philippines and was used to villages of tribal people with their own traditions, was unaccustomed to the rigid, hierarchical nature of Java. To do anything at any level, one needed permission from all the levels of government and administration above. It helped that Ann knew what she was talking about and spoke the language. "But she couldn't have gotten anywhere with that if she didn't also know how to be politically correct and formal, and at the same time charming," Raintree told me. "These were all kingdoms before they became bureaucracies within a national state. She knew how to be courtly."

Ann worried about corruption among government officials, who, Raintree said, sometimes seemed to her not to care much about ordinary people. She also noticed that the class background of government planners and administrators, who were mostly men, tended to work against poor women sharing in the benefits of development projects. The Indonesian men she worked with, mainly from the planning office and the Department of Industry, "simply did not believe that the lives of poor village women were significantly different from the lives of women of their own class," Ann would write to a colleague in July 1981. "In other words, they believed that poor village women spent most of their time at home, caring for children and doing housework, fully supported by their husbands except for a little 'pin money' they might earn doing handicrafts or selling something in the market from time to time. Given these preconceptions about the importance (or unimportance) of women's work, it is not surprising that women were seldom selected as participants in projects which could increase their income-generating abilities."

But Ann was pragmatic. She was good at recognizing a felicitous convergence of interests. She believed that improvements could be made even if they were not the top priority of the people she had to convince. The game was to enable her Indonesian counterparts to see why it was in their own enlightened self-interest to help the poor. She was an organizer, always with goals of her own. If a colleague had his own view about how things ought to be organized, Raintree said, he had to devote some energy to seeing that they were not done her way instead. In fact, he told me, "I could understand why a young man would need to go off to school in Hawaii."

On one occasion, Raintree recalled, he challenged a policy of Ann's—and went so far as to discuss the matter with the team leader. "She gave me a stern lecture about how friends don't do that," he remembered. She did not mince words. He saw her angry, too, when she believed others had been treated unfairly. For example, she had a driver in Semarang who doubled as a field assistant. As Raintree put it, "Her driver was much more than a driver." Occasionally, people unfamiliar with the arrangement had a tendency to treat the man as they might a mere driver. Ann would stand up for him, Raintree recalled, with fire in her eyes and steel in her voice. If the cultural context was such that she could express her views, she did. "Sometimes it would involve a sharp anger but not something lingering or smoldering," he said. "She spoke her mind, and that was it."

For village people, one of the biggest barriers to expanding a business, and moving out of poverty, was the lack of affordable credit—the problem Ann had stumbled on while doing the research for her dissertation. The most common source of credit was moneylenders—that is, loan sharks, as Carl Dutto described them. A trader might borrow money at four a.m., walk to the central market, buy whatever she intended to sell, take a *becak* to the suburbs, sell her product by the side of the road, pay back the moneylender at some exorbitant rate of interest, and keep whatever was left. The lenders made a killing, and their customers barely scraped by. Nearly everyone in the villages seemed to be in debt to moneylenders. Foreign development groups and Indonesian organizations such as the one for which Clare Blenkinsop worked were exploring other ways of offering small amounts of credit. By the time Blenkinsop arrived in Semarang in 1979, there were already

eight to ten thousand savers in the program run by her organization, which enabled women to become eligible for a loan by demonstrating that they could save.

The Indonesian government, too, was interested in rural credit.
To help diversify the economy, redistribute wealth, and promote
rural development, the government had mobilized the banking
system. In 1970, the governor of Central Java had used a provincial
government loan to launch a system of rural and locally run financial institutions to make small, short-term loans to rural families.
The system, known as the Badan Kredit Kecamatan, or the sub-
district credit agency, grew rapidly in Central Java. But when the
units were pressed to repay their government loans and support
themselves, many suffered high losses. There was also corruption
and mismanagement. By the late 1970s, one-third of the 486 units
in Central Java were languishing or had closed.

To help tackle the problem of credit, the U.S. Agency for International Development enlisted the help of Richard Patten, a brainy,
irascible development veteran from Norman, Oklahoma, who had
worked in East Pakistan, now Bangladesh, and in Ghana in the
1960s before moving on to Indonesia. In East Pakistan, Patten told
me, he had worked with Akhtar Hameed Khan, an Indian-born,
Cambridge-educated social scientist and development activist now
recognized as a pioneer in what is now known as microcredit—the
making of very small, or micro, loans to impoverished entrepreneurs. Khan, who had founded the Pakistan Academy for Rural
Development, had been working on ways of lending money for
small enterprises, including small shops. "We followed what he
had pioneered when we did a public-works program in East Pakistan," Patten said. "He was doing group credit through the cooperatives but then using a local bank to support it." The Agency for
International Development was interested in trying similar things

in Central Java. At first, Dutto said, the agency did not know what might work. They tried lending chicks, ducklings, and goats—to be paid back in other chicks, ducklings, and goats. They also began working with the floundering rural-banking system.

Ann, the credit adviser hired by Development Alternatives Inc., worked with Patten, the credit adviser to the Agency for International Development. From her dissertation fieldwork, Ann had found that rural industries were frequently held back by shortages of raw materials—which they often lacked because they did not have the working capital to keep them in stock. Women had an especially hard time getting even government-sponsored loans. In 1979, Ann evaluated a small credit project being carried out in ten villages in industries such as production of roof tiles, cassava chips, and rattan. In most of the villages, women as well as men worked in those industries—but not one of the one hundred twenty-nine loans had gone to a woman. The provincial development project, for which Ann was working, began providing not only capital but training in management and bookkeeping to sixty-five Badan Kredit Kecamatan banking units in Central Java. Those offices became a proving ground for new initiatives. The best of those initiatives eventually spread beyond Central Java. The system became a permanent government-run program in 1981, and the Indonesian Ministry of Finance made a large loan to the provincial government to strengthen and expand it. Looking back on the provincial development project as a whole, Silverman said it resulted in the setting up of planning bodies throughout Indonesia, which took on an important role in the allocation of government resources at the provincial level. But, he said, "the one major success we had was the small-scale credit and institutionalizing it. It was the one thing that got institutionalized in ways that are close to what was intended."

Ann's days were long and full. She worked on her dissertation before dawn, managed her household staff, saw to the schooling of her daughter. Every day, she wrote at least a couple of paragraphs to Barry, Kadi Warner remembered: "It was part of her ritual." Ann attended meetings, went into the field, spent time in the office, escorted visitors. At night, she presided over lively dinners at home. She liked running her own household, being immersed in her work, being accountable largely to herself. In her element, she was developing a big and unmistakable presence. "She was the grand lady when she was in the village, or in her house, or talking with the *bupati*," Raintree said, using the Indonesian word for a district head. "She was enormously bright; she was fluent in Indonesian; she always had a sort of twinkle in her eye. I always thought she had just swallowed a canary." Even in a difficult negotiation, she seemed to be enjoying herself. Decades later, Raintree remembered a certain look on Ann's face, a trace of which he had begun to notice in her son during the presidential campaign. After making a point, Ann would look down the bridge of her nose, her chin slightly elevated at its usual angle. In Obama, some people had interpreted that look as aloofness, Raintree said, "but when she did it, she had this puckish smile." In her work, she set goals, met deadlines, was a team player, did not bend rules, Silverman said. "This notion that she was this hippie wanderer floating through foreign things and having an adventure is not the Ann I know," he said. "In a sense, she was as type A as anybody on the team."

Ann kept much of her private life private, even with close friends. Glen Williams, who dined with her a number of times during the year they overlapped in Semarang, said he did not know at the time whether or not Ann was married. He knew that Maya's father "was the Indonesian guy," as he put it, but the subject of Lolo never came up in conversation. Ann told Silverman that she and Lolo had separated. Their marriage reminded Nancy Peluso of some other Indonesian marriages she knew of, in which husband and wife seemed to go in their own directions. "It wasn't like a real marriage," she told me. "It was just kind of a marriage in name."

Sometime in 1979, Ann and Lolo agreed to divorce. According to Maya, Ann received a phone call in Semarang from Lolo, and by the end of the call, it had been decided. I heard several different accounts of the reason the marriage ended, some or all of which could conceivably be true. According to one explanation, offered by Peluso, Ann no longer believed that she and Lolo had anything in common. She was tired of trying to arrange for them to spend time together. According to Alice Dewey, Ann knew from Lolo's doctors in Los Angeles that he had few years left to live. She knew from Lolo that he wanted more children, which she did not. So, according to Dewey, she did the practical and humane thing: She let him go. A third explanation came from Rens Heringa, who became a close friend of Ann's around the time of her divorce and who later divorced her own part-Indonesian husband. Heringa told me bluntly, "She left him—on the pretext that she had to work, which was an acceptable pretext. The real reason was that it was hopeless. He couldn't accept the way she was, and she couldn't accept the kinds of things he expected."

The divorce became final in August 1980, according to a passport application of Ann's. Lolo married the woman Maya remembered encountering in her father's home the day she and Ann had returned to Jakarta. He went on to father two more children, a son and a daughter, before dying of liver disease in 1987 at the age of fifty-two.

Ann's relationship with Maya, who turned ten in 1980, was close and affectionate. Delightful and dimply, Maya was on her way to becoming extraordinarily beautiful. In many ways, Ann treated her like an adult. She took her everywhere, in a way that some people told me was common in Indonesia. "Many hours of my childhood were spent in the homes of blacksmiths or by their furnaces," Maya has written. "When we visited the blacksmith known as Pak Marto, I would look for the reliably present feral dogs chasing chickens outside his home. . . . Mom took me to see potters, weavers, and tile makers, too." In the house in Semarang, Ann had converted a room into a schoolroom, with desks for Maya and several other children from expatriate families. Lesson manuals, textbooks, workbooks, and school supplies arrived in boxes from the home instruction department of the Calvert Day School in Baltimore. A rotating roster of parents served as teachers, meeting in various households. Kadi Warner, whom Ann enlisted to teach world and United States history, told me that the Calvert system was the oldest formal homeschooling curriculum and was highly respected. "It was the standard internationally then," she said. "If you went through that, you were prepared." But Ann was not satisfied with the arrangement for Maya, Richard Holloway recalled. "That was a source of sadness and disappointment to her," he said. "That she was failing as a mother by not giving her a better education than that."

The dilemma was not uncommon. Some expatriate families were reluctant to enroll their children in international schools for fear that they would know only expatriate children. They wanted their children to appreciate the country in which they were living and to have local friends. So they sent them to local schools. But at a certain age, a child in a local school would not receive the preparation necessary to get into a university of the sort their parents attended. "So there is a real problem," said Clare Blenkinsop, who faced the same issue later with her son. "I think that was the problem for Ann with Maya. She didn't want Maya to be cut off in some sort of international school. On the other hand, the level of education gained in anything going in Semarang was probably well below the level that was needed."

The quandary was especially difficult because Maya was half Indonesian.

In the spring of 1980, officials at the Ford Foundation in New York and Jakarta had begun talking about creating a new position in the Jakarta office. The job would entail encouraging research, at the village level, on rural employment and the role of women. Women, it seemed, were playing a critical role in keeping poor households afloat. But Indonesian government policies and programs would not reflect that reality until there were more data to prove it. Officials at Ford wanted to encourage more village-level studies. Research, they hoped, would not only help explain the causes of rural poverty, it might also suggest how to enable poor households to take advantage of opportunities the government or other agencies offered. In March, Sidney Jones, a Ford program officer in Jakarta, wrote an interoffice memo listing six people who should be sent the description of the job in case they might want to apply. Jones knew Ann through Nancy Peluso. All three of them, along with other scholars, had begun to collaborate on a possible book of articles on women's economic activities in Java, which Ann intended to edit. The six names on Jones's list had come from Peter Goethals, an American anthropologist who was a Harvard classmate of Alice Dewey's and a former denizen of the house in Mānoa. Goethals had been working on the same Agency for International Development project as Ann, but in another part of Indonesia. All six candidates were anthropologists, fluent in Indonesian, who had done fieldwork in the country. But Ann was described at the greatest length. After listing Ann's scholarly credentials, Jones concluded, "She's a specialist in small scale industries/non-farm employment and would be superb."

Eight

The Foundation

Four Americans lingered at the entrance to a teeming street market in an out-of-the-way neighborhood in Yogyakarta. It was the fall of 1981, and their little landing party must have made an unusual sight—a stout white woman, a six-foot-four-inch-tall black man, and two white male colleagues, all towering above the eddying crowd. The place was a used-book market, Tom Kessinger, the head of the Jakarta office of the Ford Foundation at the time, remembered years later. But a Westerner might have mistaken it for a paper-recycling operation. Sellers trudged in, humping inventory in fabric bundles on their backs. The market was chaotic, densely packed, and dominated by men. One year into her job at Ford, Ann was increasingly immersed in the world of street vendors, scavengers, and others who eked out a living in the informal economy, where as many as nine out of every ten Indonesians made at least part of their living. On that day, the used-book market was being forced to close, under pressure from merchants or the police. Ann was accompanied by Kessinger, who had lived for years in India, and Franklin Thomas, who had overseen the restoration of the Bedford-Stuyvesant neighborhood in Brooklyn before becoming the president and chief executive officer of Ford. "We waded into the market in a way that nobody outside the country would have," Kessinger remembered. "If you weren't someone as big as Frank is, you might even feel physically threatened. It was so dense and out of control." Ann strode into the chaos, leading the way. Thirty years later, Kessinger would remember the ease with which she unlocked the obscure logic of the place, the relationships and patterns of organization. He said, "I could see, and she communicated it nonverbally, just how comfortable and easy it was going to be."

When he had hired Ann, Kessinger had been looking for someone capable of working "close to the ground," as he put it later. The Ford Foundation, one of the leading philanthropic organizations in the United States, defined its mission as strengthening democratic values, reducing poverty and injustice, promoting international cooperation, and advancing human achievement. After going from a local to an international foundation in 1950, it had operated initially by hiring expatriates with specialized knowledge, and making them available to emerging countries trying to build democratic forms of government. By the early 1980s, countries such as Indonesia had experts and institutions of their own, so Ford was becoming a source of funding more than a supplier of outside expertise. Thomas, after ten years in community-based development in New York, believed in local talent. The Bedford Stuyvesant Restoration Corporation, which he had headed, had enlisted neighborhood people in the work of urban redevelopment. At Ford, he wanted local people engaged in every aspect of the foundation's international work. "There was an evolving sense that you probably had more knowledge in the experience of people in almost any setting than you could bring in from the outside, no matter how diligently the outsiders worked or studied," Thomas told me. Tom Kessinger, arriving in Jakarta in August 1979 to head the Ford office, had set about making contact with Indonesia's small but growing universe of civil-society organizations, in which an emerging generation of leaders was working for social and economic change. He wanted to know how those organizations could be nurtured. It was easy to find the bigger ones; they tended to be based in Jakarta and had English-speaking staffs who knew how to write reports. Harder to reach were the smaller, more numerous, less sophisticated, so-called nongovernmental organizations scattered all over the archipelago. "What Ann represented to me was getting out into the NGO circuit beyond what I could do because of my obligations and my poor Indonesian," Kessinger told me. She arrived at Ford, Thomas said, "at a time when the institutional focus had shifted from the elite to the grassroots. She personified someone all of whose ties were at a non-elite level."

Kessinger also wanted someone interested in women. There was a new focus at Ford on gender equality and the status of women. In Indonesia, the position of women had been relatively high compared with what it was in some other Muslim and even non-Muslim countries. But population pressure and technological change were pushing rural women into menial work. The extent of the problem was difficult to gauge, because there had been few studies of village women. Members of the Ford staff in Jakarta had suggested hiring someone to spend half their time as a program officer based in Jakarta, developing and managing projects addressing the need for paying work for village women. The rest of the time, he or she would work as a so-called project specialist at the Bogor Agricultural Institute, helping Indonesian researchers

analyze village-level data on women, and teaching younger scholars how to do field research. Sidney Jones, the only female program
officer in the Jakarta office of Ford at the time, invited Ann and
Tom Kessinger to dinner at her house. Not long after that, Kessinger hired Ann.

"At first impression, you would say she was easygoing," Kessinger told me. "Once you got to know her, she was really quite
intense and, in a certain sense, driven." She was serious and focused, and willing to engage with people. "But there was also a
little bit of reserve as well, which I never totally figured out," Kessinger said. "I could see that some people might see that as a kind
of snobbishness—though I don't mean snobbishness. When someone is distancing, sometimes it's personality or they're protecting
themselves. Sometimes it's read as not very open or warm. Ann had
that quality. I felt it the first evening we had dinner at Sidney
Jones's house. I was doing the interview kind of thing—not the
formal interview. I just had a sense that there were areas where I
was going to get a certain distance, not further. There seemed to be
a time when the conversation had to go in a different direction."

By January 1981, Ann was back in Jakarta with Maya and
working for Ford.

"Life in the bubble" is the phrase one longtime Ford employee
used to describe life as a Ford program officer in Jakarta. The
economy was growing, the oil industry was booming, and Jakarta
was becoming a modern city, but Ford families lived in a style that
resembled an earlier, colonial-era, expatriate existence. They were
housed in Kebayoran Baru, a quiet neighborhood of wide, shaded
streets planned by the Dutch, where Ford owned or leased a number of high-ceilinged bungalows with ceiling fans, verandas, and
gardens dense with flowering trees. The foundation furnished the
houses in teak and rattan or to the tastes of the Ford families. It

dispatched its own maintenance crew to fix toilets that ceased to flush. Ann's house was comfortable, not lavish. ("My oven has collapsed!" she wrote to a Ford support-staff member in April 1981. "I have to wire the door shut and it sprinkles flakes of rust on the food while the food is cooking." Some months later, she reported a termite infestation: "The wood is riddled with holes already and in the evening hours literally thousands of termites pour out of these holes and fly about, making the room and the back sitting area unusable.") Ford had a fleet of cars with drivers—though Ann employed her own, a man who had driven her Agency for International Development jeep in Semarang. The foundation ferried expatriate staff members in a carpool back and forth along the twenty-minute drive between Kebayoran Baru and the office. There was annual home leave for the entire family, with travel arrangements made by the foundation. There were provisions for spouse travel and "educational travel for dependent children," annual physicals and vaccinations. Children of the program staff rode a school bus together to the Jakarta International School, where—along with the offspring of diplomats, oil company executives, and missionaries—they performed in Gilbert and Sullivan operettas and recited the poetry of Rabindranath Tagore in the original Bengali. Ford arranged for enrollment and paid the tuition. "Everything seems set at the school for Maya," Kessinger, who served on the school's board, wrote to Ann in December 1980. He had, he said, "personally spoken to the Superintendent and [had] been assured that a place will be saved for her."

Ann worked three days a week in the Ford offices in a whitewashed colonial-style building with a steeply sloping tile roof on Taman Kebon Sirih (Betel Tree Garden) in Central Jakarta. Formerly a private home, the building sat squarely on a low-lying lot next to a canal. In the rainy season, brown water seeped up through the tile floors, swamping the metal file cabinets, saturating paper-work, and staining the walls. The staff fell roughly into two groups: The program staff was transient, white, and mostly male; and the administrative, clerical, and support staff tended to be permanent, Indonesian, and female. A photograph taken during Ann's tenure shows a dozen Indonesian women, all smiling and many of them dressed in batik, arrayed in front of a half-dozen mostly Caucasian men in neckties and short-sleeved plain white shirts. Floating half hidden in between is the only Western woman, Ann. Kessinger, whose title as the head of the office was country representative, had been a member of the first group of Peace Corps volunteers sent to India in the early sixties. He had worked in community development in the Punjab before returning to the United States to study history and anthropology, writing his dissertation for his Ph.D. from the University of Chicago on the social and economic history of an Indian village. He was a tenured professor of history at the University of Pennsylvania, married to an Indian, when Ford hired him in 1977 and sent him first to New Delhi. In the Jakarta office, Kessinger was a jovial presence, inclined toward the informal management style of academia, not the top-down style of the corporate world. The program officers, with Ph.D.'s in fields like comparative world history, specialized in areas such as natural resources, epidemiology, education, and traditional Indonesian culture. "There was a sense of idealism, but there was also a certain smugness of the 'best and the brightest' culture," said Sidney Jones, who went to work for Ford in Jakarta in 1977, initially in a job she said was known as "the ingenue role," because it was not expected to lead anywhere better. "You never referred to 'Ford.' It was always 'The Foundation.'"

The job of program officer required a mix of skills and talents. As Kessinger described it to me, a program officer had to talk to a lot of people, then think about the issues, then consider the context—within the Ford Foundation, in the Indonesian government, among other donors. As Jones put it, one had to think strategically about how to plant money in different places in order to bring about a desired transformation or change. "If you want to increase access to justice, for example, you think, 'Okay, we've got the legal-aid group that works with one set of people,'" she said. "'It would probably be a good idea to get a couple of really bright people trained in some kind of legal approach so that you can have those people in law faculties in a number of places. It would be good to get some judges or others to have exposure to what's done in places where there is really good access.' You put all the pieces together and you get a program."

As for herself, she said, "I just tended to take really interesting projects and fund them—without thinking very far ahead about what the end result was."

Within a week or two of starting at Ford, Ann flew to India on a trip that would end up shaping her approach to her job from then on. A young program officer in New York, Adrienne Germain, who had been working with the international program staff to increase Ford's involvement in the advancement of women, had invited Ann to join her on a trip she was taking. Unlike Indonesia, India already had a movement to improve the condition of poor working women. Ford was in contact with groups organizing street vendors and other self-employed women. Germain, who several months later would become the foundation's first female country representative and be sent to Bangladesh, had extended the invitation, she told me, "as a way of collaborating with Ann— to say, 'Look, these are the kind of women-specific programs that are going on that are really quite impressive and that you won't yet see in Indonesia.'"

They met with leaders of the Self Employed Women's Association, a then nine-year-old trade union based in Ahmedabad with roots in the country's labor, cooperative, and women's movements, which has since gone on to create a network of cooperatives and India's first women's bank. They visited the Working Women's Forum, started by a former Congress Party activist named Jaya Arunachalam, which within a decade would become not just a union of poor women but a network of cooperatives encouraging entrepreneurship by making low-interest loans. They met washerwomen, known as *dhobi*s, in the slums of Madras. Germain had first worked abroad while still an undergraduate at Wellesley College, tagging along for six months on a household survey in Peru that took her to the slums of Lima; she had strong feelings about how one should behave when working in other people's countries. Ann impressed her, Germain remembered many years later. She listened well—not to get information to do her job but because she wanted to learn. She was not, Germain said, "thinking at the top, which is where a lot of Ford was: 'Let's build our universities and let's get our intellectual capital going.'" Ann seemed to believe that you could not help people unless you learned from them first. "It was the most interactive way of being and of taking time," Germain recalled. "A lot of times, in all kinds of jobs, people didn't feel like they had that kind of time; they were there to make grants and move money. Often they didn't think much about: Could the project really be implemented the way it was? What would be the consequences? They weren't going to be around to learn the consequences. Ann was never like that. Ann was very aware that money doesn't necessarily solve problems."

What Ann saw in India left a deep impression. For years afterward, she would point to the organizations she had seen on that trip as examples of what might be possible elsewhere. Occasionally, she would use Ford grant money to send Indonesian activists to India to see for themselves. The size of the women's organizations in India astonished her. "She thought to herself, 'Why can't we do more than these itsy-bitsy NGOs? Why can't we take this to scale?'" said Richard Holloway, her friend from Semarang. Back in Jakarta, Ann wrote to Viji Srinivasan, a Ford colleague in New Delhi who had traveled with her and Germain: "The India trip certainly set my mind moving in some new directions. Could Indonesian women in the informal sector be organized a la the Working Women's Forum? (But where will we ever find a new Jaya Arunachalam?) Could a SEWA-like cooperative bank for women be organized in the Indonesian context?"

Anyone interested in the condition of poor women in Indonesia faced a shortage of data. Only a handful of Indonesian researchers were interested in women's issues, William Carmichael, Ford's vice president in charge of its developing-country programs, would write several years later in a Ford report; and most of those scholars had studied urban middle-class women. The exception was Pujiwati Sajogyo, a sociologist at the Center for Rural Sociological Studies at the Bogor Agricultural Institute. Married to one of the country's top experts on rural development and poverty alleviation, she had studied rural women in West Java in the late 1970s. The Sajogyos were "two of the more original and interesting researchers working on issues that the government thought were sensitive," Kessinger told me. Pujiwati Sajogyo's research, funded by Ford, was among the first to shed light on work patterns by gender in rural households and villages. In 1980, Ford gave the agricultural institute another $200,000 to develop detailed data on rural women outside Java and to increase the country's capacity to carry out that sort of research. Under the grant, young researchers from the provinces were to be trained and sent out to study the lives of village women. A project specialist from Ford would help analyze data from village studies and run workshops in field research for graduate students and junior faculty. The aim was to build a national network of researchers on issues involving women, increase the supply of data, and make it available to program designers and policy makers. During her first two years at Ford, Ann was the project specialist assisting Sajogyo.

Twice a week, Ann would be driven south from Jakarta to Bogor, the hill town where generations of colonials, including Thomas Stamford Raffles, the British lieutenant governor of Java during the brief British occupation of parts of the Dutch East Indies, had repaired in the early nineteenth century to escape the swelter of summer. The university lay alongside a wide boulevard, facing the Bogor Botanical Gardens, conceived a century and a half earlier by a Dutch botanist with the help of assistants from the Royal Botanic Gardens at Kew. With fifteen thousand species of trees and plants, the Bogor gardens surrounded the Indonesian president's summer palace. "I might mention that I'm in Bogor every Tuesday and Thursday at Pujiwati's office," Ann wrote in 1981 to Carol Colfer, an American anthropologist working in Indonesia, who had sent a letter proposing that she and Ann meet. "I see from your itinerary you will also be in Bogor on Tuesday, March 17. We could have a picnic in the garden."

That summer, Ann flew with Sajogyo to Sumatra, where they spent a week visiting universities, giving presentations on women and development, explaining field research methodologies, and interviewing candidates for the training workshop they planned to hold in Bogor a month later. Finding the right researchers was not simple. At the University of North Sumatra in Medan, all eleven candidates were unsuitable: Either they were from unrelated fields, such as art, or they had no experience in villages and had never done research on rural women. In Padang, the capital of West Sumatra, the university rector preferred hiring men as instructors because, he said, women went off on pregnancy leave or balked at leaving their husbands. Traveling alone in South Sumatra, Ann found that the cultural complexity of the region presented additional research challenges. There were four distinct ecological zones and fourteen indigenous ethnic groups, each with its own dialect or, in some cases, language. There were also migrants from elsewhere in Indonesia, some relocated by the government from densely populated parts of the country. The experiences of women varied widely from one ethnic group to the next; one, for example, kept teenage girls in purdah. "With all this complexity, the difficulty of selecting truly representative sample villages is enormous," Ann wrote in a report on the progress of the project.

By late September, Ann and Sajogyo had enlisted eighteen researchers from eight universities in seven provinces to meet in Bogor for the workshop in preparation for heading out into the field. Twelve were women. Ann and the Sajogyos taught seminars on a dozen topics, from theories of social structure to the role of women in small industries and petty trade. Well-known Indonesian social scientists gave guest lectures. The government's junior minister for women's affairs spoke on the connection between policy-making and research. The young researchers were to collect data on three subjects: time and labor allocation, income and expenditures, and decision-making. Each also chose a special area of interest. They would be working in Sumatra, Sulawesi, East Java, and Nusa Tenggara Timur, a group of islands in eastern Indonesia. They would be studying a half-dozen ethnic groups—from Bataks to transmigrant Javanese—in villages that made handicrafts, farmed fish, harvested forest products, and grew such things as rice, coconuts, coffee, rubber, and cloves.

Ann went into the field, too. Bill Collier, whom she had known since the early 1960s at the University of Hawai'i and who had known both of her husbands, was working on a separate study in tidal-swamp areas of South Sumatra. His team was studying agricultural systems and the condition of several ethnic groups, including indigenous Malays, Buginese migrants, and Javanese transmigrants. Ann joined the group, moving from village to village on a grid of rivers and canals, traveling by night in wooden boats in crocodile-infested waters. The group slept on the floors of village leaders' houses, built on stilts. Because the Buginese distrusted the Javanese, Collier told me, the Javanese members of the research team would insist that he and Ann step out of the boats first in every Buginese village. In one area where Ann was hoping to conduct interviews, the local leader was said to have a long arrest record for robbery and a murder, committed ostensibly with the help of his wife. He had returned from prison, and everyone in the villages deferred to him: "If you wanted to go anywhere, you had to tell him first," Collier said. The man assigned his wife and alleged co-conspirator as Ann's escort—to convince the Buginese to talk. Through flooded rice fields and swarms of mosquitoes, Ann and her escort crossed from one canal to the next on foot. "Ann ended up up to her chest in water and mud," Collier remembered. "She loved it. She could create a rapport with these people very easily, because she was sympathetic and she liked them. They realized that she was there trying to find out things to help."

Indonesia was "a country of 'smiling' or gentle oppression" when it came to women, Ann would write in a Ford memo the following spring. Extreme forms of anti-female behavior, such as infanticide or nutritional discrimination, were nonexistent or rare, but there was a "social reward system" that led middle- and upper-class women to marry early, forgo further education, and pass up careers. Educated women often stayed out of the workforce to avoid giving the impression that their husbands could not support them. Most Indonesian women worked for little money: In village industries and farming, they made about half the income of men. Yet their income was crucial to the survival of poor households— especially the one in five households on Java that were headed by women because of divorce, desertion, and the departure of men looking for work. Government programs, however, addressed women as homemakers, not breadwinners. Women were required to attend family-planning and nutrition programs, but they were rarely chosen for projects that might help them make money. As a result, young women were leaving the countryside for the cities— where they were ending up as servants, factory workers, or prostitutes. All three of those jobs involved economic and sexual exploitation, Ann said. Ford was working with grassroots organizations that focused on women, she said, but the government viewed organizing as subversive. "While Indonesia has many women's organizations, it cannot be said to have a real women's 'movement,'" Ann wrote. "In comparison with a country like India, for example, the capacity of Indonesian women to articulate their problems, organize themselves and use political or other channels to improve their condition is still minimal."

As Ann had noticed several years earlier in her dissertation fieldwork, development was not necessarily benefiting poor women. In 1982, she helped persuade Ford to award a $33,000 grant to a legal-aid organization, the Institute of Consultation and Legal Aid for Women and Families, to hold a seminar and workshop on the effects of industrialization on female labor. In preparation, a team formed by three other organizations studied women workers in fifteen factories on Java, looking at the division of labor by gender, differences in treatment, legal literacy of women workers, and enforcement of labor laws regarding women. The team leaders and their assistants were young well-trained female social scientists, one of whom later started her own organization focused on women workers. Their report quickly became "our best reference on the condition of women workers in the formal sector in Indonesia," Ann wrote afterward.

Ann was a feminist, by all accounts, but not inclined toward fiery pronouncements. As Sidney Jones described her, she could more legitimately be called a feminist than could anyone previously assigned to the Jakarta office. She had strong convictions on the rights of women. "But she wasn't at all in your face or belligerently ideological," Jones said. Two of Ann's close friends in Jakarta in the early 1980s were more immediately identified as feminists: Georgia McCauley, whose husband worked for Ford, was a former president of the Honolulu chapter of the National Organization for Women, and Julia Suryakusuma, the flamboyant daughter of an Indonesian diplomat and wife of a film director, would later quote a friend's description of her as a "feminist and femme fatale." According to James Fox, an anthropologist based in Australia and working in Indonesia, who was friendly with both of them, "Ann was never out there in the same way that Julia was, but they were close." As Fox saw it, some feminists were earnest and literal, and could constantly be teased. You could not do that with Ann, he said, because she would just play along. Her feminism was tempered, he said, by the fact that her overriding commitment was to the poor, regardless of gender. Occasionally, Ann would make jokes about feminists, said Pete Vayda, a close friend of Ann's who was working as a consultant for Ford. Which is not to say she would necessarily overlook a remark she considered demeaning.

"Have a good weekend, honey," said one Australian consultant.

"Don't call me honey," Ann growled in response.

"Okay, sport," the consultant countered cheerily.

On another occasion, Ann challenged a table full of Indonesian activists, all men, with whom she was dining, because she felt they were being rude to the waitress.

"Excuse me," a younger Indonesian friend recalled Ann saying. "You guys make me feel uncomfortable. I'm sitting here and you're doing nothing to me and yet I feel badly. How do you think she felt?"

What drove her?

In the eyes of her children, there was something soft and a bit naive about their mother. In *Dreams from My Father*, she comes off as a romantic, a dreamer, an innocent abroad. Amid the secrets, the unacknowledged violence, the corruption of Jakarta, Ann is "a lonely witness for secular humanism, a soldier for New Deal, Peace Corps, position-paper liberalism." Twenty years after the end of her first marriage, her chin trembles when she speaks to her college-age son about his father. Her wistful expression at a screening of *Black Orpheus* seems, to her son, a window into "the unreflective heart of her youth." In later life, she travels the world, working in villages in Asia and Africa, "helping women buy a sewing machine or a milk cow or an education that might give them a foothold in the world's economy," as Obama describes her work. She stares at the moon and forages through markets of Delhi or Marrakech "for some trifle, a scarf or stone carving that would make her laugh or please the eye." At times, she seems almost childlike.

Maya, too, described her mother to me as what she called "a softie"—a person of acute sensitivity and empathy who would be overwhelmed with feeling at the sight or even the prospect of other people's suffering. In the company of her family, she might weep at a newscast, Maya said, and she could barely watch movies in which children were hurt. "She could be naive when speaking about this country and what people were ready for . . ." Maya said. "There was that sense—like, 'Why can't we all get along?' And, you know, there was a touch of the flower child in her." Perhaps Ann was simply an optimist; perhaps she refused to be cynical. But, Maya said, "it seemed perhaps a little naive at times—this failure to comprehend that not everyone would necessarily have good motives or benevolent intentions."

When I asked President Obama if he saw his mother as naively idealistic, as his book seemed to suggest, he paused a while before answering, then said, "Yes, I do and did see her that way, in part— but not in a pejorative sense. I mean, my mother was very sophisticated and smart. In her field of study and her work, she was deadly serious about what she was doing, willing to take on a lot of sacred cows, and really committed. So as a professional, she knew her stuff. There was a sweetness about her and a willingness to give people the benefit of the doubt, and sort of a generosity of spirit that at times was naive. . . . Now, I like that about her. That's not a criticism; there's a wonderful quality about that. But there's no doubt that there were times when she was taken advantage of in certain situations. And she didn't mind being taken advantage of. Part of the idealism was, 'You know what? If somebody makes me pay five times what the going rate is at the market for this little knickknack that I think is neat, that's fine.' There's an idealism and naiveté embedded in that. But I don't see that as a criticism. I see that as part of what made her special—and also part of what made her resilient. Because I think she could bounce back from disappointments in a lot of ways."

Friends and colleagues described her differently. Many remembered Ann as tough, sharp, and worldly. Most said they had never seen her cry. She was more open than many people, both intellectually and emotionally. She was unusually curious: She wanted to understand the reasons for things. At one point, for example, she became interested in the relationship between Indonesians and the relatives some of them exploited as servants, Pete Vayda remembered. "It was the kind of thing she was very interested in—some kind of injustice based on something structural or cultural," he said. "It was not a matter of saying these were evil people, but something systematic about exploiting poor relatives from the countryside." Her convictions, he said, arose less out of emotional responses than out of empirical data. Her sense of injustice was sharp but informed—not a sentimental reaction. He could not recall having heard Ann "give any passionate speeches about the injustices of the world." She would just comment, rather matter-of-factly, "I'm looking into this." She was fully aware of corruption, the government restrictions, the cynicism of elites. She knew all about people exploiting one another, and she did not romanticize any of those things. At the same time, she believed it was not impossible to make life in Indonesia better. "She saw the good and the bad everywhere," Vayda said. "She was smart about it. She realized these were things she had to accept if she wanted to make a difference." He said he had no evidence that correcting injustices was what drove her—but if something could be corrected, that was a bonus.

"Other people talk about her warmth and compassion and generosity," Vayda said, with some impatience, reflecting on characterizations of Ann in the media during the presidential campaign. "All that's true. But I haven't seen that much about how funny she was—and how hardheaded."

What was striking, James Fox said, was not her passion but her authority.

"Ann had lived how many years with poor people?" he said. "She didn't have to parade it, it was just there. When she talked, she talked as if she knew the villages of Java. You knew she knew.

With friends or colleagues, apparently in Yogyakarta,
about 1977 or 1978

It was a kind of mission, but she didn't put up a flag to parade it." At the same time, he said, "she just couldn't stand some of the bullshit that comes from an expatriate who's been in the country a week and knows the answer to everything. Ann could be very tough. She didn't suffer fools who pretended to know what they didn't know."

To some in the Ford Foundation office, she came off as more of an advocate.

"She was a very tough person, and I mean that in a good sense," said Terance Bigalke, a Ford program officer in Jakarta. At Ford, she did not go out of her way to "nuance" her positions, he said. "In an office setting, you often say things where you're making your point but very carefully choosing your words," he said. "That wasn't her style." She seemed to believe people should be able to take the full force of her opinions; she was ready to do the same in return. Most people seemed to respect her for it, Bigalke said, even if they might not have taken such an undiplomatic stand. They may even have found it endearing. "They could feel how passionately she felt about the issues she was working with," he said. "It wasn't an academic exercise for her, it was something she was really committed to."

Or as Tom Kessinger put it, "It wasn't just a professional job. It was something a little more personal."

One of the Indonesians with whom Ann worked most closely was Adi Sasono, the son of Muslim social activists from Pekalongan on the north coast of Central Java, who had been a student leader at the time of the overthrow of Sukarno. Trained as an engineer and educated in Holland, Sasono had worked in the corporate sector until the mid-1970s, when he had quit and, with a group of young intellectuals who saw themselves as Islamic reformers, formed an organization to explore alternative approaches to development in Indonesia. By the time Ann met him, Sasono was the director of the Institute for Development Studies, an independent organization with a full-time staff of thirty. He was organizing squatters and scavengers in the cities and encouraging the growth of rural cooperatives. Sasono, who would go on to become a minister in the Indonesian government after the fall of Suharto in the late 1990s, wanted to find ways of allowing "development without displacement"; he wanted to integrate the sprawling informal economy into city planning. His ideas were so attractive, Richard Holloway of Oxfam told me, that many of the international-development people wanted to work with him. "Of all the Indonesians I worked with, he was the strongest in terms of a conceptual framework for what he was doing," said David Korten, who was working for the U.S. Agency for International Development in Indonesia at the time and has since become a critic of economic and corporate globalization. Korten recalled "how far he was ahead of most of us in understanding the dysfunctions of the 'modern' development sector and why it so inexorably increases the marginalization of the majority of the population. He saw the bigger picture that most of us were missing."

It was assumed, Sasono suggested, that rapid industrialization and the exploitation of natural resources were the best route to economic development and high employment. But industrialization was failing to absorb the growing labor force in the cities. Poverty was increasing, and the gap between rich and poor was widening. The benefits of growth were not trickling down. In Jakarta, people were squatting in cemeteries, encamped beside garbage dumps, crowded in shanties alongside railroad tracks. The government was demolishing makeshift settlements to make way for high-rise buildings and the widening of roads, and the police were confiscating pedicabs to clear streets for cars. There was talk of shipping vagrants to a nearby island. Shantytowns, demolished one day, were being reborn the next. "They were doing constant battle with authorities," Bigalke remembered. "Police were needing to be bribed to allow people to continue setting up their stands on the street." Sasono made the case for a broad-based, decentralized approach to growth—"for the people, by the people, and with the people." Even without government help, he believed, the poor would prosper on the strength of their energy and wits. Sasono was a figure not unlike Saul Alinsky, the author of *Rules for Radicals: A Pragmatic Primer for Realistic Radicals* and the father of community organizing in the United States, Richard Holloway told me. Alinsky wrote that book, he said, for those "who want to change the world from what it is to what they believe it should be." Community organizing, of course, was the line of work that Barack Obama would take up in Chicago just a couple of years after Ann began working with Sasono in Jakarta. Alinsky's phrase, about wanting to change the world, echoes what Craig Miner, the historian, had told me about Kansans—that they were people who said, "You're not okay, I'm not okay, and I know how to fix it."

Through Sasono, Ann widened her circle of acquaintances to include a diverse group of labor activists, reformers, people in cultural organizations, and organizers from the slums. Her fieldwork in the handicraft villages and on the provincial development project in Central Java had convinced her, like Sasono, of the vitality of the informal sector, and the value of development from the bottom up. "She was very interested in demonstrating what a significant contribution to the overall economy the informal sector was making," Bigalke told me. That way, the informal sector might be encouraged by the authorities rather than stifled. Ann and Sasono, along with others, traveled together to Malang in East Java to visit the largest grassroots women's cooperative in Indonesia, the Setia

Budi Women's Cooperative, which had been set up exclusively to meet the financial needs of women. They attended seminars and workshops in Jakarta, Semarang, and Bali. "They got along well together," said her close friend Rens Heringa. "With him, she could really talk—politics and social and economic problems, that kind of thing." Holloway said, "She was friendly with Adi professionally and possibly personally. Of course, you don't express emotion in Java. So whatever emotion they had was always concealed. They hung around a lot together. It would have been talked about a bit. But no big deal." Through Sasono, Ann told Holloway, "I'm able to find really impressive people that I respect greatly, who are Indonesians and not privileged foreigners like myself, but who are working with down-and-out and poor people."

Ann had a strong sense of right and wrong about people abusing other people, Holloway had noticed. She knew wealthy women in Jakarta, some educated abroad, who "talked up a great talk about democracy," Holloway said, then went home and gave their own servants no wages, poor food, and abysmal accommodations. He had been struck by what he described as Ann's "vituperation about high-class Javanese women treating servants badly." That sort of thing was a fact of life in Indonesia, he said. "But she was not prepared to just slough that off and say, 'That's how Indonesia is.' She would get angry about it." To encounter Indonesians who felt passionately about challenging such injustices was emboldening. Holloway said, "She would, I think, feel justified in this because, 'I'm not just a foreigner getting angry, there are people like Adi getting angry. This is an Indonesian response, not a foreign response.'"

It was an important point, Holloway added.

"There was always a danger that you would become overidentified with the problems of the people you were working with," he said. "When that happens, you exaggerate the nature of their problems in a way that's meaningful to you but not to them. They have accommodated such problems in their view of life; for you to go on about it seems naive or foolish."

Ann played an unusual role during that period: At a time when fledgling independent-sector organizations offered just about the only opportunity for the exercise of democratic values, Sasono told me, Ann served as a catalyst and a bridge. The Suharto government tolerated a limited amount of activity. But the organizations had a tendency, Bigalke said, "to kind of carve out their own little territory and not be all that interested in interacting with others." Rarely did one group try to bring others together. "In a way, Ann was doing that through the various grants that she had, and then bringing people together at her home for dinners in the evening, having the kinds of social interaction that we had with the institutes that we were giving grants to," Bigalke said. Sasono, who had been impressed as a young man by the stories of American democratic institutions as told in booklets distributed by the United States Information Service to libraries all over Indonesia, said he learned about pluralism from Ann's example.

"Bridging is not an easy job, because she has to understand the ideas of many people with different ideas," he said. Being an anthropologist, she talked to people as partners, not "as target beneficiaries." Her involvement was emotional, not simply intellectual. Those discussions, Sasono said, gave people ideas and courage. Many became activists in the reform movement that eventually brought the government down. A few, such as Sasono, went on to work in the governments that followed. "Development, like democracy, is a learning process," Sasono said. "People have to learn to have freedom, on one side, and also responsibility, the rule of law, social discipline. It must be done through a social learning process.

That's what we learned from both Ann Dunham as well as David Korten, because both come from a society that has learned from democracy in more than two hundred years."

More important than projects, he said, was the selling of ideas.

In mid-1982, Ann made several field trips to tea plantations in the mountains of Java. An Indonesian organization, the All-Indonesia Labor Federation, had proposed to the Ford Foundation a project aimed at improving the welfare of female tea plantation workers. It was also intended to increase the participation of women in labor organizations. Traveling with women, some of whom she had met through Sasono, Ann talked with plantation owners, managers, and pickers. She kept detailed notes, full of observations about the meddling of managers, the hardships faced by the pickers, the comfortable lives of the owners. "She is a Sundanese and she also lives on the plantation in a large comfortable home with diesel-powered electricity, stereo and cassette collection, etc.," Ann wrote of the owner of a plantation between Jakarta and Bandung, where heavy ash from an erupting volcano was falling. "She provided us with a lavish lunch, but attempted in various ways to obstruct our free discussions with her workers." Managers tried to orchestrate the interviews—handpicking the workers and sitting in on the conversations. "We overcame this by rearranging chairs, splitting up and moving in amidst the workers for private conversations," Ann wrote. The area was Islamic, and the women said they were "diligent in praying," Ann wrote. None had ever been to Jakarta or Bandung. None had completed more than third grade. Only two out of seventy-five they met with could read or write. Most could not understand Bahasa Indonesia, the national language. "Claimed school costs prohibitive," Ann wrote. "Includes contributions of rice to the teacher."

Accompanying Ann on one of those trips was Saraswati

Sunindyo, a young organizer newly graduated from the University of Indonesia in Jakarta with a degree in sociology. "My line about Ann is, 'She found me in a slum when I was organizing,'" Sunindyo told me when I interviewed her in Seattle, where she was living. Sunindyo was organizing the residents of a squatter settlement in Jakarta for an organization run by Sasono. Later, she moved to Bandung, where, she said, she lived in a shack in a community of scavengers she was organizing into a cooperative. She and Ann met at a meeting of independent and grassroots organizations. "She was this big American woman," Sunindyo remembered, referring to Ann's presence more than her size. "She is a big woman with very little ego. She's not playing the role of an expatriate—not 'I'm an American, I read lots of books, therefore I know.' She worked for the Ford Foundation, but she didn't act like someone who was going to dictate what Ford wanted." Instead, Sunindyo said, Ann "would listen and listen and listen. She was interested in how people are doing things. Rather than, 'Okay, this is a story from another place that I read about. . . .' We all read lots of books, but we don't have to show it. That's Ann. She saw potential in people. And when they needed a push, she really pushed."

In September 1982, Sunindyo traveled with Ann and several younger women to a plantation in the mountains southeast of Bandung. They were housed for the night in a Dutch-period guesthouse with an antique wood-burning stove and a veranda overlooking the adjacent valley and what Ann described as the "tea-covered hills beyond." The bathroom Ann shared with one other woman, she wrote in her field notes, was the size of the bathroom used by many of the workers, as well as their children. To speak with workers, Ann and the others were taken to where women were picking tea. Sunindyo, wanting not simply to gather information but to help out, fell in beside one picker and began picking with her, dropping tea leaves into her basket. The skin on the faces of the pickers was cracked from the weather and the cold.

"And politely, very politely, Ann asked one of the women, 'May I see what's in your lunch box?'" Sunindyo remembered.

There was only rice and *sambal,* a paste made from ground red chili peppers.

"So, we asked, 'What else are you going to eat?'" Sunindyo recalled.

"The leaves," the woman said.

The trip to the tea plantation with Ann was important to Sunindyo. "For us, young women at that time, it was really empowering—in the sense that we were learning from her," she said. "We just watched, said, 'Okay, that's it, that's how.'" To have Ann recognize their commitment and treat them as friends emboldened them to return to their work in their organizations "knowing that we are in this together," Sunindyo said.

"There is Ann, who works for the Ford Foundation," she said. "We see Ann as one of us."

Ann's circle of friends in Jakarta kept expanding. There were anthropologists, artists, activists, academics, curators, writers, development consultants, and filmmakers, among others. Yang Suwan, a Chinese-Indonesian anthropologist educated in Germany and newly returned to Jakarta, had done studies on women in development in West Sumatra and East Kalimantan. She and Ann shared a fascination with Indonesian crafts and textiles. Rens Heringa was studying a group of isolated villages on the northeast coast of Java where women made batik from hand-spun locally grown cotton. In October 1981, in the hot period before the rains broke, she and Ann took a three-day car trip along the northeast coast of Java to visit those villages. They stopped along the way to explore a series of saline ponds where the owners, many of them of

Arab descent, trapped shrimp and harvested salt. Wahyono Martowikrido, the archaeologist whom Ann had known in the early
and mid-1970s, was back at the National Museum in Jakarta. Ann
Hawkins, who had known Ann in Semarang, had moved to Jakarta to work for UNICEF, around the corner from the Ford
Foundation offices. By crossing an old Dutch canal on jerry-rigged
boards, she and Ann would meet from time to time for lunch. Pete
Vayda, living in a Ford bungalow near Ann's, dropped in regularly
for breakfast and rode to work in Ann's car. Her long dining room
table was a gathering place, often arrayed with packages of home-
made Indonesian snacks. "Please, take these," Yang Suwan remembered Ann saying. "You'll help the poor women if you eat the
snacks." Often, Ann had guests. After Vayda introduced her to a
graduate student of his who was doing fieldwork in East Kalimantan, the student, Timothy Jessup, became a regular guest when he
was in town. Was there a place in Jakarta to play squash? Vayda
asked Ann. Soon she had arranged, through Lolo, for Vayda to
become a member of the Petroleum Club.

Ann could be found at parties at the East Jakarta home of Ong
Hok Ham, a Chinese-Indonesian, Yale-educated historian and
public intellectual. Newspaper editors, academics, artists, foreign
reporters, foundation program officers, and diplomats with duty-
free privileges were regularly invited. The parties served as a kind
of salon and a source of inside information and political gossip. "He
collected people he found interesting," said John McGlynn, an
American translator of Indonesian literature who first encountered
Ann in the early 1980s. "He wanted intellect, he wanted argument.
I was told you can count on Ann for some of that." Ann was
a member of a group McGlynn referred to as "the white women in
tablecloths"—expatriates with a taste for wraparound batik skirts.
Ann's laugh was full-throated and spontaneous, "a cross between a

chuckle and a neigh." But her speaking voice was soft—as Heringa put it, "almost Javanese. It was as if she was telling fairy tales. In that way, she had adapted fully." On several occasions, she gave lectures on topics such as textiles and Indonesian ironworking traditions as part of a series organized by the Ganesha Society, a group of mostly expatriate volunteers at the National Museum. At other times, she could be found at exhibitions and plays at the Taman Ismail Marzuki Arts Center, where some of the performances were known to be, as James Fox put it, "pushing the edge of things."

"If you knew Indonesian culture, if you knew what was being said, you could recognize the game," Fox said. "But you had to know the language well enough, you had to know the way things were being communicated. Of course, Ann did. Her Indonesian was excellent; it was almost like a native's. She could pick those things up. So either at events like that or parties we'd have with Indonesians, you could participate. In the expatriate community, you would almost have to spell it out and they'd never get it. You'd tell them the simplest thing, and it would be a revelation. Ann was one of those rare birds who knew how things were. She had an edge to her. She was feisty. She had a huge sense of humor, I thought. It was honed to be subtle. She could make a joke without appearing to. It was innuendo."

It was, perhaps, almost Javanese.

"Are you aware that our friends are all people living in more than one culture?" Ann marveled to Yang Suwan on one occasion, being driven home one evening in Jakarta. "We are so lucky to know both cultures. This problem about ethnicity, about race—it is not a problem for us."

Ann's closest female friend was Julia Suryakusuma, the "feminist and femme fatale." On the surface, the two women made an unlikely pair. A diplomat's daughter born in India and educated at the American high school in Rome, Suryakusuma was tall and beautiful, and twelve years younger than Ann. Colorful and out-spoken, she prided herself on being, as she put it, "naughty and rebellious." She had married Ami Priyono, an Indonesian film di-rector who was fifteen years older, when she was barely twenty. James Fox considered her "some of the best company in Jakarta," and Rens Heringa described her to me as "a person one gets into trouble with." Ann was calm and measured. Julia was volatile. "The ideas were squirting out of her imagination," Timothy Jessup said. "It was interesting to see them talk, because Julia would be waving her hands around. Ann would be calm, and Julia would be getting very excited. She liked to make an impression and shock people. Ann liked to make an impression in a different way." Yet they were both bright and unconventional, and not terribly inter-ested in conforming. "Ann used to say that I was from another planet," Suryakusuma told me. "Well, it takes one to know one." They shared a scholarly and personal interest in the condition of Indonesian women. They occasionally fought over handicrafts. They went to parties together, hung out, critiqued each other's re-lationships with men. ("You know, Julia, you're overqualified for him," Ann once told her.) "We shared our innermost secrets, our fears and desires," Suryakusuma told me. The friendship was inti-mate and turbulent. "She put up with a lot of shit from me," Suryakusuma said. There were periods when they did not speak.

During one of those periods some years later, Ann sent Suryaku-suma a letter that, at least at this distance, seems remarkable in its blend of frankness, respect, and bruised affection.

> Friends often ask me about you, Julia. . . . Frankly, I don't know what to say to them. The situation is made more myste-rious because I am not even sure what you were angry about.

I <u>THINK</u> you were angry because I suggested you patch up your quarrels with Garrett and Rens, but I am not even sure about that. If that <u>is</u> the case, I can only say that, as an old friend, I felt I had the right to give you an honest opinion.

It has been more than 7 months since we last talked, Julia. I haven't called you because I felt I should respect your wish to break things off. Also, I don't like you in your arrogant bitch mode, and I did not want to run the risk of encountering you in that mode again. (Who in the hell did you think you were talking to, anyway, Julia?).

That said, I do of course miss you, and I miss the whole family as well. After all, we were best friends for almost 10 years. I hope things are going well for all of you. Will you be moving into your new house soon? . . .

Have a good holiday. Regards to Ami. Love, Ann.

Yet on another occasion, Ann wrote, "Wanted to write and let you know how much I enjoyed our time together in London. . . . I realized when we were there how much you actually mean to me. In a world where most people are such bloody hypocrites, your spirit shines like a beautiful star! I never have to go through a lot of crap with you, so to speak. Sounds corny, but I mean it. I love you a lot, kiddo."

With many of her friends, Ann kept the details of her private life private. Even with some who knew her well, she revealed little about her childhood, her parents, even her marriages. On the subject of her sex life, she was discreet even with close friends—or so they led me to believe. But opportunities for romance did not end with her second divorce. Carol Colfer, who was also a single American woman in her thirties working in Indonesia, said she and Ann used to talk about people hitting on them. "It was very common," she said. "A lot of Indonesians like white skin. And, of course, she had quite white skin. We would joke about people bothering us and thinking we were going to be these wildly sexually active folks. We weren't very wild." If Ann confided on a regular basis in anyone, it appears to have been Suryakusuma. "We were both very sexual," Suryakusuma told me. "We talked a lot about sex and our sex lives." Ann was sensual, Suryakusuma said. She took pleasure

With Ong Hok Ham, Julia Suryakusuma, Ami Priyono, and
Aditya Priyawardhana, the son of Julia Suryakusuma and
Ami Priyono, July 1989

in, among other things, food and sex. Rens Heringa said she and Ann shared an astrological sign, Sagittarius, thought to signify an adventurous spirit. "I never was interested in Dutch guys, ever," Heringa said. "She never was really interested in white guys." According to Suryakusuma, "She used to say she liked brown bums and I liked white bums."

Ann's secretary at the Ford Foundation, Paschetta Sarmidi, noticed that Ann's eyes "glittered" at the mention of a certain Indonesian man who worked for a bank near the Ford offices.

"You like Indonesians," Sarmidi observed tentatively. "The first time, you married an African. The second time, you married Lolo. Now you like the man from the bank."

"She smiled," recalled Sarmidi, who pressed no further.

Ann loved men, but she did not claim to understand them, Georgia McCauley, who became a close friend of Ann's in Jakarta in the early 1980s, told me. McCauley, who was fifteen years younger than Ann and a mother of two small children, remembered once asking Ann for advice about men. "She said, 'I'm so sorry, I have no idea. I just have nothing to offer you. I haven't learned anything yet,'" McCauley told me. "She was befuddled by them. They were interesting to her; she had this intense curiosity. Her relationships had not worked out. Like many women, she didn't understand men. She was a cultural anthropologist, it was a kind of *topic*: 'Interesting, but don't know!'"

Life in the bubble had its downside for an unmarried American woman with a half-Indonesian daughter at home and a half-African son in college thousands of miles away. In a community made up largely of married men with wives and children at home, Ann was an anomaly. "You're more subject to gossip," said Mary Zurbuchen, who had become a single parent by the time she returned to Jakarta in 1992 as the Ford Foundation's country representative. "People might have wondered who she was and who she was hanging out with. They might have noticed things." After attending a meeting of high-ranking Ford people from all over the world, Nancy Peluso remembered, Ann remarked that nearly all the participants were male, and those who were not male were mostly unmarried or childless. "She was really the odd person out,"

Peluso said. Ann's home life "imposed different kinds of constraints on her life that Ford was simply not cut out to understand."

Suzanne Siskel, who joined the Ford Foundation as a program officer in Jakarta in 1990, ran into Ann at a party in 1990 shortly after accepting the job. "She looked at me," Siskel told me. "She said, '*Hmm*. You're going to work for Ford? Get ready for the eighteen-hour workday.'"

The logistics of managing Ann's household could be complex: "Barry will stay in Indonesia +/- one month and then return to New York via Honolulu, taking Maya with him and dropping her off at her grandparents for the rest of the summer," Ann wrote to her boss, Tom Kessinger, in April 1983, laying out the family's travel plans for the summer after Barry's college graduation. "This will count as her home leave. I will either go to Hawaii at the end of the summer to pick her up, staying two weeks as my home leave, or I will have her grandparents put her on a plane to Singapore and I will pick her up there. We will do our physicals in Singapore at that time." For work, Ann traveled often: New Delhi, Bombay, Bangkok, Cairo, Nairobi, Dhaka, Kuala Lumpur, and throughout much of Indonesia. On at least one occasion, she appealed to Ford to rewrite its spouse travel policy to cover dependent children. "This is particularly relevant for single parents who do not have another responsible adult in the household to handle child care during periods of extensive travel," she wrote in a memo to New York in December 1983. On the other hand, the cost of living in Jakarta, combined with a Ford salary and benefits, made it possible to be a single mother in a high-powered, travel-intensive job in a way that might have been more difficult in the United States.

"You managed," Zurbuchen said. Even if barely.

The Jakarta International School, where Ann enrolled Maya,

was both extraordinary, in its community and curriculum, and extraordinarily exclusive. Founded by international organizations, such as the Ford Foundation, that put up money in return for shares, it served the families of those institutions. The grounds of the new campus in South Jakarta were landscaped with tropical flowers. There was a swimming pool, air-conditioning, a theater with plush upholstered seats, where students performed plays by the likes of George Bernard Shaw. The faculty was international. The student body comprised fifty-nine nationalities, with the United States and Australia contributing the most. Parents were accomplished and ambitious for their children, and there was an abundance of nonworking mothers available to, say, sew kimonos for a production of *The Mikado*. The school played a powerful and positive role in shaping the worldview of its students. "They came to easily transcend the notion that national identity is the normal referent for looking at people," Tom Kessinger said of his two sons. "And they found early on that friendships take many different forms, particularly over time." One group was glaringly absent, however. Under Indonesian law, Indonesian children could not attend. When Kessinger wrote to Ann, telling her that Maya's enrollment had been approved, he added that the only hitch was that the school would need copies of the first page of Maya's passport and of Ann's work permit: "They need them to satisfy Government of Indonesia regulations for all students, and are somewhat concerned because she obviously carries an Indonesian surname." In that way, among others, the school stood apart. "It was like a satellite on its own," said Halimah Brugger, an American who taught music there for twenty-five years. Frances Korten, who joined the Ford Foundation office as a program officer in 1983 and had a daughter in Maya's class, recalled, "That kind of insularity of the foreign community was something that Ann, I think, frankly, more than the rest of us, felt was really not good. . . . To have her child going to a school that Indonesians couldn't attend, I think, was an affront."

It was not easy. Ann wanted Maya to have an English-language education, and Maya would have been ill equipped to leap into an Indonesian school for the first time at age ten or eleven. In preparation for entering the Jakarta International School, Ann had made sure that Maya's homeschooling included English. But Maya felt, as she put it, some "discomfort being the only Indonesian in the Jakarta International School." It was a discomfort of which Ann was surely aware. "I think batik-making was the only Indonesian thing that I did," Maya remembered. "I remember taking choir and singing 'Tie a Yellow Ribbon Round the Old Oak Tree.' We did *Pygmalion* and British history." Hoping to gain acceptance, she brought in photographs of American relatives she did not even know. "There were a couple of mixed kids like me," she said. "No full-blooded Indonesians, except folks who worked there. Some. I certainly felt like I was in two different worlds: the world of Indonesia that I knew, populated by Indonesians, and then the world of JIS, which was basically an expatriate school." Ann worried that the nature of her work would affect Maya's shot at social acceptance. "Ann said Maya's friends thought Ann's job was rather odd—going into the field, talking with poor people," Yang Suwan told me. When Maya had friends coming over for the night, Yang recalled, Ann seemed uncharacteristically anxious. The Indonesian snacks would disappear from the dining room table. "Suddenly, there are steaks and soft drinks," remembered Yang. She would say, teasingly, "Ann, this is not locally made!" Ann also worried about Maya's exposure to the excesses of some of her more privileged, jaded classmates. Richard Holloway remembered Ann observing, in some distress, "I'm afraid that this comes with going to an international school, because most of the kids there have too much money."

Ann wanted Maya, like Barry, to be a serious student. "She hates me to brag, but I am forced to mention that she made high honors this term," she wrote to Alice Dewey in February 1984. She made her expectations clear. "Ann was pretty strict with her," Rens Heringa remembered. "I think she needed to be. Maya was too pretty for her own good. Ann talked to her, took her to task—to do her homework, to be a serious student, to not do the things that many of her classmates did." She worked hard to pass on her values. On one occasion, she arranged for Maya to accompany a friend of Ann's who was doing research in a slum area of Jakarta, then was upset when the colleague's methods fell short of Ann's exacting standards. Ann herself took Maya into the field and traveled extensively with her outside the country. In April 1984, Ann used her annual home-leave allowance instead for what she called a "grand tour" with Maya to Thailand, Bangladesh, India, and Nepal. "I had to spend five days en route at an employment conference in Dhaka, but the rest was vacation and great fun, despite beastly dry season weather and dust storms in North India," she wrote to Dewey late that month. "Saw lots of Moghul palaces and forts, rode elephants, rode camels, bought heaps of silk and clunky silver jewelry and useless gew-gaws very cheap—altogether a most satisfying trip."

Ten months earlier, Ann and Maya and a group of Ann's friends had traveled to Bandungan, a hill resort near Semarang in Indonesia, to watch a total solar eclipse over Central Java. The government had campaigned for weeks to convince Indonesians to stay inside with their windows covered in order to avoid being blinded by the sight of the eclipse. The countryside was eerily empty, many Javanese having taken to their beds in fear. The group drove past mosques packed with men, all turned toward the interior, praying. From Bandungan, they made their way to a place where nine small eighth- and ninth-century Hindu temples sit one thousand meters up in the foothills of Gunung Ungaran. Reached by a trail through a ravine and past hot sulfur springs, the place offered one of the most dazzling views in Java, to the volcanoes in the distance. "We sat on the edge of the escarpment and watched the shadow of the eclipse rushing across the plain beneath us and engulfing us," recalled Richard Holloway, who had gone along on that trip. The horizon turned red, according to a later description, "and in the half-light distant volcanoes usually obscured by the glare of the sun became visible. For the four minutes of total eclipse, the sun, almost directly overhead, looked like a black ball surrounded by a brilliant white light."

Ann remained in regular contact with Maya's father, Lolo. They spoke often by phone and met for lunch, according to Paschetta Sarmidi, the secretary who worked with Ann. "They tried to take care of Maya together," Sarmidi said. But Lolo's second marriage had changed Maya's relationship with his family. His new wife was young and "not secure enough to bring me into the family—and certainly not Mom," Maya said. "We stopped going to all family functions. There was a complete loss of contact." Maya continued to see her father on his own, but he never took her to see his family or play with her cousins. Ann complained to at least one friend that Lolo, like a stereotype of a divorced parent, was lavishing Maya with luxuries, toys, and sweets. "That particular thing really irritated her," her old friend Kay Ikranagara remembered. "She felt that he had grown up without material things, and now he put so much importance on material things. He was conveying this to Maya."

One evening, shortly before dinnertime at the house in Kebayoran Baru, a group of young activists was gathered around Ann's dining room table, working on a project, Yang Suwan recalled. There was a knock at the door. Yang went to open it and found a man she had never seen before with his arms full of jackfruits and packages. He was there to see Maya, he announced. When Maya ran in and hugged him, Yang was startled. She glanced back into the dining room. Ann's expression had grown uncharacteristically dark. "I had never seen Ann's face so changed, so not friendly," Yang said. When Lolo left after ten minutes, the young people chided Ann, saying she should have invited him to dinner. After all, he was Maya's father. "She looked so annoyed," Yang remembered. "She didn't want to talk."

Ann's visits with Barry were inevitably infrequent. When she went to work for Ford in early 1981, he was in his sophomore year at Occidental College in Los Angeles. That fall, he transferred to Columbia University in New York City. At least twice during her nearly four years at Ford, Ann arranged for him to fly to Indonesia to visit. "I would like to use my educational travel for dependent children this summer to have my son, Barry, come out to visit us," she wrote to Kessinger in May 1981. Barry spent July in Jakarta, then went on to Pakistan to visit a friend from Occidental on his way back to the United States. A week before leaving Jakarta, he sent a telegram to Nancy Peluso, Ann's friend, who had offered him her apartment on West 109th Street in Manhattan: "DO WANT THE APARTMENT WILL ARRIVE AT LATEST AUGUST 24 IN CASE COMPLICATIONS WIRE MOM." The following summer, Ann and Maya visited him in New York City. And in May 1983, after graduating from Columbia, he flew again to Indonesia for a month, stopping in Los Angeles and Singapore to visit friends. "After Barry arrives I would like to take a week or ten days off," Ann wrote to Kessinger in April. "If I can get reservations (this is right after the eclipse and right after JIS gets out), we would like to go to Bali."

Richard Holloway, Ann's friend from Semarang, recalled arriving to stay at Ann's house and being startled to encounter Barry for the first time.

"There was this young black lad pumping iron in her garden," Holloway remembered. "Very good-looking, great body, polite, personable."

"'This is my son, Barry,'" he recalled Ann saying.

"'Nice to meet you.'"

Women, however, told me that Ann spoke often to them about Barry.

"Never did we get together where we didn't hear, right up front, the first thing, what Barry was doing," said Georgia McCauley. If Ann had received a letter from him, Yang Suwan said, she would be in a good mood all day. Saraswati Sunindyo, who had described Ann as "a big person with little ego," said that little bit of ego pertained to her son. She would show his photograph "and say how handsome he is," Paschetta Sarmidi, Ann's secretary, said. "She spoke of Barack Obama a lot of times a day."

"You married an African?" Sarmidi recalled asking.

"Yes."

"Is he very black?"

"Yes!"

"How is Barry? Does he have his father's skin?"

"Yes."

"Is it like my skin?"

"No," Ann answered. "Your skin is like a Hispanic. But Barack Senior, he is very black. Barry is very handsome. And he is very smart, Paschetta. My boy is brilliant."

By February 1984, during his first year out of college, Barry was working for Business International Corporation, a small newsletter-publishing and research firm that helped countries with foreign operations understand overseas markets. Ann reported on his progress to Dewey.

> Barry is working in New York this year, saving his pennies so he can travel next year. My understanding from a rather mumbled telephone conversation is that he works for a consulting organization that writes reports on request about social, political and economic conditions in Third World countries. He calls it "working for the enemy" because some of the reports are written for commercial firms that want to invest in those countries. He seems to be learning a lot about the realities of international finance and politics, however, and I think that information will stand him in good stead in the future.

In November 1982, after receiving a call from an aunt in Kenya telling him that his father had been killed in a car accident in Nairobi, Barry telephoned Ann in Jakarta with the news. She had been divorced from Obama for eighteen years and had not seen him since that Christmas in Honolulu eleven years earlier. But when the younger Obama delivered the news of his father's death, he wrote in his memoir, he heard his mother cry out. Ann telephoned Bill Collier, perhaps the only person she knew in Indonesia who had also known the elder Obama. Collier, a classmate and friend of Obama's at the University of Hawai'i, told me that Ann's sadness was unmistakable. It was clear, he said, that she still felt strongly about Obama. Julia Suryakusuma found Ann in her office on the verge of tears. "I just heard the news that Barack's father died," Suryakusuma remembered Ann saying. Then she broke down and wept.

"I always got the impression that she was critical of her husbands," Suryakusuma said, "but I had the feeling she still loved them in a certain way."

By early 1984, Ann was at a crossroads. She had spent six years fulfilling her graduate course requirements and doing the field-work necessary to graduate with a Ph.D. But she had yet to take her comprehensive exams, complete a dissertation, and sit for its defense. The nine-month leave of absence she had requested from the University of Hawai'i in 1979 had stretched into five years. "The major reason for the delay in my return to Hawaii is the need to work to put my son through college," she wrote to Alan How-ard, the chairman of the anthropology department, in March 1984. "I am happy to say that he graduated from Columbia in June, so that I am now free to complete my own studies." Her contract with Ford was set to expire in late September. "I will either not extend it, or extend it but request an educational leave of absence for nine months (one school year)," Ann told Dewey in a letter that Febru-ary. "If I do not need to be physically present in Hawaii during the whole time, it might be better for me to stay in Indonesia through the end of the year. The deciding factor will probably be finances." If she could land a part-time fellowship with the East-West Center, she and Maya would return to Honolulu for the 1984–1985 aca-demic year. If not, she might accept an offer from Pete Vayda, who was returning to the United States, to take over the lease on his house in Bogor. "This would be an ideal, quiet place to work and finish up my thesis draft and the house is available very cheaply," she told Dewey. She hedged her bets. She asked Ford for a ten-month leave of absence, applied to schools in Hawaii for Maya, and approached the East-West Center about a fellowship. At the same time, she began looking into applying for a one- or two-year ap-pointment as a visiting professor in the rural-sociology department at Cornell University, specializing in women in development. It was a long shot: A Ph.D. was a prerequisite for the job. She let Alice Dewey know she had listed her as a reference on applications for fellowships from several foundations and funding agencies. "If anyone asks, you can tell them that I am good with dogs," Ann said.

Meanwhile, she went to some lengths to make it clear to Dewey, still the chairman of her dissertation committee, that she was swamped with work.

> Maybe you remember that I am handling projects for Ford in the areas of women, employment and industry (small and large). Jakarta was made the Regional Southeast Asia office last year, so that we are also working in Thailand and the Philippines. This year I have major projects for women on plantations in West Java and North Sumatra; for women in kretek factories in Central and East Java; for street food sellers and scavengers in the cities of Jakarta, Jogja and Bandung; for women in credit cooperatives in East Java; for women in electronics factories, mainly in the Jakarta-Bogor area; for women in cottage industry cooperatives in the district of Klaten; for hand-loom weavers in West Timor; for shop girls along Jl. Malioboro and market-sellers in Beringharjo (still tentative); for slum dwellers in Jakarta and Bandung; for street food sellers in Thailand. . . .

During Ann's tenure in the Jakarta office, Ford had backed the first women's studies center in the country, a fledgling research center at the University of Indonesia. Ann had successfully made the case for an early affirmative-action program for Indonesian women—a scholarship program aimed at getting more women trained in the social sciences and working in the upper levels of university faculties and the civil service. Smaller grants had gone to translating into Indonesian, for use in universities, a key text by Ester Boserup, a Dutch economist, on the role of women in development; paying for fellowships for female graduate students doing dissertations on women in home industries; supporting a conference to familiarize the leaders of grassroots organizations with women's issues; and sending top staff members from the women's cooperative in Malang to India to learn from the women's cooperatives and trade unions there. The Bogor project, which continued for some years afterward, had laid the groundwork for a network of Indonesian researchers experienced in the study of village women. It had generated what Ann called, in a 1983 report, "a great deal of useful and surprising data, which forces us to change some of our basic perceptions about Indonesian women." Java was atypical, as it turned out. Rural women on Java worked long hours, often in multiple occupations, though their hourly earnings were low. Elsewhere, women worked few hours, and needed money but had few opportunities to make it because they lived in places with few roads, means of transportation, or markets. Under such circumstances, development planning needed to be decentralized— tailored to each province, even each village. Pujiwati Sajogyo, who went on to serve for a time as a consultant to the Indonesian government's Ministry for the Role of Women, helped shift the government's focus away from simply the health and domestic roles of women to include women's need for income and paying work.

In the end, Ford did not renew Ann's contract. She had been in the Jakarta office for nearly four years, which, several Ford people told me, was becoming the standard tenure after which program officers moved to another country or moved on. Kessinger was interested in trying someone new in Ann's job. Ford was increasingly a grant-making organization, not an operating foundation. No longer were several hundred Ford staff members scattered all over, say, India, teaching in management schools, serving in government ministries, working in agricultural research. Program officers sat behind desks, conceived areas of activity, designed grants, wrote memos justifying what they wanted to do. To Kessinger, Ann seemed less comfortable in the office than she was in the field. Some people were good at one thing, some at the other, he believed. Few were good at both. "I felt that from an institutional point of view, she'd probably given us what she could give us," he said.

Kessinger also believed that Ann should complete the work needed to get her Ph.D. Not infrequently, graduate students drifted away from writing their dissertations because they needed money and found paying work, he knew from his years as a professor. When he had started graduate school, the average time from enrollment to a Ph.D. in history was nine years—in large part because students married and needed to support their families. Ann was lucky in that she had found work that not only paid well but that she loved. But that kind of good fortune made it even harder for people to go back and finish. Those who never did, Kessinger was convinced, went on to regret it. Your Ph.D. was your union card. "Get a union ticket," Ben Finney, the University of Hawai'i anthropologist, advised his students. "Become a qualified anthropologist. Then you can get your own grants or jobs." If Ann ever wanted to work in a university, she would need a doctorate. Furthermore, as Kessinger saw it, there was something selfish about carrying out fieldwork and doing nothing with it. In the village in India where he had done his fieldwork, the first questions were always: Why are you here? Why is anybody interested in that? The people you studied expected you to finish. Kessinger told Ann as much. Looking back later, he did not know how she took his tough love. She said, at least, that she saw his point.

"She felt she had to do it," her friend Rens Heringa recalled. "And she did it."

She would go back for a year, she seems to have imagined. She would return to Honolulu in time to register at the University of Hawai'i in late August and would stay through the spring semester. She would audit whatever basic theory courses were offered, take her comprehensives, and defend her dissertation before the end of the spring term. To support herself and Maya, she hoped to find a research or teaching position. "Something in the areas of peasant studies, women's studies or applied anthropology would probably be most suitable," she wrote to her department chairman, Alan Howard. She asked Dewey to look out for a two-bedroom apartment or house-sharing arrangement on a good bus route or within two miles of campus. Then she set about packing up her life in Jakarta—finishing up evaluations on several grants, clearing out her office, moving out of her house, finding homes for her animals. She would stop in Singapore with Maya for two days for insurance physicals. She would make one last visit to Yogyakarta and her villages, on which Dewey would join her. She suggested Dewey pass up the opportunity to make the return trip to Hawaii with her and Maya. "After nearly nine years in Indonesia, I will probably need to hire a camel caravan and an elephant or two to load all our baggage on the plane, and I'm sure you don't want to see all those airline agents weeping and rending their garments," she wrote. Her sea freight shipping allowance of three thousand three hundred pounds, she said, "should about cover my batik collection."

At a farewell party at Yang Suwan's house in Kebayoran Baru, Yang told Ann to choose anything in the house as a farewell gift. In the years they had known each other, Yang had made a point of bringing Ann handicrafts from remote reaches of Indonesia that Ann had not visited. She admired Ann's knowledge and never dared give her anything second-rate. Yang had built up her own collection, too. One of the most beautiful pieces in it was a sarong by Masina, a batik artist from Cirebon on the north coast of Java, where the mixing of Javanese, Sundanese, and Chinese influences had produced a rich culture and a distinctive style of batik. The pattern on the sarong was *mega mendung,* or rain clouds in reds and blues, dyed naturally in just the right weather. The sarong hung on a wall in her house. On the day of the party, the house was filled with Ann's friends—Julia Suryakusuma, Wahyono Martowikrido, Pete Vayda, and many others. When Yang made the offer of any object in the house, Ann spun on her heel without a moment's hesitation and pointed to the sarong, displayed on the wall directly behind her.

"This!" she said.

Perhaps Ann had had her eye on that batik for a long time, Yang thought later. After all, Ann knew everything you had in your house. Ann knew her friends, too, Yang thought, fondly.

"She knew I could never say no."

In early July, a shipping company packed up Ann's possessions: batiks, ikats, *wayang* puppets, wood carvings, wall decorations, paddy-field hats, ten boxes of books, three wooden chests, one trunk of clothes, a rattan sofa, five rattan tables, two rattan cabinets, a rattan bed, kitchen utensils, one mirror, and so on. The total weight fell well short of the 3,300-pound limit.

Then she and Maya headed for Honolulu, leaving Indonesia behind.

"It wouldn't have surprised me if she had stayed forever," Sidney Jones, Ann's colleague, told me one afternoon in Jakarta, where she was still working a quarter of a century later. "I got the sense that she was permanently enamored of the place. It's probably the same thing that I feel: This is where a particular formative period of your life took place, it's where your friends are, it's the place that you've made a second home. And it eventually becomes your first home."

Nine

"Surviving and Thriving
Against All Odds"

Honolulu was a comedown. Ann went back to the University of Hawai'i, where she had first enrolled as an undergraduate twenty-four years earlier. She rented a modest two-bedroom apartment in a cinder-block building not all that different from the one she had left behind in 1975. Maya was accepted by Punahou, the school to which Barry had returned from Jakarta alone in 1971. Madelyn Dunham helped make up the difference between Maya's partial scholarship and her tuition. Once again, Ann was living a couple of blocks from her parents. At the university, she sat in on Alice Dewey's course on economic anthropology, reviewing material she had surely already learned. Having never learned to drive, she commuted by public bus or on foot. Without savings, she was in no position to buy a house that might have served as a base for future operations, a repository for her collections, a gathering place for her children and for her friends—that is, a home on the scale of the roomy, bustling households to which she had grown accustomed. The anonymity of urban America, even Honolulu, felt alien after the warmth and intimacy of Ann's life in Jakarta. In her tiny household of two, she was without servants for the first time in years. Fearless abroad, Ann seemed vulnerable at home. She wanted Maya, who had roamed Jakarta at night, to be at home in Honolulu by dark. Eager to go out with friends, Maya would hesitate, worrying about her mother. "She seemed lonely, perhaps?" Maya told me. Ann would have loved a companion, Maya said, but she had too much dignity to go to great lengths to find one. Instead, she worked on her dissertation and planned her escape.

"I sympathize with your desire to get back out there in the real world, writing something with an impact on more people," Ann wrote to her friend Julia Suryakusuma, who was doing graduate work in the Netherlands. "I've made the decision to stay based in Hawaii so Maya can graduate there, but it has not been the most thrilling two and a half years of my life, let me tell you."

On January 1, 1985, Ann opened a spiral notebook she had begun keeping toward the end of her time in Jakarta. It was already filled with methodically numbered lists of all sorts under headings that included "Work + Employment," "Health and App," and "Personal and Travel." There were lists of vegetarian dishes, topics for future articles, calories burned per hour of various activities. One list of debts, titled "Owed to Folks," comprised fifteen entries, including "Punahou $1784" and "$2000 deposited in account by Mom." There was a handwritten schedule of daily activities ranging from what appears to be meditation at five a.m. and straightening up the apartment at seven-thirty a.m. to "read w/ Maya" at nine p.m. and "read and slp" a half-hour later. "People List" contained 216 numbered names, the first five of which were, in order, Maya, Adi, Bar, Mom, Dad. The notebook suggested a woman trying hard to be organized, struggling to be responsible about money, looking for a job, thinking about her children, worrying about her weight, reflecting on her past, sorting out her future. On New Year's Day, she turned in the notebook to page 103 and wrote a list of challenges to herself, without elaboration, under the heading, "Long Range Goals."

1. Finish Ph.D.
2. 60K
3. in shape
4. remarry
5. another culture
6. house + land
7. pay off debts (taxes)
8. memoirs of Indon.
9. spir. develop (ilmu batin)
10. raise Maya well
11. continuing constructive dialogue w/ Barry
12. relations w/ friends + family (corresp.)

If Ann had imagined she could wrap up her dissertation in nine months, as she had told the university, she was mistaken. Eighteen months after returning from Jakarta, she passed her comprehensive exams, having submitted a list of two dozen theoretical issues in anthropology and archaeology that she was prepared to discuss. But her dissertation, on five peasant industries, had ballooned to nearly seven hundred pages. It was already twice as long as many Ph.D. theses, and it was far from finished. "But I'll definitely be through and out of here when Maya graduates in June," Ann wrote to Suryakusuma. A year later, she was wishing she had chosen a smaller topic. Her enthusiasm was waning. "I don't find I care very much about it," she wrote again to her friend. "The creative part was over long ago, and it's just a matter of finishing the damn thing." It was not an uncommon problem. Financial support for graduate students in anthropology was hard to come by. Jobs in international development would turn up, promising good pay plus expenses. Graduate students, burdened with credit card bills, would accept, figuring they could finish the dissertation on weekends. Repeatedly, Ann appealed to the university for patience. "I regret the delay, but hope you can once again hold the fort for me till I get back," she would write several years later to Dewey. Ben Finney, a member of Ann's dissertation committee, recalled drafts "of this and that" coming in and Dewey "pulling out her hair. 'It's too long!'" Dewey received in the mail from Ann a postcard of a painting by Picasso, *Interior with a Girl Drawing*. In the painting, a brown-haired woman wearing a garland of flowers draws blithely on lemon-colored paper. Another woman slumps over a table nearby, burying her face. "Rather a nice Picasso I picked up at the Museum of Modern Art en route," Ann wrote in the letter attached. "I call it, 'Ann writing her dissertation on yellow tablets while Alice waits patiently (I hope) in the background.'"

Ann's parents had little understanding of Ann's professional passions. Stanley, nearing seventy, had never found work that he loved. Retired from selling insurance, he now devoted himself to crossword puzzles and television game shows such as *The Price Is Right*. He started projects—photo projects, albums, a family tree—that as often as not went unfinished. He had an immense repertoire of jokes, at which his granddaughter cringed while dutifully laughing. Madelyn, by contrast, loved her work and did it well. By the time Ann returned to Hawaii in 1984, Madelyn had risen to become one of the first female vice presidents at the Bank of Hawaii. Her marriage to Stanley did not seem, at least from the outside, to have improved with age. They bickered and sniped and took refuge in separate bedrooms. Madelyn drank. Occasionally, Ann told a friend, Madelyn would rent a hotel room in Honolulu where she would spend a solitary vacation. "Well, you know how Mother and Father are," Ann would say to her uncle Ralph Dunham after her father's death, some years later. "They fought all the time, but they really loved each other." Ralph Dunham agreed: As far as he could tell, they couldn't live with each other, or without. Ann sometimes wondered if Madelyn was reminded of Stanley when she gazed on her restless, voluble, dark-haired daughter. "I don't think either one of her parents read her dissertation or really even knew what it was about," Maya told me. "So there was a whole side of her adult life that remained a mystery to them. There was a difference in interests and in manner and in temperament that was difficult to bridge."

At the same time, Madelyn made it possible for Ann to live the life she chose.

"Our mom was the one who gave us the imagination and the language, the storytelling, all of those things," Maya told me. "And those things are really important. . . . But I think that if my grandmother had not been there, in the wings, making sure that we had savings accounts and school tuition taken care of and that sort of thing, maybe I would have felt more torn about the way that I was raised. As it was, I could feel free to love my childhood unabashedly and to love growing up in all those different places with all these different languages and flavors. And so on some level, I would say that our grandmother gave our mother the freedom to be the kind of mother that she was."

As Ann's list of long-term goals suggested, she was not especially interested in staying put. In May 1986, less than two years after returning from Jakarta, she moved to Pakistan on a six-month contract to work as a development consultant on a rural-credit program in the Punjab. The following summer, she was in Illinois, presenting a scholarly paper at an academic meeting and visiting Barry in Chicago. Next, she was in New York visiting friends with Maya, who was looking at colleges. From there, Ann flew to London for three days en route to Pakistan. ("Any chance you could fly over and spend some time with me in London?" she had asked Suryakusuma in a letter. ". . . It would be great if we could do London together. . . . If you are still planning to go to India in September, could we meet in Delhi? I'd rather see you in Delhi than Bombay just because I like the city better, but Bombay might also be possible. . . . You could also come over to Pakistan. . . .") Back in Pakistan, she spent three months completing the consulting contract she had begun a year earlier, then returned to Honolulu, stopping off in Jakarta. The dissertation would be worth the wait, Dewey believed. "Ann would run out of money and go take a job," she recalled. "Not washing dishes. She was building up more data. So she would come and go constantly. We knew she was the kind of student who was going to end up knowing three times more than we did—in our specialties. So we just let her go."

Ann took Maya with her when she could. In 1986, they traveled together to India en route to Pakistan, stopping in Delhi, Agra, and Jaipur. In Pakistan, Maya stayed with Ann for three months, studied Mughal dancing, and accompanied her into the field. They took a six-day driving trip from Islamabad to the border of China along the Karakoram Highway, the highest paved international road in the world, following the Indus River gorge, passing through the tribal areas of the Pathans, Gilgitis, and Hunzas to the place where the Hindu Kush, the Himalayas, and the Karakoram Range converge. Pakistan was fraught with difficulties, said Michael Dove, an American anthropologist and friend of Ann's from Java, who worked in Pakistan from 1985 to 1989 and saw her there during that period. Bombs fell in marketplaces and around the house in Islamabad where Dove and his wife were living. Dove said he and his wife were kidnapped by armed Pathans in the upper Indus River gorge. "It was the opposite of Indonesia," he recalled. "It was a difficult culture, much more violent. Everyone had a gun." In border areas, people kidnapped foreigners to raise cash. It was difficult to be a Western woman in Pakistan without a husband. Simply walking alone in public was problematic.

Ann wrote to Suryakusuma:

Pakistan is an interesting experience but I do not love it the way I love Indonesia. For one thing, the level of sexism is almost beyond belief. Even the most innocent acts, like getting on an elevator with a man, riding with a male driver, or talking with a male colleague in your office are subject to suspicion. Since almost all marriages are arranged, and all Pakistani men are sexist, many educated Pakistani women choose to remain single (in Pakistan that means virgins for life!) The people are also quite puritanical in general, although the intellectuals somewhat less so. I did make some good friends when I was there, however. One of them was my field assistant, a young woman who was active in a feminist organization in Lahore.

Ann had been hired to work on the design and initiation of the pilot phase of the first credit project for women and artisan-caste members carried out by the Agricultural Development Bank of Pakistan, the country's largest development institution. In the Punjab, where she was working, Ann observed that village people fell into three classes. Feudal, landowning families lived lavishly in hilltop villas and sent their children abroad to the best universities.

Small landholders lived in walled mud compounds and farmed tiny plots. Artisan-caste members, including blacksmiths and weavers and other craftspeople, made products for the landowning families, to whom they were indentured, in return for raw materials and a small share of grain. Some artisan-caste members, however, had cut their ties with the landlords. They were buying raw materials and selling their products in the markets. Ann interviewed carpet weavers, pottery makers, blacksmiths, leather workers, tailors, and others during her first six-month stay. She talked with branch managers of banks. She surveyed buyers, suppliers, and intermediaries in Lahore. When she returned a year later, she conducted training courses for sixty-five extension workers, including the first women, who would work with the artisans. She also made recommendations for increasing lending to poor rural women. Over a two-year period, she told Dewey in a letter, the program made loans to nearly fifteen hundred artisan families and landless or near-landless agricultural families. "So there are some satisfactions in a job pretty well done under difficult field circumstances," she said.

Details of the pleasures of Pakistan she saved for Suryakusuma, her flamboyant friend from Jakarta. In one letter, dated August 28, 1987, she wrote:

> I am now ensconced in the Canadian Resthouse on the canal bank in beautiful Lahore. . . . They don't have any guests at the moment, so I'll be able to stay here at least till October 10 and maybe longer. Meanwhile, I have the whole upper floor to myself, with an enormous verandah that looks out over flowering tree tops, a cricket lawn and the canal beyond. It's a perfect place to drag a blanket out to about 6:00 AM and sit and meditate with nothing between me and God but the sky. (My,

I am waxing romantic today.) It's also a good place for a cup of coffee in the evening with friends once the weather cools down a bit. Summers in Delhi and Lahore are ferocious, and everyone with money leaves and goes to London or at least to a hill station, but the weather should be perfect by the end of September when you come. . . . Three or four days a week I drive by jeep from Lahore to my project area about one and a half hours from here. I spend all day in our regional office or in the project villages, getting back to Lahore, hot and dusty, about 7:00. Usually, I stop at the Hilton on my way home and throw myself in their rooftop pool to wash the dust away. After 2 or 3 fresh lime sodas I begin to feel human again. Two of my Pakistani women friends are also brave enough to swim there in the evenings (braving the glares of all the male guests who feel they should be in purdah), so I often don't get home till 9:00. In the village, on the other hand, I have made good friends with a family of blacksmiths (6 big boys, and 4 girls, all very "healthy" and strong, like you would expect peasant blacksmiths to be), and I usually stop for a meal or tea (with lots of sugar and buffalo milk) with them a couple of times a week. So my life is full of contrasts as usual.

Ann's approach to matters of the spirit was eclectic. She would meditate in Buddhist monasteries and make small offerings in the Hindu communities that she visited. When she had a kris made for herself in Java, Maya said, she went through the ritual of sleeping with it under her pillow—a process through which a kris is thought to communicate with its owner through dreams—and having her dreams interpreted. "It was important to just sort of acknowledge that everyone had something beautiful to contribute spiritually," Maya told me. "She always counseled us to be very open-minded, to have deep respect for everyone's religions, to recognize that every religion had something good to offer." According to others, she was skeptical of organized religion and ceremonial excess. Don Johnston, a Southern Baptist from Little Rock, Arkansas, and a colleague of Ann's in the early 1990s, said she seemed at that time to be leaning toward deism or Unitarianism—the religion of the church in Bellevue, Washington, she attended as an adolescent. God, she thought, could be found at the intersection of many belief systems. "As anthropologists, we tend to talk about religion more as ritual practice and part of human society," said Nina Nayar, who became a close friend of Ann's several years later. "Rarely do we converse about belief in God. I would not say Ann was a Christian or a Hindu or a Buddhist. I would not put a label on her. But she had a general interest. And I think she probably had more spiritual stuff in her than most people who profess to be religious and faithful. She never once used words in my presence about being atheist or agnostic. She was not a woman of labels. The only label she would not shun was the label of anthropologist."

In *The Audacity of Hope,* Obama describes his mother, despite her professed secularism, as "in many ways the most spiritually awakened person that I've ever known." Without religious texts or outside authorities, he says, she worked to instill in him the values that many Americans learn in Sunday school. She possessed, too, "an abiding sense of wonder, a reverence for life and its precious, transitory nature that could properly be described as devotional." She would occasionally wake him in the middle of the night, as a child, he writes, to look at the moon or have him close his eyes as they "walked together at twilight to listen to the rustle of leaves. . . . She saw mysteries everywhere and took joy in the sheer strangeness of life."

In the late summer of 1986, Ann arranged for Maya to fly to

Jakarta, on her way back to Hawaii from Pakistan, to visit her father. Lolo Soetoro had been hospitalized in Jakarta with the liver disease that had been diagnosed a decade earlier when Maya was a small child. Though Ann had been led to believe by his doctors, during his hospitalization in Los Angeles, that the disease would cut short his life, Lolo had lived another seven years. Now he was gravely ill. Maya, having just turned sixteen, flew by herself to Jakarta, where relatives met her at the airport and took her to the home of her uncle Trisulo. Lolo, released from the hospital, spent a week with her in Trisulo's house. He was more talkative than Maya had remembered. He asked about her school, her favorite subjects, and her friends. He brought photographs of himself that he wanted her to keep. There were moments of affection and tenderness. But their time together felt awkward to Maya. "I felt a teenage resentment that he hadn't been present in a more meaningful way and that he had left the rearing of me to Mom," she remembered later. "I was sort of feeling like I wanted him to be sorry about that." Later, she would come to regret not having stayed longer. But she had been away from Hawaii for three months, and she was impatient to go home. It never occurred to her that her father might be dying—and that he might know it. Afterward, she wrote him a long letter from Hawaii and tried to send it in time to reach him before his birthday on January 2. She wanted them to have a meaningful relationship, she told him in the letter; she wanted to know him better. But the letter was waylaid in the Christmas rush, she told me, and did not arrive as planned. In the meantime, a family member telephoned from Indonesia to say that Lolo had fallen into a coma. In early 1987, he died.

The house in Menteng Dalam, to which Maya and Ann had returned from Hawaii in 1975, went to Maya (and was sold some years later, with the proceeds going to help pay for her graduate-school education). To protect Maya's rights, Ann stopped in Jakarta on her way home from Pakistan the following November. The house was being rented by Dick Patten, whom she had gotten to know while she was working on the provincial planning project in Central Java in 1979 and 1980. Patten, who had extensive experience in credit systems in Indonesia, had gone on to work as a consultant to one of the largest banks in Indonesia on a program not unrelated to the work he and Ann had done earlier. The aim of the new program, run by a state-owned bank called Bank Rakyat Indonesia, or the People's Bank of Indonesia, was to make small loans on a broad scale to low-income rural households throughout the country. At a time when the term *microfinance* was not the household word that it has since become, the Bank Rakyat Indonesia project, launched in early 1984, had gotten off to a remarkable start. By late 1985, the bank had made nearly one million small loans, ranging in value from a few dollars to a few hundred dollars. It would soon be initiating new loans at a rate of 120,000 a month. The program held the potential to benefit small enterprises of the sort Ann had studied as an anthropologist, worked with as a development consultant, and tried to help in her years at Ford. So in the summer of 1988, after Maya graduated from Punahou with plans to enroll at Barnard College in the fall, Ann moved back to Jakarta to work with Patten on what was quickly becoming the most successful commercial microfinance program of its kind in the world.

Once again, her dissertation would have to wait.

"Anyway, they are paying me well and I need to fill up my bank account again. (How's that for revolutionary fervor?)," she wrote to Suryakusuma in August 1988.

The credit program had arisen out of the ruins of an earlier effort at rural lending. During the 1970s, Bank Rakyat Indonesia had set up a network of 3,600 small banking units for the purpose of channeling government-subsidized credit to rice farmers under the country's push for rice self-sufficiency. Lending under that program had peaked in the mid-1970s, after which operational losses had ballooned. So it had been phased out, leaving the bank with an extensive network of fully staffed loan offices with little to do. With the encouragement of the Ministry of Finance and advice from the Harvard Institute for International Development, with which Dick Patten was affiliated, the bank had tried something new.

From the beginning, anthropologists had shaped the new credit program. Marguerite Robinson, an American anthropologist who had done fieldwork in India and spent twenty years teaching, had joined the Harvard institute and been sent to Indonesia to work with the Ministry of Finance. James Fox, the anthropologist from Australia whom Ann had known in Jakarta in the early 1980s, had worked with Robinson and Patten advising the bank. From anthropological fieldwork, including Ann's, they knew that rice farming was just one of many economic activities in Indonesian villages that needed credit in order to grow. They also knew, from village studies, that government-subsidized credit, under the old system, had reached only a small fraction of villagers. It needed to be more widely accessible. So, working with the finance minister, the consultants began exploring a program of unsubsidized commercial microfinance. The bank would lend money for any reasonable economic activity, not just rice farming. The program would soon operate without an ongoing subsidy; instead, it would charge interest at the market rate. The market rate was nearly twice the old rate. But most villagers, if they borrowed money, did so through loan groups or moneylenders, who charged in excess of one hundred percent interest on an annual basis. Even with an interest rate of thirty-two percent, it was argued, the new program would be an improvement.

The project took off. Within two years, with the help of a microsavings program, the new general credit program was self-sustaining. By 1989, the bank had 2.7 million rural savings accounts; it had made as many as 6.4 million loans to 1.6 million borrowers. The microfinance program would become the biggest and most lucrative part of the bank's operations. In 1999, Fox called the program "probably the single largest and most successful credit program of its kind in the developing world."

Ann joined the team in 1988 and worked on and off over the next four years as a research coordinator and consultant under three separate contracts funded by the World Bank and the U.S. Agency for International Development. Ann had what Patten lacked—an intimate knowledge of Indonesian villages. Working with teams of staff researchers from the bank, she designed and carried out what might be described as customer surveys and market research, the results of which were used to fine-tune and measure the success of the microfinance program. She spent weeks at a time traveling with her teams on field trips through Java, North Sumatra, South Sulawesi, and Bali, meeting with bank branch managers and interviewing customers for hours on end. The teams examined how customers were using the money they had borrowed. They gauged its impact on households and rates of employment. They studied repayment rates by gender, estimated the scope of unmet demand, and tracked the rates at which customers were either keeping up with or falling behind on their payments. The consultants used the studies—original research at a time when there was little like it—to refine the microfinance program and to convince the bank not simply to continue the experiment but to expand it, increasing the size of the loans. For every million rupiahs that the bank loaned, Ann told Kamardy Arief, the bank's chief executive officer, her research showed that one additional job was created.

"Ann provided a justification from the field for the approach of commercial microfinance," said Don Johnston, who joined the Harvard group in early 1990 and worked closely with her and Patten. "She was showing that this was something that was benefiting the customers—not something the banks were doing out of desperation. That left Dick and me free to worry about the operational side. We had our ammunition to deal with outsiders, and we had the information that gave us confidence that the basic product approach and expansion direction we were taking was right. So then we could worry about fighting the internal battles . . . to keep the institution on track."

The microfinance program was an extraordinary success. In June 1990, it was making 115,000 loans a month with a value of $50 million and an average loan size of $437. It was soon a major source of the bank's growth. During the East Asian monetary crisis of the late 1990s, when the repayment rate on the microloans remained higher than that of the small, medium, and corporate customers of the bank, the program helped the bank weather the crisis. As of 2009, the bank operated more than four thousand microbanking outlets in Indonesia. It had 4.9 million microloan customers and 19.5 million microsavings customers.

"If you work in the development racket, you're lucky at the end of ten years or twenty or thirty to be able to look back and say, 'I think I did more good than harm,'" Richard Hook, who was hired as an adviser on the Bank Rakyat Indonesia project the same year as Ann, told me. "The non-successes are all too numerous. Often you inflict collateral damage, albeit unwittingly and unwillingly. This project met Indonesian needs. It was based in a massive Indonesian institution—a state-owned commercial bank. It was run by Indonesians. We were external advisers. The concept was making small loans to low-income rural people. The conventional wisdom was you won't get repaid and these people don't know how to handle a loan, they were too innocent of sophisticated procedures and financial know-how to know how to handle credit. We didn't believe that. A number of Indonesians didn't, either. We worked together and made this project work. That was just such a delight."

Patten was brilliant, creative, and not necessarily easy to get along with. Akhtar Hameed Khan, the microcredit pioneer whom he had known in East Pakistan in the 1960s, once described him as "the finest development worker I have ever met." The son of a successful midwestern banker, he had grown up on a daily regimen of meat and potatoes so rigid, his daughter told me, that it drove him to swear off potatoes for life. He had spent most of his adult life in East Pakistan, Ghana, and Indonesia—a long way from Norman, Oklahoma. A divorced father of three, he inhabited the persona of an inveterate bachelor. He liked people who did not need to talk all the time, and he hated the sort of questions that began with "Don't you think . . ." He was hardworking and occasionally napped on the office floor. For a time, he lived in a house with a two-story cage that served as home for a black Sumatran gibbon— until the gibbon terrorized various neighbors and found its way into the electrical wires above the street, necessitating a neighborhood-wide power shutoff. Patten was opinionated and blunt but not without compassion. After three months as office manager, Flora Sugondo went to him in tears, saying she wanted to quit because, working for Patten, she had become convinced she could do nothing right. Patten apologized, persuaded her to stay, and vowed never to treat her that way again. When Johnston, a graduate student in economics at Harvard, arrived in Jakarta for a temporary stint as a research assistant in Patten's office, Patten gave him a paper to edit, and Johnston "marked the hell out of it in red ink," as he put it. Patten was thrilled. Johnston was suddenly the permanent project assistant. "When I got there, everybody was so happy," Johnston told me. "I was one of the few people who could work productively with Dick."

Ann was another. Patten valued Ann's ability to recognize what kind of research would be useful in building the microfinance program. They shared a certain midwestern straightforwardness and a fascination with Indonesian culture and Indonesian people. Patten operated the house in Menteng Dalam as a kind of guesthouse for expatriate consultants. During periods when Ann was between contracts or not renting a house of her own, she stayed there. She treated Patten like a favorite uncle, said Johnston, who lived in the house. Sometimes she called him her surrogate father. There might be as many as ten or twelve people at the table for dinner—pot roast or meat loaf, and vanilla ice cream for dessert. Patten kept the lights dim and the radio tuned to the BBC. He liked Bach—"up and down music," as Ann dismissively called it. Patten found her good company and entertaining. Once, he told me, Maya telephoned Ann from Yogyakarta, where she was taking time off from college and working for a travel company, leading cultural tours in Java and Bali. An older, unmarried American tourist, who happened to be a teacher, had arranged to have a blind masseur come to her hotel. The woman had become hysterical, accused the masseur of molesting her, and had him arrested. Maya wanted her mother's advice. "First, give the teacher a good, hard slap," Patten remembered Ann saying. "Then go to the police station and make sure nothing happened to the masseur."

Recalling the story, Patten laughed.

"It's so entertaining and so indicative of the way she thought: *Just worry about the masseur.*"

Ann's methodology in the field was meticulous. She designed novella-length questionnaires to be used as a guide for interviewing potential customers about matters ranging from working-capital turnover periods to the number of relatives employed without pay. For inexperienced research assistants, she appended handy tips. "Has the Respondent ever been inside a bank before?" one question asked. If not, why not? If the respondent answered that he or she was afraid of banks, the interviewer was to find out why. "This is an important question, so take whatever time is necessary to discuss it with the Respondent," Ann wrote. Another question required that the interviewer fill out a chart with ten vertical columns under headings such as "type of account," "maximum amount of savings," and "use of withdrawals." The interviewer was to list every savings account the respondent had had in the previous seven years, as well as other deposits through savings-and-loan societies, credit unions, and other organizations. "If the Respondent has any savings in kind, for example in a rice bank, list this also, but give a rupiah value underneath," Ann's instructions said.

She had an unusual ability to adapt. With bankers, she came across as professional, methodical, and not the least bit eccentric. With older Indonesians, her accent and diction took on a precision that Don Johnston thought sounded faintly Dutch. Arriving in a village for the first time, she transformed herself into the beloved visiting dignitary—her bearing regal, her silver jewelry flashing, her retinue in tow. "She was clearly the queen bee of the entourage," recalled Johnston. "Then she gets there and they realize, 'Oh, this is not just a foreigner but this is a foreigner who can speak Bahasa Indonesia, and who knows a lot about what we're doing and who wants to talk to us about this stuff. And she has some connection to this big bank, BRI, but she's not a banker, so I don't need to be scared of her.'" She was even deft in her dispensing with inevitable Indonesian comments about her physical dimensions. When a boatman professed trepidation about whether the personage boarding his boat was going to sink it, Ann switched, humorously, to the role of the grand lady: How dare you! There was

Interviewing bank customers, with colleagues, about 1989

showmanship involved, but she was never inauthentic. "Ann was a genuinely complex person who had a really varied background," Johnston said. "So she could legitimately tap those different experiences to build empathy with different people." It made them want to line up and tell her their life stories.

On a field visit to village banks in the district of Sleman in 1988, Ann proposed a short detour to the village of Jitar, the home of a respected kris smith whom she knew. According to Ann's account, she was traveling with three carloads of bank colleagues and local government officials. At the smith's house, he invited the group inside for tea. Members of the group, laughing loudly and making raucous jokes minutes before, fell silent, sat formally, and then addressed the smith, Pak Djeno, with deep respect and deference. When Ann said she wanted to buy a small kris, the smith brought out four blades. "A deadly hush came over the room, and even whispering ceased," Ann wrote later. For days afterward, her colleagues discussed the encounter. "The very fact that I had known a keris smith and had purchased a keris also caused a change in their behavior toward me. They began to show me some of the deference they had shown to Pak Djeno, speaking with greater respect and formality. Somehow, a little of his magical power had managed to rub off on me."

Ann combined the discipline of a workaholic with a personal warmth that her Indonesian colleagues and subordinates described to me as maternal. She was not a practitioner of "rubber time": If she had an appointment, she was never late. In the field, she might start work at nine a.m. and not wrap up until thirteen hours later. She would stay with an interview long after colleagues were ready to move on. She traveled with a Thermos and took her coffee black, no sugar. "Coffee is my blood," she said; if she ever got sick, she said, she wanted intravenous coffee. She rarely seemed to get enough sleep. She tested survey questions on herself first, to feel what a respondent might feel. She would never risk insulting her host by declining food. When the manager of a bank branch in South Sulawesi threw her a surprise birthday party, including karaoke, she launched gamely into "You Are My Sunshine." In the town of Garut, she turned her attention to a girl of no more than seventeen who was serving dinner to members of the team at their hotel. Ann asked her about her family, her marriage, her education.

How much was she paid? Was it enough? Then, when dinner was over, she slipped the girl money.

On occasion, a misunderstanding across some cultural divide left Ann rattled. On a visit to a village in Sulawesi in 1988, an irate local official pursued Ann and her group, shouting furiously in a local language that none of them understood. He appeared to believe the group had failed to obtain his permission to enter the area. The confrontation subsided after some local residents intervened in the group's defense. But late that night, Ann remained upset and was unable to sleep. She asked a bank colleague, Tomy Sugianto, to accompany her on a walk around the outside of the hotel where they were staying. The hour was about one a.m., Sugianto told me. Ann, visibly exhausted, was on the verge of tears. She seemed haunted by the memory of the local official's fury and whatever misunderstanding had provoked it. She felt wrongly accused. "She only wanted to know why the man was so angry," Sugianto remembered, "and what we did wrong."

To her younger colleagues, she was Bu Ann—Bu being an affectionate abbreviation of the honorific *Ibu,* a term of respect for mothers, older women, and women of higher status. She treated them, they felt, as family. If she went out to lunch in Jakarta, she would order an extra meal for her driver, Sabaruddin, and his family. She helped pay for his five-year-old daughter's surgery and for repairs to the roof and the doors on his house. In the town of Tasik Malaya, she pointed out to her team that the village chief, a successful businessman, had started out as a peddler—evidence that anything was possible. To her young research assistants, she emphasized accuracy, rigor, patience, fairness, and not judging by appearances. "Don't conclude before you understand," Retno Wijayanti recalled Ann saying. "After you understand, don't judge."

She even tried her hand at matchmaking. In the fall of 1989, the

bank hired a willowy twenty-four-year-old woman named Widayanti from Malang in East Java, who was soon assigned to help Ann
and Don Johnston with a survey of potential microfinance customers. Ann quickly discovered that Widayanti was a Pentecostal
Christian. Johnston, the son of a church musician in Little Rock,
was a Southern Baptist. Widayanti began to notice that whenever

*With Tomy Sugianto (left) and Slamet Riyadi (right),
from Bank Rakyat Indonesia, in Tana Toraja,
South Sulawesi, 1989*

she asked Ann a question about the survey, Ann would say, "Oh,
just ask Don." Did Widayanti know that Don had once been a
Sunday school teacher? Ann asked her. To Johnston, Ann talked
up Widayanti's intelligence, her command of English, her honesty
and strong principles. To Flora Sugondo, the office manager, Ann
confided that she wanted to match up Johnston and Widayanti.

In October 1993, Ann was a guest in Malang at their wedding.

That *Ibu* quality was useful, Julia Suryakusuma told me. "Ann was a very intellectual person, but she didn't come across as being that," she said. "That whole *Ibu* quality took away the threat of being a pioneer, a professional, efficient. It took away the edge." Occasionally, however, Ann found the role of surrogate mother tiring. "I get so tired of having to mother people myself—for example, all my research assistants at BRI—that I actually enjoy being on the receiving end of a little mothering once in a while," she confessed to Suryakusuma in a letter.

Not long after Ann returned to Indonesia in 1988, Suryakusuma's husband, Ami Priyono, asked a young Indonesian journalist, whom he knew, to see if he might help out a friend of Priyono's. A few days later, a secretary in the Bank Rakyat Indonesia office called the journalist, I. Made Suarjana, a reporter in Yogyakarta for *Tempo,* an independent newsweekly, and set up an appointment for him to meet Ann at the Airlangga Guest House in Yogyakarta, where she would be staying on a trip for the bank. Arriving at the hotel, Suarjana was startled to find that the person he was meeting was Caucasian and a woman. From the name, Sutoro, he had expected an Indonesian man. They got along immediately. Soon, he was driving Ann to Kajar, to update her dissertation research in her spare time. Occasionally, she would ask him to visit other villages for her in her absence. They dined together on her visits to Yogyakarta, eating tempeh and *sayur lodeh,* an eggplant stew that she loved. They went to batik exhibitions and visited the ninth-century Hindu temples at Prambanan, northeast of Yogyakarta. For Ann's birthday, she asked Suarjana to go with her to Candi Sukuh, a fifteenth-century temple on the steep, pine-blanketed slopes of Gunung Lawu, three thousand feet above sea level on the border of Central and East Java. The temple, which Ann had known of for years but had never visited, was known for, among other things, its humorous, *wayang*-style carvings, stone penises, and other indications that it may have been the site of a fertility cult. The temple reliefs also included a scene of a smithy with the same double-piston bellows still used in Kajar. To drive to the temple, Ann arranged to rent a car. When it arrived, she and Suarjana were amused to discover that it was a white Mercedes—the car of choice for government officials and newlyweds.

Suarjana was twenty-eight the year he met Ann—one year older than Barry. Ann was turning forty-six. For an Indonesian man, he was tall, nearly six feet, with a taut, high-cheekboned face that reminded Ann of Mike Tyson, the heavyweight boxing champion. He was the fifth of seven children of a Balinese poet, journalist, and politician, Made Sanggra, who had been a nationalist fighter against the Dutch. (The name is pronounced *mah*-day.) Suarjana had grown up in Sukowati, a crafts center in Bali, where his mother had a business buying and selling Balinese clothing. The family was Hindu. As a child, Suarjana had learned Balinese dancing, music, and woodcarving. He had studied Indonesian language and literature at university, married in his early twenties, and become a father three years before he met Ann. His relationship with Ann, he told me, was "a romantic-intellectual relationship," the exact nature of which, he said, would remain between them. The connection was deep, he said, and rooted in shared interests. There was no limit to what they could talk about, no difference that could not be bridged. She volunteered little about her past and, on a visit to Honolulu, even stopped her father from showing Suarjana photographs of her when she was young. She never directly told Suarjana her age. When the question arose by chance in a conversation, she refused to answer—then handed him her passport. Intellectually, the relationship changed him. Perhaps Ann was changed less by him than he was by her, he said. But he was sure he'd left a mark.

They talked about Indonesian art and culture, gender roles in Bali, the reasons for declining production in Kajar. Were government programs flawed in concept or in implementation? Was there a relationship between the salaries of government ministers and corruption? Ann was the scholar in their conversations; Suarjana was the cynic. She spoke from the head; he spoke from the gut. "Oh, Made, *please*," she would complain, in exasperation. She was also the optimist, her mind always bending toward practical solutions. She would assert nothing, it seemed to him, without evidence to support it. She had the spirit of a teacher, a *jiwa guru*. Whatever Ann knew that Suarjana did not know, she would offer to teach him. She gave him a four-volume set of books on English grammar and usage. "How far did you study?" she would invariably ask. Then she would administer a pop quiz on the spot. She corrected his essays in red ink in his spiral notebook. She insisted each of them speak the other's language. If he spoke to her in Bahasa Indonesia, she might refuse to answer at all. She recommended him for a workshop for journalists at the East-West Center and paid his tuition at an English language institute at the University of Hawai'i. From her example, Suarjana said, he learned how to be open-minded and to recognize shades of gray. He learned to look at batik differently, too: In his mind, its importance was no longer strictly cultural and economic. Woven unmistakably into textiles were the lives of the people who made them.

"You're an eccentric," Ann told him. He was not sure what the word meant. But it was a compliment, he was sure of that.

If Ann had a weakness, he thought, it was that she too easily trusted strangers. Her generosity and her compassion got the better of financial good sense. On one occasion, a man came to her, professing to represent a nongovernmental organization and asking for money, Suarjana told me. She gave him two million rupiahs, or roughly twelve hundred dollars, of her own money—and never heard from him again. She was not especially concerned about money. Once, Suarjana suggested that the price of a batik she was considering buying at an exhibition was too high. "It's only paper," she said blithely, before allowing him to talk her out of the purchase on the grounds that most of her money would go to the dealer, not the craftsman. She was not ambitious or acquisitive, at least in the usual sense. She would have liked to have learned to drive so she could have driven Suarjana around Hawaii without having to rely on her father. She would have liked to have found a way to afford a house in Bali where friends and her children could stay. As the latest deadline for her dissertation closed in, Suarjana threatened to end their friendship if she did not finish. When she finally did finish it in 1992, and he congratulated her for it, she told him, "I did it because I wanted us to remain friends."

To those who knew her well, Ann seemed happy with Suarjana. Rens Heringa met her and Suarjana for dinner in Yogyakarta. "It had just started," Heringa remembered. "She was all rosy and happy, and it was quite funny and nice." Ann ordered spaghetti, which Suarjana loathed, and joked that it was his favorite food. She called over a street singer to sing "Bésame Mucho."

Bésame, bésame mucho,
As if tonight were the last time.

In a letter to Suryakusuma, who was skeptical of Suarjana's motives, Ann downplayed her feelings. "I never said I was a woman in love . . ." she protested. "I like him a lot. He has a place in my heart." Suryakusuma believed Ann could be too open, too trusting. In a letter that Suryakusuma read aloud to me, but did not give me, she told Ann: You have a big capacity to love, but you often love uncritically. ("I know I benefit," Suryakusuma wrote.) She told Ann that one of the nicest things about being her friend was that Ann was not judgmental: "You take people as they are, with all their faults." But, Suryakusuma said, often one's strong point is also

In the early 1990s

a source of vulnerability. Your capacity to love, she told Ann, leaves you open to being used by others.

The attention of a much younger man was flattering, Heringa told me, but it cannot have been simple. Indonesians made jokes about older women who went around with younger men. Hotels expected couples to be married. "Ann didn't give a damn," Heringa told me. "She was much less concerned about what people thought

than I was. She just could not have cared less." In the spring of
1990, Ann and Suarjana spent several months together at the
University of Hawai'i, where Suarjana took part in the English-
language institute in which Ann had helped him enroll. They lived
in a dorm at the East-West Center, where, according to Suarjana,
they had separate rooms. He cooked Indonesian *soto*—a souplike
dish with bean sprouts, scallions, cellophane noodles, lemon slices,
hot chili, egg slices, and so on—for Ann's parents. They took a
short vacation to the Big Island. Ann reported to Suryakusuma that
she had enjoyed their domestic arrangement. They had had only
one fight—over his tendency to turn off her fan without asking
first. They enjoyed collaborating on the chores and the shopping—
the novelty of which, Ann confessed, was wearing off for her.
"After all, God surely intended me to be a *Nyonya Besar*," she wrote
to Suryakusuma with mocking self-knowledge, using a term for
"mistress of the house."

Ann's work at Bank Rakyat Indonesia had delayed, once again,
the completion of her dissertation. In early November 1989, she
asked Dewey to run interference for her with the university. "Have
just returned from a long, hard trip to North Sumatra with my
field team," she explained. There had been delays getting into the
field, she said, "and it has been necessary for me to do more hand-
holding than anticipated. My field workers are sharp, but most are
economics or business majors who have never worked with village
people before." In mid-December, she returned to Hawaii for
Christmas. Maya, having finished her job as a tour guide, was back
in Honolulu, staying with a University of Hawai'i professor, with
a temporary job lined up waiting tables in a Japanese restaurant.
"Barry is also coming at Christmas with a new girlfriend in tow,"
Ann wrote to Dewey. "He is still enjoying law school and writing
pro-choice opinions on the abortion issue for the Law Review."

Ann's dissertation committee, headed by Dewey, and the chairman of the anthropology department agreed to submit an extension request to the graduate division. "So now I must make some hard decisions about finishing my degree vs taking a new job," she wrote to Suryakusuma in January. Bank Rakyat Indonesia had agreed in principle to giving her a two-year contract, but she did not know whether the bank would wait several months while she finished. "My family and friends all say to finish my degree, but there are also practical considerations if I take several months off from work," she wrote. Among them were the usual financial pressures. To Dewey, Ann wrote, "Am sending a money order for the $1000 I borrowed from you some time back. You can take out interest in batiks or other goodies when I get back."

In early 1991, Dewey persuaded Ann to narrow the focus of the dissertation to metalworking, with particular attention to blacksmithing, the forging of iron and steel to make tools. That meant dropping four other peasant industries—basketry and matting, clay products, textiles, and leather—about which Ann had gathered data over the course of a decade and a half. Soon, she was firing off chapters to Honolulu. "Since narrowing the topic to blacksmithing and metal industries, everything is going much better," she wrote to Dewey. Ann's office rented a house for her in her old neighborhood, Kebayoran Baru. "I thought if I went to Jogja I would end up eating lesian with Made on *Jalan Malioboro* every night and never get anything done," she told Dewey. (*Lesian* appears to be a misspelling of *lesehan*, a Javanese word meaning to sit on the ground or on a mat, usually with one's legs folded back. *Makan lesehan* is to eat in that position, often at a low table.) In her spare time, she could not resist rounding up even more data, driving with Suarjana to Klaten, where, she exulted to Dewey, "there are iron and brass casting industries which date from the Dutch period (they used to make spare parts for the sugar factories and railway locomotives). Absolutely fascinating!" The following fall, she was back in Hawaii for two months, finishing her dissertation. On November 10, with her draft due at the end of the month, she handwrote a short note in Indonesian to her former research assistant, Djaka Waluja. She had heard from the village headman in Kajar, through Suarjana, that Waluja had been in the village. If he had any new information, Ann asked, could he send it along?

Ann's opus weighed in, at the end, at one thousand forty-three pages. She had completed the dissertation, "Peasant Blacksmithing in Indonesia: Surviving and Thriving Against All Odds," almost twenty years after entering graduate school. She had paid for the typing of at least one draft in barter, Dewey would remember: rattan furniture from the house in Kebayoran Baru.

Drawing on data from the fields of archaeology, history, metallurgy, and cultural anthropology, Ann described the occupation as it was seen by the smiths themselves. She recounted the early history of metalworking industries in Indonesia, with its "unbroken line" tying the culture of the Early Metal Age to the present-day smiths. She discussed metalworking technologies, types of bellows, the layout of the smithy. She examined the class position and social status of smiths. She devoted one hundred pages to Kajar, and another seventy to smithing villages in the Minangkabau highlands in West Sumatra, Tana Toraja in Sulawesi, Central Java, Bali, and South Sulawesi. She looked at the future of metalworking industries against the backdrop of economic trends, critiqued government programs, and looked at the implications of her findings for future development. Although economists and bureaucrats had been predicting the demise of village industries since the late nineteenth century, she wrote, she had found that employment in those industries had increased. Social scientists who saw that increase as a sign of a crisis in the agricultural sector were assuming, incorrectly, that agriculture was more profitable than other occupations. In fact, metalworking was more profitable than agriculture in a number of villages she had studied. For that reason, villagers considered metalworking their primary occupation, agriculture only secondary.

I asked James Fox, a respected anthropologist who had worked in Indonesia over a twenty-year period, what he made of Ann's dissertation. Fox, who had degrees from Harvard and Oxford and had taught at Duke, Cornell, and Harvard, was a professor at the Research School of Pacific and Asian Studies at the Australian National University when we spoke. He said he held the view that anthropology, as a discipline, was too fashion-driven: Anthropological theory had a half-life of five years, and graduate students tended to gravitate to the latest theory. Ann, he said, did something unfashionable. She produced an ethnography of the sort Fox believed would be a reference point for many years. "Ann's book will be a monument into the next century," he said. "You can get into it, and you can get a glimpse of life in a certain period. You can't do that with a lot of anthropological theory. It's momentary. It might be stimulating, but it doesn't last long."

When a redacted version of the dissertation was published by Duke University Press in 2009, Michael Dove, the Yale anthropologist and Ann's longtime friend, wrote in a review that her study of Kajar "is one of the richest ethnographic studies to come out of Java in the past generation. This sort of long-term, in-depth, ground-level study, once the norm in anthropology, is increasingly rare." Ann had concluded that development in the villages she studied was held back not by a lack of entrepreneurial spirit but by a lack of capital—the product of politics, not culture. "Indonesia exemplifies the truth that often the disadvantaged do need not assistance but fair play, not resources but the political control over resources," Dove wrote.

Ann signed the dissertation S. Ann Dunham. On the dedication page, she wrote:

> dedicated to Madelyn and Alice,
> who each gave me support in her own way,
> and to Barack and Maya,
> who seldom complained when their mother was in the field

On February 8, 1992, less than two weeks before Ann was to defend her dissertation, Stanley Dunham died. He had been diagnosed with prostate cancer more than a year earlier. His condition had deteriorated, his brother said, to a point where he was unable to walk. He was buried at the National Memorial Cemetery of the Pacific, or Punchbowl National Cemetery, a rolling green landscape of finely tended lawns flecked with gravestones overlooking the Pacific. His death hit Ann hard. The tensions between them, which had marked earlier years, had subsided. She had talked about him, at least to some, as the family's emotional glue. "When she talked about her mother, it was with admiration," Don Johnston, her colleague, said. "But clearly her stronger emotional bond was with her father."

Two years earlier, Obama, at age twenty-eight, was elected president of the *Harvard Law Review*—"its first black president in more than 100 years of publication," as the Associated Press reported on February 5, 1990, the day after the election. That initial article, in which Obama was said not to have ruled out a future in politics, made no mention of his parents. An article in *The New York Times* the following day mentioned them briefly—a former Kenyan government official and "an American anthropologist now doing field work in Indonesia." A longer article a week later in *The Boston Globe* went into greater detail. "What seems to motivate Barack Obama is a strong identification with what he calls 'the typical black experience,' paired with a mission to help the black community and promote social justice," the *Globe* reported. It described "his unusual path, from childhood in Indonesia, where he grew up, he says, 'as a street kid,' to adolescence in Hawaii, where he was raised by his grandparents." The article dwelt at some length on the influence of Obama's father, who, it said, was born in Kenya, "studied at Harvard and Oxford and became a senior economist for the Kenyan government." In high school, the article said, Obama began a regular correspondence with his father, "whose heritage was to be a major influence on his life, ideals and priorities." One of Obama's most valued possessions, the article said, was the passbook that his grandfather, a cook for the British before Kenyan independence, was required to carry. "He said that even though his heritage is one-half white, and although he has had a mixture of influences in his life, 'my identification with the—quote—typical black experience in America was very strong and very natural and wasn't something forced and difficult,'" the article said. Of Ann, it said little more than "His mother, who is white, is a Kansas-born anthropologist who now works as a developmental consultant in Indonesia."

In an even longer article in the *Los Angeles Times* a month later, Ann was described simply as "an American anthropologist" and "a white American from Wichita, Kan."

The marginal role to which Ann was consigned in those accounts did not go unnoticed. She had raised Obama, with the help of her parents, after his father had left for Harvard when Obama was ten months old. She had been his primary parent for the first ten years of his life. She had returned to Hawaii to live with him when he was in middle school. She had moved back to Hawaii from Indonesia for several months during his senior year. Yet in those accounts, Obama had been "a street kid" in Indonesia, then sent back to Hawaii to be "raised by his grandparents." Yang Suwan, Ann's Indonesian anthropologist friend, recalled Ann returning to Jakarta around the time of the *Harvard Law Review* election. As always, she was extraordinarily proud of her son. But on another level, she seemed crushed.

"'His mother is an anthropologist,'" Ann told Yang, quoting an article she had seen. "I was mentioned in one sentence."

The new girlfriend Obama had brought with him to Hawaii the previous Christmas was different from Ann. A young lawyer from Chicago whom Obama had met while working as a summer associate at the law firm of Sidley Austin, Michelle Robinson had grown up on the South Side of Chicago and had returned there after graduating from law school. Her father, Fraser Robinson III, a descendant of slaves, had been employed as a maintenance worker and later a foreman in a city water-filtration plant; her mother, Marian, had stayed at home with Michelle and her brother when they were young. The family was hardworking, churchgoing, and close-knit. As an undergraduate at Princeton and as a law student at Harvard, Michelle Robinson had been active in black student organizations. She moved systematically through her life, making sensible, carefully considered decisions, each building to the next. "I would say Michelle is much more like our grandmother," Maya told me. "And I would say that my mother and my grandmother really were also opposites." After the Christmas visit, Ann reported back to Suryakusuma. "She is intelligent, very tall (6'1"), not beautiful but quite attractive," Ann wrote of Robinson. "She did her BA at Princeton and her law degree at Harvard. But she has spent most of her life in Chicago." Ann, who prided herself on raising her children to have a global perspective, described Robinson as "a little provincial and not as international as Barry." But Ann liked her. "She is nice, though," she said. If Robinson and Obama were to marry after he graduated from law school, Ann told Suryakusuma, she would not be unhappy.

Graduation rolled around.

"I would have liked to go for the graduation, but both Barry and his girlfriend recommended that the family skip it," Ann wrote to Dewey from Jakarta. "Apparently hotels are a problem and the law school graduates with everyone else so that you can hardly find your kid."

When Ann told Made Suarjana that Obama was graduating from Harvard Law School, he said, "So he's going to be a billionaire." Ann corrected him: No, she said, he wants to return to Chicago and do pro bono work. Because Suarjana knew that Obama was interested in politics, and because he felt he knew something about American public life, he said, knowingly, "Okay, so he wants to be president."

To his surprise, Ann began to weep.

It was the only time, he told me, that he saw her cry. He was uncertain what it was about the idea of her son one day running for president that brought her to tears. He thought maybe it was fear: What would it mean to be a man with an African father running for president in a country riddled with the racism Ann must have encountered when she had married the elder Obama? Maybe it was protectiveness: Every facet of a candidate's life, professional and personal, would be unearthed and subjected to scrutiny. Maybe it was the anticipation of loss—a mother's loss compounded by whatever regret she might have had about the years they had spent apart and the distance that almost inevitably was widening between them.

"No, not this time," she answered, according to Suarjana. "He's going to be a senator first."

Had they already talked about it? Suarjana wondered later. If Obama was to be "a senator first," perhaps Obama and Ann had discussed what would follow. Obama must have thought about running for president, Suarjana said, or Ann must have thought about his running. What role had she played in cultivating that ambition? Suarjana had been struck by the respect with which Ann treated Obama. It reminded him of the way a mother treated the eldest son in a Javanese family, preparing the boy from an early age to one day inherit the role of father and backbone of the family. Ann's relationship with Obama seemed different from the relationships between mothers and sons that Suarjana had seen in American movies. Conversations between her and Obama, occasionally recounted to Suarjana, had a certain gravity. When Ann recounted stories about her daughter, she sounded less formal and more relaxed. That made sense, Suarjana thought, because Ann and Maya had lived closely together for many years. Nevertheless, he could not help but notice the depth of Ann's admiration for her son.

His life decisions, it seems, carried more than the usual freight.

"She felt a little bit wistful or sad that Barack had essentially moved to Chicago and chosen to take on a really strongly identified black identity," recalled Don Johnston, Ann's colleague at Bank Rakyat Indonesia. That identity, she felt, "had not really been part of who he was when he was growing up." Ann felt he was making what Johnston called "a professional choice" to strongly identify himself as black. "It would be too strong to say that she felt rejection," he said. But she felt, in that way, "that he was distancing himself from her."

At the same time, Ann's example could be discerned in some of Obama's choices. Barry had left Hawaii far behind him when he had planted himself first in New York City and then in Chicago—just as Ann had done when she had made Indonesia the center of gravity in her life. His community organizing work paralleled some of her development consulting work abroad. Then, after all of Ann's efforts to secure for him the best education and impress on him the importance of living up to his potential, he had flourished at Harvard.

"So that experiment I was talking about earlier?" President Obama said when we talked, referring to his account of his confrontation with his mother during his senior year in high school. "Turns out she was actually onto something."

Ten

Manhattan Chill

Ann, at fifty, straddled hemispheres. She was an American citizen who had lived in Indonesia for more than half of her adult life. She had a doctorate from the University of Hawai'i based on work done over two decades in Java. She had a career in Asia but a family in the United States. Her mother, Madelyn, turning seventy, was a widow living alone in Honolulu. Barack, at thirty-one, was a lawyer in Illinois, writing his first book and engaged to a woman rooted in Chicago. Maya, twenty-two, was an undergraduate majoring in English at the University of Hawai'i. Ann longed to live closer to her children and had begun dreaming of grandchildren. But she could live more comfortably in Indonesia, on a development consultant's salary and benefits, than she could ever afford to live in Hawaii, and her work had a degree of impact in Indonesia that she could not begin to match in the United States. As long as she had a job, she could keep renewing her visa and continue to live in Indonesia. She even toyed with the idea of making it a more permanent base. She thought about one day having a house in Bali, if she could come up with the money; it would be a place where she and her children and their friends could alight. But as a foreigner, she could not own property, she could only lease it. As an expatriate, one heard unsettling stories of sudden lease cancellations, mysterious property claims, precipitous departures. If she could park everything that was important to her in another country, the risks might be fewer. But Ann did not have the luxury of maintaining homes in two places. She never wanted to fall out of love with Indonesia because of some catastrophe she could ill afford, she told Garrett Solyom. An American consular official in Bali had once told the Solyoms ominously, "If you're at an age where you don't have the money or connections to be able to get out of here at a moment's notice when you need to, you shouldn't be here."

In mid-1992, Ann made the decision to move back to the United States. Barack was to marry Michelle Robinson at the Trinity United Church of Christ in Chicago in early October—an event to which Ann looked forward with great pleasure. On a visit to Chicago in advance of the wedding, she got in touch with Mary Houghton, the president of ShoreBank, a bank holding company that Houghton and others had founded in the early 1970s in an effort to show that banks could play a constructive role in low-income black neighborhoods. Houghton, who had also advised microfinance organizations, had met Ann at a party in Jakarta in the late 1980s and remembered her warmly as "forthright, sharp-tongued, opinionated, happy." When Ann contacted her, they agreed to meet for what Houghton remembered years later as an agenda-free brunch in downtown Chicago. Ann's contract in Jakarta was to wind up the following January. She was moving back to the United States and would need a job. Houghton offered to put her in touch with a nonprofit based in New York City whose interests seemed aligned with Ann's. Conceived during the first United Nations World Conference on Women in 1975, the organization, called Women's World Banking, had set out to promote full economic participation for low-income women by helping them develop viable businesses. Toward that end, it offered support, training, and advice to several dozen microfinance organizations in Asia, Africa, Latin America, and elsewhere, which in turn offered credit and other financial services to women producers and entrepreneurs. The original board had included Ela Bhatt, the founder of the Self Employed Women's Association, whom Ann had first encountered during her eye-opening trip to India in her first weeks at Ford. Women's World Banking was governed by women and run by women and existed first and foremost for the benefit of women.

In mid-September, Ann received a letter from Women's World Banking, alerting her to a job opening. Embarking on a monthlong trip to Hawaii and the mainland, Ann sent off her résumé and a letter asking to be considered. In New York, she met with the president of Women's World Banking, Nancy Barry, in a French restaurant near the organization's offices in Midtown Manhattan. Barry, a Harvard Business School graduate in her early forties, had worked at the World Bank for fifteen years before becoming president of Women's World Banking. Smart, charismatic, and driven, she was a product, she liked to say, of both the decentralized culture of Women's World Banking and the command-and-control ethos of "the World Bank of Men." At Women's World Banking, she wanted to influence the policies of banks around the world to better serve the poor. Ann had more experience with poor women than anyone in the Women's World Banking office, Barry could see. She had also influenced the design of the services offered by

Bank Rakyat Indonesia, which ran the largest self-sustaining microfinance program in the world. At their first meeting, Barry found Ann's size jarring, she told me. The staff of "Wild Women's Banking," as it had occasionally been called, was so young and attractive that it had been suggested Barry had a "looks problem." But she was impressed by Ann's intelligence, experience, and independence of mind. She could see that Ann had a sense of humor, the ability to laugh at herself, and the charm to win people over. So Barry offered her a job that had not previously existed: coordinator for policy and research. In many countries, government and bank policies favored big over small businesses, the formal over the informal sector. They favored male clients, who owned property, over women, who did not. Governments also placed restrictions on the activities of independent-sector organizations in ways that held back microlending, limiting loan sizes, rates of interest, and the outside funding those organizations could receive. Ann's job would be to help Women's World Banking and its affiliates persuade policy-makers to change all that. "This was not like we had a position for a policy coordinator," Barry told me. "But in my mind we had a whole agenda waiting to happen if we had the right person."

Moving to New York City for the first time was not easy at age fifty. Ann arrived in Manhattan in late January 1993 during a cold snap so bitter that her lungs ached when she breathed. Three weeks into her stay, a truck bomb detonated in the underground garage beneath the World Trade Center, injuring a thousand people and killing six. Ann, with a starting salary of $65,000 a year, had expected to be able to find a two-bedroom apartment for about $1,500 a month within walking distance of the offices on West Fortieth Street. But because two-bedroom apartments were renting for more than $2,000, she was forced to settle for an antiseptic one-bedroom in a forty-story tower near the United Nations for $1,550.

She parked most of her books and belongings in storage in Hawaii, for which she paid another $250 a month. (A "wardrobe inventory" she put together around that time listed a remarkable forty-eight skirts, half of them marked "sm" and apparently not in use.) Women's World Banking paid for two weeks in a hotel near the office while Ann looked for an apartment, but she got stuck there for ten extra days, at her expense, waiting for the credit clearance needed to sign a lease. She spent $8,000 on housewares and furniture from Pier 1 Imports, and another $1,500 on winter clothes. She had never worn panty hose in her life, she told friends. The small amount of savings she had accumulated dwindled, and her credit card debt rose. Afraid of the subway system, she spent money on cabs. *"Aduh! Aduh! Aduh!"* she would say, falling back on an Indonesian expression of pain in the face of the rushing crowds. Ann missed Indonesia. The best Indonesian restaurant in New York seemed no better than the lowliest *warung*. From her room on the twenty-sixth floor of the hotel, she gazed at the sky, remembering the full moon in Bali and wondering why she had traveled so far from Made Suarjana. She told herself she would stay in New York for two or three years, then move to Bali. Suarjana could start a civil-society organization or a publishing house, and she would look for work as a consultant.

Life at Women's World Banking was consuming. The two dozen employees were mostly young, female, unmarried, and childless. Driven by devotion to "the mission" and an esprit de corps cultivated from the top, they toiled long hours in an office culture that more than one of them remembered years later as having the intimacy and intensity of a dysfunctional family. Barry pegged the pay and benefits to those of other not-for-profits; she scrimped, she told me, only on vacations. The staff was international and impressively credentialed. Kellee Tsai, the daughter of immigrants from

Taiwan, had come straight from a financial analyst's job at Morgan Stanley, putting away her pearls and lipstick and fully expecting a cohort of hirsute women in vintage clothing. Instead, she found hyperarticulate women in saris and handcrafted jewelry, and Christmas parties catered by a high-end Upper West Side boîte. The financial products and services coordinator was a young Australian woman with an MBA from Harvard who had run the Australian government's food aid program in Ethiopia. The regional coordinator for Africa was a Kenyan-born, British-trained accountant who had been the first in her peasant family to go to university. The communications coordinator, a British-born lawyer, had grown up in Pakistan and Iraq, where she could remember having watched her mother water-skiing on the Tigris in a bikini. Other staff members were Indian, Ecuadorean, Colombian, Canadian, American, Honduran, Haitian, Ghanaian. The calendar was crowded with conferences in foreign capitals such as Tokyo, Accra, and Mexico City. "In many ways, it was one of the most dysfunctional organizations I've ever worked in," said Nina Nayar, who worked at Women's World Banking as Ann's assistant. "But I have never felt such warmth, such passion, such excitement. It was like a soap opera: You're crying, you're laughing, you're celebrating, you miss people, you love people, you hate people, and you know that this is all psychodrama, but you're so hooked on it that you have to be there every day at three o'clock to see this thing."

Office space was tight. Despite her seniority, Ann doubled up in a small, dark room in the back of the building with Kellee Tsai, who was a few years older than Maya. Accessible only through a windowless word-processing zone nicknamed "the bunker," the room had back-to-back desks and a view into the wall of the next building, a few feet away. Women's World Banking had not lavished attention on developing well-oiled office systems; if a person needed something done, she might be best off doing it herself. Ann, for the first time in a long time, was without secretarial assistance. "She couldn't type to save her life," one colleague remembered. And on matters technological, she was the opposite of self-sufficient. An aspiring Irish-born playwright named Donald Creedon, who had worked as a Manhattan doorman before learning word processing, served as "computer coordinator." He devoted his time to helping staff members get their computers to do what they wanted. Ann, wedded to an outdated version of word-processing software, needed constant assistance. Creedon, ensconced in the bunker, would hear her cry out in frustration. "Then she would call my name—without moving," he said. "The expectation was probably, 'You can come and help me type this thing. Because I need help.'"

Ann's office became a magnet for younger colleagues. When she was stuck on a piece of writing, she might be found holed up back there—like the village elder, Creedon thought—telling stories. They were not about her but about people she had met, worlds she had known, absurdities she had witnessed. Stories sprang from her head fully formed, many of them endowed with the clarifying wisdom of myths. Younger women would find excuses to wander down to word processing for a chat. With her glasses on a chain around her neck or perched on the tip of her nose if she was reading, Ann seemed perpetually on the verge of smiling. She was mischievous and witty. She worked her dark, shapely eyebrows for emphasis, her toothy grin for punctuation—sometimes the tip-off that she had made a joke at the expense of someone present, who might catch on a minute or two late. "Maybe because she was an observer, she saw how ridiculous things could be," recalled Brinley Bruton, a young program assistant in the office. "I remember her literally sitting back and wiping tears away from her eyes because she was laughing so hard. She had that kind of laugh—a belly laugh."

One of Ann's stories—at least as one colleague remembered it years later—concerned a group of village women from Africa and Indonesia. On some earlier occasion, Ann had invited them to get together to talk about their lives. During a discussion of similarities and differences, the Indonesian women mentioned an unusual practice: After childbirth, a woman would put a salt pack in her vagina, ostensibly to restore its firmness. The practice was painful, the women conceded. But it was thought to help women remain "young" for their husbands. The African women were incredulous: Why would a woman willingly inflict pain on herself? "The Indonesian women—or so Ann told the story—asked, 'What do you do, then, to be able to continue to please your husbands?'" recalled the colleague who was present. "The African women all rolled about laughing and said, 'We find a bigger man!'"

Sometimes, Ann was the anthropologist in the field, with Women's World Banking as her village. She could capture the essence of a personality in an anecdote, even in a subordinate clause. "She would not be the type who would do well in a conventional organization, because she was very straightforward in her views on everything and often did it with humor—humor that had a bite," Nancy Barry told me. Ann toyed with the idea of writing a murder mystery set at one of Women's World Banking's global meetings, during which sleep-deprived staffers pulling all-nighters in the service of the mission occasionally almost came to blows. It was said that a delegate had returned to her home country after one global meeting and promptly expired. A recurring topic of conversation in the office concerned who would be the murder victim in Ann's book, some of her colleagues told me. Others, however, said the victim was to be Barry; only the identity of the murderer remained up for grabs. "Of course, it could have been anyone," Ann confided conspiratorially to Creedon. "Because, God knows, there were enough people who had a motive."

Several younger women in the office told me that in those days, they wanted to be Ann. Her assistant, Nina Nayar, an Indian woman then in her mid-twenties, had an undergraduate degree in anthropology, a master's in South Asian regional studies, and experience working in Ahmedabad with the Self-Employed Women's Association. The child of supportive but protective parents, Nayar told me that Ann, by example, taught her how to live. To Nayar, Ann seemed unconcerned about society's opinions about working women, single women, women who married outside their culture or tradition—women who, as Nayar put it, dreamed big and pursued their dreams and were fearless in the pursuit of adventure and knowledge. Ann did not seem, at least to Nayar, to feel that marriage as an institution was essential or even particularly important. What mattered was to have loved passionately and deeply, to have had lasting relationships, to have lived honestly and without pretense. She never spoke of her marriages as mistakes or failures; they had simply worked out differently than expected. Nor was she haunted by decisions she had made. "The past was her past," said Wanjiku Kibui, Ann's Kenyan colleague, whom Ann affectionately referred to as her in-law. "But it was not a prison." When Nayar told Ann that she intended never to marry, Ann suggested Nayar was simply trading one orthodoxy for another. Ann advised Nayar to remain open. Niki Armacost, who became the communications coordinator, said of Ann, "She was the opposite of uptight. It was like, 'Oh, interesting! So *that's* how those people live.' I think she was a very principled person, but she was not a judgmental person. She had a set of principles, and tolerance was one of the principles. But she didn't lecture people about those things."

Business trips became field trips. When Ann and Nayar traveled together, it was Nayar's job to make sure Ann could get coffee at five a.m., as soon as she got up. In Jakarta, Ann took Nayar into the *kampung*s and in pursuit of the best street food: "Oh my God, my taste buds have finally come alive!" Nayar remembered her saying. In other cities, there were outings to anthropological museums and art museums and shops specializing in silver jewelry: "I will have to starve for the rest of the month, but I had to get this silver and turquoise thing," Ann would say, according to Nayar. "Isn't it magnificent?" Several younger colleagues suggested to Ann that they should all live together in Bali. "We talked about Alice Dewey's house, so we said, 'Ann, why don't you set up a house for us in Bali and we'll come there and do our dissertations together?'" Nayar recalled. "'You can be one of our readers. We'll take care of you and you can take care of our dissertations.' She thought it was a brilliant idea." Ann was a mentor to several younger women, but she had her limits. On the elevator one day, Brinley Bruton, who had been trying her hand at fiction, asked Ann if she would read one of her stories. "Which was, in fact, 'I want you to read this story and tell me it's wonderful,'" Bruton remembered. Unapologetically, Ann declined. "I came out of it feeling a little hurt," Bruton told me. "But in retrospect, I have respect for her. She wasn't going to pretend."

Ann arrived at Women's World Banking during the long lead-up to the United Nations Fourth World Conference on Women, which was to be held in Beijing in September 1995. To organizations like Women's World Banking, the conference offered an opportunity to promote their agenda. Discussions of the status of women had tended to focus on matters like health, education, and reproductive rights. But women made up the majority of the economically active poor in the world. Over the previous two decades, institutions had begun offering financial services for low-income women producers and entrepreneurs. As a result, their enterprises had flourished and the role of women in the economy had grown. Yet even the leading microfinance institutions were reaching only a tiny fraction of the women who could benefit. Women's World Banking saw the conference, and a parallel forum for nongovernmental organizations, as a chance to change the policies of governments, banks, and donors so that financial services to the poor could grow. Ann made the case to Barry that Women's World Banking ought to play a role in organizing many of the disparate microfinance institutions into a movement. If a coalition of organizations could agree on an agenda and demonstrate the contributions of low-income women to economic development, it could catapult the issue of microfinance into a prominent place in the "platform of action" that would eventually be endorsed by the nearly two hundred countries expected to be represented in Beijing.

Barry was skeptical about Ann's suggestion of a coalition. She saw the other organizations as competitors vying for the favor of a finite number of donors. Women's World Banking had worked hard in its early years to differentiate itself from the others, defining itself in part by what it was not. That is, it was not like Grameen Bank in Bangladesh, one of the largest and most successful financial intermediaries focused on the rural poor; it was not like ACCION International, another microfinance organization with a network of lending partners. Barry, who had been on the board of Women's World Banking during those early years, had been influenced by what she later called "that kind of insular, go-it-alone, we-are-the-best, we-are-different mentality." She doubted that some groups would be willing to collaborate. She worried that time would be wasted trying to bring together organizations with divergent interests. Instead, she favored what she described as a more unilateral approach—that is, one in which Women's World Banking was in charge. "It kind of made me nervous," she told me. "Even though I'm a big believer in building coalitions—coalitions that *we* lead, if you know what I mean."

Barry was "a pretty tough character to deal with," she told me, looking back on those years with a degree of self-knowledge and candor that was striking. She had grown up in a Catholic family in Orange County, California. One uncle was a priest who had marched with the labor leader César Chávez. A great-aunt was a nun. A graduate of Stanford and Harvard Business School, Barry had worked in Tanzania for McKinsey & Company, the management consulting firm, before going to work for the World Bank for fifteen years. At Women's World Banking, she was bent on results. She took dissent personally. Small things—say, the wrong word in a business plan—could set her off. She felt she had to manage everyone—the funders, the board, the affiliates. "It wasn't like Women's World Banking was the leader of the network," she told me. "*I* was the leader of the network. So I was like the big brain, and everybody else was feeding into the big brain." Younger women on the staff, swept up in the mission, tended not to challenge Barry. "If you're a young twenty-five-year-old and you're working with somebody that is working on something supercompelling, with unbelievably interesting people and with a mission to die for, you're a net learner, so you're kind of into it for at least ten years," Barry said. "By the time you get ten years into it, hopefully you actually know that I'm a good-hearted person and you've learned how to manage me. But for Ann, who was also very strong-headed and strong-willed, I think it was not fun."

Ann was not afraid to take on Barry. She had little patience with the shorthand that is useful and necessary in corporate life for selling an idea, and she was unwilling to make any claim—about, say, loan repayment rates and women—without the data to back it up. She preferred to acknowledge what was not known, then go find the answer. "She would sell an idea by saying, 'Well, we don't know the answer. That's why it's important that you fund us,'" Nayar remembered. "There was no halfway. In the business of development, academics have a very limited role. You can't indulge in spending weeks and months on research. Oftentimes, deadlines are what we're led by. Ann didn't live by those rules. She would say, 'If I have to get this thing ready, I am going to research it, I'm not just going to give you sound-bite stuff. If it's got my name on it, it has to be right.' It used to drive us crazy. We had to push Ann to do something. There would be much 'Oh, c'mon, Ann. Get it over with.' But I understand. She would never produce anything that she was not proud of."

The confrontations between Ann and Barry became, to Nayar, the clash of the Titans. "I had the luxury of being in on all their meetings," she said. "It was horrible. I can understand Nancy, because I'm very much a can-do, will-do, do-it-now person. But I also related to Mother Ann." Barry needed justification for the policy statements the organization was making. "For instance, 'Women are good clients.' Okay, what are the ways that we can prove that?" Nayar said. "Ann would want to write a dissertation. And Nancy just wants, like, 'For example, boom, boom, boom.'" According to Nayar, "Ann would say, 'I can't whip things together into nonsensical bullet points. I need to have justifications for all my bullet points. So that's a paragraph!' And Nancy says, 'Cut it down, cut it down.'" Colleagues joked that Ann had been in Asia too long. She had a different sense of time, and instead of arguing, she preferred to debate or discuss. Over time, it seemed to Nayar, the conflict forced Ann to become more confrontational and assertive. "Both are demonic once they get on their high horse," Nayar said. "God can't turn them around. It was just two very strong women."

At other times, Ann seemed to fret about not meeting Barry's expectations. "Nancy would be harping on her: 'Are you done with that yet? You're still working on that?'" Kellee Tsai, Ann's office mate, remembered. "Nancy had her in tears so many times, it was horrible."

As Barry herself put it, "Because of my pigheadedness, you actually had to be pigheaded to get your way." Each person in the office had her own approach. Wanjiku Kibui, the regional coordinator for Africa, would call Barry out, in a way that Barry appreciated, when she was, as Barry put it later, "misbehaving." Niki Armacost, the communications coordinator, would find a better time. "Ann would just stay," Barry remembered. "She would stay and fight." On the question of the coalition of microfinance organizations, she would not back down. In a series of long, uncomfortable meetings with Barry, Ann insisted that Women's World Banking use its influence for a greater good. To do otherwise would be small-minded and selfish. "We have to be grown-ups now," Barry remembered Ann saying, in effect. "She would have used language like that." Intentionally or not, Ann made Barry feel guilty: "I don't think she was ever mean-spirited or nasty, but she could not have been more direct about what was at stake and why it was the right thing."

Eventually, Barry relented. In October 1993, Women's World Banking joined two dozen other microfinance organizations to form the International Coalition on Women and Credit. Its aim was to influence the opinions of policy-makers at a series of regional conferences leading up to Beijing. Coalition members would hold workshops, publicize the successes of microfinance and microenterprise, make policy recommendations, and lobby delegates.

Finally, they would all converge on Beijing. At Barry's insistence, Women's World Banking became the secretariat for the coalition. It fell to Ann, as the policy and research coordinator, to marshal the data needed to back the claims that the coalition would be making and to take the lead in dealing with the other organizations.

That was not simple. The organizations were not merely competitive, they also differed as to how best to deliver financial services and the type of clients it was most important to reach. Now they were expected to put aside their differences and support a common objective. "It became like an infiltration," Barry recalled. "If you picture all these regional and global meetings put on by the UN for the year or two in preparation for Beijing—complete chaos, all of these NGO leaders, strident, doing their thing, not at all respectful. If I'm in health, I don't want microfinance to get primacy. Ann got all these coalition members showing up to these regional meetings around the world and getting the health and education people saying one thing: 'The poor woman has to have an income. Then she can pay for education.' So that whole bottom-up approach, getting disparate players to act to common cause? She pulled it off."

Ann believed in it, said Lawrence Yanovitch, director of policy and research at FINCA, also known as the Foundation for International Community Assistance, a leader in village banking in Latin America, who served on the executive committee with Ann. That was simply her nature: She had little ego, he said, and she cared about the issues first. Barry told me, "She could be kind of a fat lady with big hair and a bohemian, but she was trying to do the right thing for the right reasons. And she did it with great intelligence and very strong rigor in terms of preparation and methodology and thinking through strategy."

At the same time, the secretary general for the Beijing conference asked Women's World Banking to chair an "expert group" on women and finance, to be made up of forty representatives of microfinance networks, development banks, government leaders, and others. In addition to Barry and Ann, the group included Dick Patten, Ann's friend and longtime colleague; Ela Bhatt from the Self Employed Women's Association; Muhammad Yunus, the founder and managing director of Grameen Bank, who would win the Nobel Peace Prize in 2006; and Ellen Johnson-Sirleaf, who would go on to become president of Liberia. In September 1993, Women's World Banking sent every member of the group an unusually detailed questionnaire on women and microfinance. The questionnaire bore the unmistakable marks of Ann's research methodology—a total of ninety-two questions, few of them amenable to short answers. ("I think we even had a conflict over the questionnaire," Barry told me. "Something I really know how to do super-well is moderate meetings and create a process where you get consensus in a very robust and detailed way out of a messy process. So I'm very results-oriented. My recollection is Ann would have loved to have gotten more stuff from everybody.") Two hundred pages of responses poured in to the Women's World Banking office. Ann and Nina Nayar, working with Barry, distilled them into an interim report. That report went out to every member of the expert group, along with profiles of leading microenterprise institutions and an analysis of government budgets and the flow of donor aid. Finally, the expert group met over five days in January 1994 to hash out and endorse a final report and recommendations—a framework for how to build financial systems that work for the poor.

"That was considered a huge achievement in the world of microfinance," recalled Niki Armacost. "No one had talked about common standards before. No one had talked about the kinds of criteria that you need to evaluate microfinance organizations, or the policy constraints, or the challenges they would have to deal with, or why it was important to be lending money to women. None of that had been put together before. So it was a seminal document."

Outside the office, Ann was increasingly worried about money and her health. When she had moved to New York, she had understood that she would not be able to live as well as she had in Jakarta. But she had hoped to get by, she wrote in a memo to Barry eight months after accepting the job, "modestly but decently, in a manner suitable for a grownup, meet my basic family obligations, and still save a small amount toward Christmas, emergencies or the future." That had not happened. After less than a year, she was spending more than she was making. She was sinking ever more deeply into debt. After taxes, she expected to take home just $41,000 of her starting salary—a figure she expected to shrink the following year, when she would be eligible to claim fewer exemptions and deductions. The monthly payments on her ballooning credit-card debt had doubled to $600 a month. In her memo to Barry, she had asked for a raise. "To make a long story short, in the seven months I have been at Women's World Banking, I have been forced to exhaust my savings and I am now going further into credit card debt at the rate of about $500 a month in order to just get by," she wrote. "There is no possibility of saving even a penny. Clearly I cannot continue this way, no matter how devoted I am to Women's World Banking or the mission."

Money was not Ann's only worry. She was more overweight than ever, her skin was pale, and her abdomen and lower legs were swollen. When she walked any distance, she would pant and become short of breath. By the summer of 1994, it had become painful to walk. When Maya and others urged her to see a doctor, she seemed to procrastinate and make excuses. She attributed her symptoms to menopause. "You, my in-law, will see when you reach my age," she said to Wanjiku Kibui, her Kenyan colleague, laughing it off. Though Ann appeared to fear little in life, she was uncomfortable with doctors, especially gynecologists. Once, she had told a friend that she had rejected a physician's suggestion that she consider a hysterectomy to address a problem of heavy bleeding. "The indignity of it!" the friend remembered her saying. The prospect of the procedure seemed to violate her sense of privacy and self-respect. She was also morbidly afraid of cancer. On at least a dozen occasions, Nayar recalled, Ann brought up the subject. "If you're going to get it, you're going to get it," she would remark at the slightest reminder of cancer—passing a cancer-awareness ribbon or discussing a new health insurance policy requiring Pap smears. "If it gets you, it gets you."

"The only thing I'm really afraid of in life is to die of cancer," she told Nayar.

"Why do you say that?"

"Well, my father died of cancer."

"A lot of people's parents die of cancer," Nayar would reassure her. "So you're in a high-risk category. You have to take precautions."

It was as if she did not want to know, Nayar thought, or maybe she thought she knew and did not want to see it in writing. Around the time of a review of the benefits package at Women's World Banking, Ann became especially agitated. She had no savings, and she was worried about her health. "I think she realized that if she was going to get sick—even if she was going to get old—this was not the job that was going to help her," Nayar said. "And she would have to think about that rather than depend on her children."

In late June 1994, Ann wrote Barry a letter giving notice that she would be resigning. For months, she had been considering leaving. She had a sense, she told Don Johnston, her former colleague in Jakarta, that Women's World Banking was spinning its wheels— "rushing off to a lot of different places, doing a lot of different things, but not making a really strong impact on women's access to finance anywhere," as Johnston put it. Having finally completed her dissertation, she wanted to get it published. She had prepared an application for a postdoctoral grant to cover the cost of three months in Indonesia updating the research and nine months at the East-West Center revising the dissertation for publication. But she had also been contacted by Development Alternatives Inc., the firm in Bethesda, Maryland, that had hired her for her first big job as a development consultant fifteen years earlier. Development Alternatives wanted to bid on a project aimed at strengthening the Indonesian State Ministry for the Role of Women. To have a shot at winning the contract, the firm would need a certain kind of team leader—ideally a woman, fluent in Indonesian, with the combination of authority and sensitivity that it would take to be accepted by the minister and her staff. "It had to be someone who was basically Indonesian—but an American," said Bruce Harker, who was working for the Bethesda firm, developing technical assistance contracts in Indonesia. He had known Ann in Java. She seemed to him the only person who could do the job. He knew she was torn about whether to be living, at that period in her life, in Indonesia or the United States. But when the firm contacted her, she seemed excited by the job opportunity and eager to return to Indonesia. The base pay was $82,500, well above the $69,550 she was making, before taxes, after her first year at Women's World Banking. In addition to health insurance, the benefits included a housing allowance and a car. "After much agonizing, and lengthy discussions with family and friends in the US and Indonesia, I have decided to accept the position," Ann wrote to Nancy Barry. "I have enjoyed my time in New York, and I have added a lot to my store of professional knowledge, particularly in the areas of policy work and institution building for NGOs. I will leave WWB with great affection for the organization, and all the people working here. I hope there will be opportunities for us to meet and cooperate in the future. (Who knows? Perhaps we will all meet at Beijing.)"

Ann seemed to have a feeling that she was running out of time, Nayar told me. Ann told her, "I just need to go home."

Before she left, Ann made one last trip for Women's World Banking. In July, she flew to Mexico City for the global meeting of the Women's World Banking network. She seemed worn out by the travel, but she rallied when she arrived. Nayar was struck by Ann's ability to connect with people across regional and cultural differences. "It was not just the Asians," Nayar said. "It was the Africans, because they saw her in her muumuus and her trinkets, and she fit right in to the Mama circle—the West Africans with their scarves and all that." Nayar was also reminded of Ann's effect on men. The Mexican organizers had hired "these stunning, drop-dead-gorgeous male models," as Nayar remembered them, to serve as hosts to the several hundred women. Ann had always been flirtatious, Nayar said. A glimmer in her eye expressed eloquently her interest and delight in men. "These boys were eating out of her hand," Nayar remembered. "They weren't looking at us, they were all around Ann. I think she was probably one of the most sensual women I have met in my life. Size didn't matter, it was what was inside. She just exuded woman."

The young male host assigned to Ann's group turned out to be an anthropology major, fluent in English, who did modeling on the side. Soon, he, Ann, and Nayar were in a taxi, heading to an archaeological dig. Ann took Nayar to the Frida Kahlo Museum at

Casa Azul, the house in Coyoacán where Kahlo had grown up and later lived with Diego Rivera. At the National Museum of Anthropology, Niki Armacost recalled, Ann stopped in front of an exhibit illustrating human evolution. "There was an Africa grouping, an Asia grouping," Armacost told me. "She was talking about the Africa grouping. The image they had up on the wall was this incredibly curvaceous African woman who had this huge, curvy bum. And we're all so—kind of unshapely. And she said, 'You know, it's very interesting, because when the white explorers found these African women and took them back to Europe, that's when the bustle started!'"

On an outing to Teotihuacán, the vast archaeological site northeast of Mexico City that was the largest city in the pre-Columbian Americas until it was suddenly and mysteriously abandoned, Ann wanted to climb the Pyramid of the Sun, one of the biggest pyramids in the world. Worried about her stamina, Nayar suggested instead the Pyramid of the Moon because it was smaller but offered dazzling views of the bigger pyramid and the majestic expanse of the Avenue of the Dead. Against the backdrop of a sacred mountain to the north, the two women, a generation apart, ascended together. "It was so hard for her to climb this thing," Nayar remembered years later. "I really thought she was going to pass out or fall. There was no way I was letting her go up on her own. She was also a little afraid of heights. But she was going to do it. And she did it."

Two months earlier, Ann had gone to see a physician with a private practice in obstetrics, gynecology, and infertility on the Upper East Side of Manhattan. She had been given the doctor's name by another physician, who had retired, and had made an appointment for a gynecological checkup. She told the doctor, Barbara Shortle, that she had a five-year history of heavy and irregular periods, for which previous doctors had put her on hormone-replacement therapy. Twice, she said, she had received a dilation and curettage, a procedure commonly done to diagnose the causes of abnormal bleeding. Each time, she said, the test had turned up nothing. Shortle, who had a particular affection for Hawaii, took a liking to Ann, but she also suspected Ann was seriously ill. From the extent of the bleeding, Shortle thought she might have uterine cancer, a rarity in Shortle's practice, which could in many cases be treated successfully with surgery and radiation, depending on the grade of the tumor. Shortle jotted her hypothesis in her notes. She recommended a physical exam, a Pap smear, a pelvic ultrasound, a mammogram, and, most important for a diagnosis, another dilation and curettage, which could be used to rule out uterine cancer. The D&C would have to be done in a hospital, and would for that reason take up the better part of a day at a critical time when the staff at Women's World Banking was especially busy. Ann went ahead and had the physical, the Pap smear, the pelvic ultrasound, and the mammogram, as well as a breast ultrasound, at the radiologist's suggestion.

"I completed all of those tests," Ann would write to Shortle a year later in connection with an insurance claim, having never seen her again, "except the D and C, which I postponed for work-related reasons."

Eleven

Coming Home

In late November 1994, Ann's driver, Sabaruddin, picked her up from the modest little house on a narrow street in Jakarta where she had been living since returning to Indonesia. In the used car she had bought with the transportation allowance from her new employer, they rumbled south toward Ciloto, a resort town in the highlands an hour and a half outside the city. For three months, Ann and her team of consultants had been preparing for a three-day retreat at which the staff of the State Ministry for the Role of Women was to come to grips with its mission—embedding a commitment to gender equality deep in the government of the fourth most populous country in the world. To some friends, Ann had described her new assignment as a dream job. But it had quickly proved far more frustrating than she had chosen to dwell on in advance. The bureaucracy was sluggish and resistant to change. There was not enough money in the consulting contract to cover all the work Ann felt was needed to do the job properly. Within a month or two, she was exhausted, overworked, and not feeling well. Bruce Harker, who was overseeing the project from the office of Development Alternatives Inc. in Bethesda, had been taken aback, during a visit to Jakarta, when Ann, appealing to him for more money for the project, had broken down in tears. Yet there she was on the first afternoon of the workshop in Ciloto, delivering a paper on international trends in gender and development. Attendance at the workshop was slightly lower than hoped: Even the minister had begged off, sending word that she had been called to the palace for a meeting with President Suharto's wife. By the time Ann left Ciloto a day or two later, her vague feeling of unease about her health had been superseded by a sharp pain in her abdomen, which she was no longer able to push from her mind.

The job in Jakarta had sounded promising enough in New York City the previous spring. With the approach of the United Nations conference in Beijing, the Asian Development Bank, an international development bank with its headquarters in the Philippines, had decided to make a grant to the Indonesian government for the purpose of strengthening and increasing the influence of the State Ministry for the Role of Women. The bank had invited consulting companies to bid on a contract to provide technical assistance—advice on shaping a strategy, training the staff, and setting up databases to measure the ministry's impact. In a joint venture with an Indonesian firm with connections to the Suharto family, Development Alternatives Inc. had bid and won. But in last-minute negotiations, the amount of money available to the team leader for work activities had been reduced, Harker told me. His company had become, in effect, the subcontractor, leaving Ann, the team leader, working for a firm that did not have control over the budget. From the beginning, the going was rocky. In Jakarta, Ann found herself working out of a dark, dingy office in the Ministry of the Environment without easy access to the ministry she was advising. There were the usual technological aggravations, including cell phone service that seemed not to cover the office where she worked. The ministry staff was inexperienced—and in some cases uninterested—in complex questions involving gender. Recruited from other agencies, many of the staff members needed training—and might move abruptly, without warning, to another ministry at any time. "We found it very frustrating, because there was no interest," Mayling Oey-Gardiner, a demographer who was also a consultant to the ministry, told me. Without a critical mass of support, she said, little could be done. Furthermore, the task was huge. Ann's responsibilities ranged from preparing an assessment of the ministry to working with other ministries on a program to "mainstream" a concern about gender equality into everything from planning and budgeting to evaluation. She was expected to work with local governments on a plan for improving their cooperation with the women's ministry, and she was responsible for preparing a series of reports, including a final one that would give future direction to the ministry and suggest additional projects for the development bank. In Ann's previous jobs, when money had been needed for work activities, it had been found. But this time around, that was not the case. So when Harker arrived in Jakarta a few months into the contract to conduct an interim review, Ann turned to him, in desperation, for help.

"The tears were a surprise," Harker remembered. "Who's accustomed to having a fellow professional start crying in a private meeting over a disagreement about money? It should have told me how much stress she was under. What I took from that experience was what I would take from practically anyone: This is a person who is exhausted, who is extremely frustrated, and who is struggling. To this day, I don't know if there were struggles in her personal life that made her especially concerned about the personal-expenses side of it. That was an issue that led to tears. I don't know what it was anymore—about the housing, the car, not having enough gas money. These are little things that I had long since, in my own life, paid out of my own pocket. I was taken aback by some of it."

Ann had found a small, sparsely furnished house in a *kampung,* a villagelike neighborhood within the city, where her neighbors were largely Indonesian. The street was so narrow, and space so tight, it took geometric precision for Sabaruddin to park Ann's car in its allotted space. The house had a little living room with a bedroom off it, a study, a bathroom, and a kitchen. There was room in the back for the one woman she employed as her *pembantu.* (The Indonesian word means "helper" but is variously translated as house staff, housekeeper, or servant.) Rens Heringa found the place to be "a poky, uncared-for little house" in a neighborhood very different from where Ann had lived earlier. Gillie Brown, a younger British woman whom Development Alternatives Inc. had retained in Jakarta to handle financial management and records, as well as other matters, called the house "an incredibly humble sort of place." But Ann was not like other consultants—those who spoke no Indonesian, lived in "smart houses," and relied on Brown to make arrangements. Brown felt a certain affinity with Ann, though Ann was twenty years her senior. Brown had left the United Kingdom in her mid-twenties with her husband and their three children—a three-year-old, a two-year-old, and a five-week-old baby. They had gone to live in a village in Bangladesh, then on a rice farm in southern Somalia. Trained as an engineer, she had grown accustomed to working in professional settings dominated by men. It seemed to Brown that the humble house was what Ann had wanted—to live surrounded by Indonesians, buying her food on the street. To Brown, Ann seemed to feel she had come home.

Some of Ann's oldest expatriate friends, including Nancy Peluso, had returned to the United States, but she picked up her friendships with Julia Suryakusuma, Yang Suwan, and others where she had left off. Made Suarjana, the young journalist Ann had first met in Yogyakarta in 1988, had moved by himself to Jakarta in February, though he would move with his wife and two children to Bali the following December. He saw Ann occasionally in Jakarta in 1994, he told me. When I asked him if he thought that Ann would have liked to have made a life with him, he told me she knew he was married. Her closest friends, however, did not remember Ann telling them that Suarjana had a wife. They told me they doubted that she knew—or if she did, that she must have believed the marriage was effectively over. Several, including Rens Heringa and Alice Dewey, used almost identical language in describing what Ann had told them about what had become of her relationship with Suarjana. "She told me that she felt that in the end, the difference in their ages was too large," said Heringa, who spent time with Ann in the Netherlands in late 1993 and in Jakarta in late 1994 and early 1995. "They'd had a lovely time, but she didn't want to hold him back from having a full social life in Indonesia. Because she knew she was going to leave, what was going to happen to him? She sent him away. He got married."

Late one night during the last week in November 1994, Bruce Harker, in his bed in Potomac, Maryland, received a telephone call from Ann in Jakarta. Ignoring the time difference, which she well knew, she must have felt the call could not wait. She had been having abdominal pains for some time, she told him, and the pain had become so severe at the workshop in Ciloto that she had returned to Jakarta to see a doctor. The doctor, a gynecologist at a clinic that specialized in treating expatriates, had concluded that Ann had appendicitis and had referred her to a surgeon at Pondok Indah Hospital, a high-end medical center in a wealthy neighborhood of Jakarta. Faced with the prospect of surgery, Ann was trying to decide whether to stay in Jakarta or fly to Singapore. For routine procedures, many longtime expatriates were comfortable with the best Indonesian hospitals. They did not consider themselves foreign enough to automatically mistrust Indonesian doctors. Furthermore, Ann had friends in Jakarta, as well as her *pembantu* and her driver, to help her out if she stayed. But other expatriates, and even some Indonesians, automatically went to Singapore for hospitalization, especially for anything major. Gillie Brown, who had taken her daughter to Singapore for an appendectomy, urged Ann to go there, too. "I thought she was nuts, staying in the country," Brown told me. On the other hand, Harker had once had hip surgery in Singapore, he told Ann, which had been done so badly that it was later redone in the United States. "She wanted to know whether there was airfare and accommodations for her to go to Singapore in the budget," Harker remembered. "I said, 'Look, here's the deal. We didn't budget an appendectomy. You've got health insurance, that's taken care of. We can cover the airfare. We can cover a few hundred dollars.'"

Ann chose to stay in Jakarta. On November 28, 1994, the day before her fifty-second birthday, a surgeon at Pondok Indah removed her appendix. Three days later, she returned home to recuperate in her housekeeper's care. The incision healed promptly, she would tell her insurance company in a letter some months later, but the abdominal pain returned. Her surgeon advised patience, because recovery could take several months. When the pain became too much to bear, she returned twice to the medical clinic, where she saw two internists as well as a gynecologist she had not previously seen. According to her account to the insurance company, doctors at the clinic told her she had an abdominal infection and prescribed an antibiotic. After two and a half weeks on the drug, she felt no better. Meanwhile, she had returned to work after a week of resting at home. To some friends, she said simply that her recovery was going slowly. In e-mails and conversations with Nina Nayar, she seemed unconvinced by the diagnosis. She was lethargic and weak. When she ate, she felt immediately full. A masseuse to whom she had gone for a massage declined to continue, Ann told Dewey. "What is wrong with you is serious," the masseuse warned.

On December 13, Ann met Rens Heringa at a Protestant church guesthouse in Jakarta where Heringa was staying, having arrived six days earlier on a two-month visit from the Netherlands. Ann was more distraught than Heringa had ever seen her. She was in constant pain and barely able to digest food. Weeping, she was certain that the diagnosis of appendicitis was wrong. "She said, 'I have cancer,'" Heringa told me. "I said, 'Ann, how do you know?' She said, 'Well, I feel it.'" She reminded Heringa that her father had died from cancer—as if it was contagious or inherited. Heringa tried to reassure her. She told Ann about her own six-month recovery from an appendectomy in the late 1960s in Surabaya in East Java. She encouraged Ann to get a second opinion, but Heringa tried above all to calm her down. "Listen, this is because your father just died," Heringa recalled saying. "Don't get things in your head. Have yourself diagnosed, absolutely. But try not to be carried away."

On Christmas Day, Heringa told me, she met Ann and Made Suarjana for lunch. The occasion was not festive. Ann, for whom food had always been a source of great pleasure, ate almost nothing. "She clearly was in pain," Heringa remembered. "Made was as concerned as I was. We both felt pretty helpless." Five days later, Ann made an appearance at the birthday party of Ong Hok Ham, the historian. Three weeks later, she and Heringa made a plan for lunch, which Heringa's diary showed was canceled. "Isn't it strange, though, how we continued our regular routine of meeting at restaurants, almost denying what was going on with her?" Heringa said to me, after going back over her datebook. "It looks as if she was of two minds."

In late January, Bruce Harker, in Maryland, received a second late-night call. This time, Ann sounded scared. She had had the appendectomy, she told him, and pain medication had got her through the recuperation. But the pain in her abdomen had returned with ferocity.

"How urgent is it?" Harker asked.

"Urgent," Ann said. "I've got to get out of here and go home to Hawaii."

Ann was afraid to board a flight to Honolulu without knowing that her employer would reimburse her for the cost of the ticket. At fifty-two years old, she did not have what Harker later called "the screw-you resources"—the financial freedom to do what she needed to do and take her chances. When she had asked her younger colleague Gillie Brown if the project had the money to cover the flight, Brown had referred her to Harker. By the time Ann reached him, she seemed to have made up her mind to leave. Harker understood. In that situation, a foreign resident in a place she loved would suddenly feel like she was in a world of strangers—no matter how much affection she had for the culture and the people.

"You have to do what you have to do," Harker remembered telling her. "I can't authorize you to go—that's not something I can do without doing some homework. But just because I can't authorize you to go doesn't mean you shouldn't. Between you and me, two friends talking, I can't authorize you and buy you a ticket, but if you go home, you've made the strongest possible case for being reimbursed. Plus, you'll get the care you want."

Ann slipped out of Indonesia quietly, keeping her fears to herself, for the most part. When she met with Gillie Brown to brief her on how to fill in as team leader, Ann reassured her: "You'll be fine. It'll only be a couple of weeks. I'll be back." She told Julia Suryakusuma, who had postponed a planned birthday party for Ann, that she would be returning quickly. "Don't be long," Suryakusuma said. "You promised to help me with some stuff." Ann called Made Suarjana and told him simply that she was going to Hawaii for a checkup, which seemed reasonable enough. Yang Suwan, who had planned a celebratory birthday meal with Ann, was puzzled by not being able to reach her by phone. From late November on, Yang's calls to Ann's house went unanswered. Once, a man picked up the phone and explained simply that Ann had put off her birthday. On another occasion, he said Ann was very sick, but he did not say with what. A few days after that, Yang heard that Ann was no longer in Jakarta. It seemed unlike Ann not to explain, Yang thought, but Ann had always moved within multiple but separate circles of friends. Perhaps that was how she wanted to live, Yang figured. In which case, she should respect Ann's wishes.

Rens Heringa, however, glimpsed Ann's terror. The two women had been close friends for more than a decade and had many experiences in common. Both had grown up in the West and married Indonesian men whom they had met at university. Both had followed their husbands to Indonesia, raised children there, and eventually divorced. Both were anthropologists with an interest in handicrafts, Heringa specializing in textiles. Each had visited the villages where the other had done her fieldwork. They had circles of friends in common. The afternoon before Ann left Jakarta, in a torrential downpour of the sort that besieged the city during the rainy season, Heringa took a taxi to Ann's house. To Heringa, it seemed as if the world were weeping. The little house seemed bare. There were crates, half packed for shipping. "It was horrible," Heringa told me. "We felt sure we wouldn't see each other again. She was in a bad way. This was just sad, very sad, because we had to say good-bye."

On January 25, 1995, twenty-seven years after first arriving in Indonesia with Barry to join Lolo, Ann left for the last time. Madelyn Dunham met her in Honolulu and arranged for her to be taken to the Straub Clinic and Hospital. Several days later, she was seen by a gastroenterologist, who concluded within a week that her problem was not gastrointestinal. Next, she was referred to an oncologist, who, in the second week in February, diagnosed her illness as third-stage uterine and ovarian cancer. According to her correspondence with her insurance company, the disease appeared to have spread in her abdomen. She underwent a total hysterectomy and was sent home on Valentine's Day to recuperate in Madelyn's apartment, in her care. Once Ann had recovered from the immediate effects of the surgery, she embarked on a series of six monthly chemotherapy treatments intended to, as she described it, eradicate remaining traces of the cancer and prevent further spread.

Maya, who had graduated from the University of Hawai'i with a bachelor's degree, had spent the fall of 1994 traveling in the southwestern United States and in Mexico, largely out of contact. After injuring a knee while hiking, she had spent several days in a bar at the Grand Canyon, drinking coffee and reading novels by William Faulkner, Tony Hillerman, and Ernest J. Gaines. There, in the bar and using a pencil, she had filled out an application to the graduate school of education at New York University. Several months later, in Mexico City, she had telephoned her grandmother in Honolulu and discovered that she had been accepted into a master's degree program. Moving to New York City in late December, she had found a job as a bartender to cover her rent while going to graduate school. After a week on the bartending job, she received a call from Madelyn. Ann had returned from Jakarta, Madelyn told her. The appendicitis had turned out not to be appendicitis. It was cancer.

Barack, meanwhile, was in Chicago, juggling multiple callings. At the time of his mother's diagnosis, he was three years out of law school and an associate in a Chicago law firm that specialized in civil rights cases; he was teaching part-time as a lecturer at the University of Chicago Law School; his memoir, *Dreams from My Father,* which a literary agent had encouraged him to write after the *Harvard Law Review* election, was scheduled for publication in August 1995; and he had begun maneuvering toward possibly running for public office for the first time. The indictment in August 1994 of the congressman from the Second District of Illinois, Mel Reynolds, had prompted the state senator from Obama's district, Alice Palmer, to explore a bid for Reynolds' seat. By the time Palmer announced her candidacy for Congress in June 1995, Obama had already laid the groundwork for his campaign to fill her seat. On September 19, 1995, he announced officially that he was embarking on his first political campaign—a run for election to the Illinois State Senate.

In Honolulu, Ann pressed on gamely. According to her correspondence, Barry helped her with insurance forms and letters in the immediate aftermath of her surgery. After a short time, she moved into an apartment in the same building as her mother and attempted to get back to her life. Her hair fell out, but otherwise she seemed to tolerate the treatment. She attended concerts and seminars at the university, having acquired a collection of colorful turbans and scarves. "She seemed as cheerful as ever," said Michael Dove, the anthropologist Ann had known in Java and Pakistan and who was now at the East-West Center. "She even looked the same as ever, except, I think, she'd lost her hair and was wearing a scarf." She insisted on going to a traditional Hawaiian feast known as a luau with her old friend Pete Vayda and his wife, when they arrived in Hawaii on vacation. She went on walks at Ala Moana Beach Park with the Solyoms—and with Maya when she visited. Georgia McCauley, her friend from Jakarta who was now back in Hawaii, saw her weekly. Madelyn's sister Arlene Payne telephoned regularly from North Carolina and sent books—mostly French authors, at Ann's request, notably Proust and Sartre.

Ann also continued to work. When Alice Dewey dropped by the apartment, she would find Ann at the computer. Gillie Brown sent the progress reports on the project in Jakarta for Ann to edit. Ann dispensed wise advice to Brown. Despite her youth and inexperience, Brown had been thrust by Ann's departure into the role of team leader. She was ambitious to make headway and impatient with the rigid code of female behavior inculcated by the Suharto government. In her first meeting with the state minister for the role of women, Brown received what she would later remember as a lecture on the importance of lipstick—which she was not wearing. As the daughter of a Welsh farmer, she knew that farmers looked after their cows well for a reason: Cows brought in income. It seemed to Brown that Suharto attended to the welfare of Indonesia's women like a farmer tended his herd. That was why the health and education statistics for women in Indonesia looked so good. When she would complain to Ann that nothing in Indonesia was changing, Ann would laugh. "If you can see progress on gender issues over a ten-year period, you're doing well," Ann would say. Ann's advice to the younger woman on dealing with people was unfailingly practical. "She'd always laugh first and say, 'Why don't you do it this way . . . ?'" Brown recalled. With older Indonesian women of high status, Ann suggested Brown try backing off. She could see, in a way that Brown did not, that change would eventually come. "Don't just get frustrated and unhappy," Ann seemed to be saying. Focus on where you can make a difference. Accept that progress takes time.

Quietly, Ann also emboldened Brown to examine the ground rules in her own life. Brown was a married mother of three and the "supplementary income earner" in the family—the role to which married women in Indonesia were consigned by law, Brown told me. Coming from a conservative area in West Wales, Brown felt she had pushed the barriers to their limits. To have claimed even more independence—to have wanted things for herself, such as a career and an identity independent of that of her family— would have felt selfish. Ann inspired Brown, through their telephone and e-mail discussions of the limits on the lives of Indonesian women and through her comments on Brown's reports, to reconsider her own life. "I think Ann was, in the subtlest of ways, trying to say, 'Well, actually, you have these constraints in your own life . . .'" Brown told me. "I think there was a mutual respect in trying to live our lives differently. She was sort of saying, 'There's more: There's you.'"

Ann's compensation for her job in Jakarta had included health insurance, which covered most of the costs of her medical treatment. She had even had a physical in order to qualify—an examination she said had required six separate office visits in Jakarta. Once she was back in Hawaii, the hospital billed her insurance company directly, leaving Ann to pay only the deductible and any uncovered expenses, which, she said, came to several hundred dollars a month. To cover those charges as well as living expenses, she filed a separate claim under her employer's disability insurance policy. That policy, however, contained a clause allowing the company to deny any claim related to a preexisting medical condition. If, during the three months before starting work, a patient had seen a doctor or been treated for the condition that caused the disability for which they later wanted coverage, the insurance company would not compensate the patient for lost pay.

In late April, a representative of the insurance company, CIGNA, notified Ann that the company had begun evaluating her disability claim. (According to CIGNA, the disability policy was underwritten by Life Insurance Company of North America, a subsidiary of CIGNA.) In the meantime, the representative suggested that Ann find out if she was eligible for benefits under the Social Security system. Ann had already been told by Social Security Administration officials in Honolulu that she was not eligible: She had not earned enough credits in the previous ten years to be eligible for Social Security disability income, and she was ineligible for benefits under the Supplemental Security Income program for disabled people with limited resources because she owned an asset worth more than $2,000, an Individual Retirement Account. In response to the letter from CIGNA, Ann sent back copies of letters from the Social Security Administration and a half-dozen other documents that CIGNA had requested, along with a four-page letter that included a detailed chronology of her illness. "During the three months before joining DAI, the only doctor I consulted was Dr. Barbara Shortle, a New York gynecologist," Ann wrote in the letter. "Dr. Shortle gave me a routine annual examination in May 1994, including pap smear and pelvic exam. She sent me to a laboratory for a mammogram and pelvic ultrasound. On the advice of the radiologist of the laboratory, I also had a breast ultrasound. None of these tests indicated that I had cancer. The pelvic examination indicated that I had an enlarged uterus, but this is a condition which I had had for about five years previously."

Ann's letter did not mention the one procedure, the dilation and curettage, she had omitted to have.

By late June, CIGNA had made no decision on Ann's disability claim. The company was waiting to hear from Shortle, a representative told Ann. Ann faxed a letter to Shortle, whom she had not seen since her appointment thirteen months earlier. She explained that she was being treated for ovarian cancer in Hawaii and that her disability claim had been held up for months while CIGNA investigated whether her cancer was a preexisting condition. She said she had given Shortle's name to CIGNA, which, in turn, had faxed Shortle a request for information. Two weeks later, CIGNA sent another letter to Ann, addressed this time to "Mr." Dunham. Among other things, the letter said, "If we do not receive either the requested information or some communication from you within 30 days from the date of this letter, we will assume you are no longer claiming benefits under your Long Term Disability Plan."

In one of several drafts of a response to CIGNA, Ann coolly leveled a pointed objection.

> Since I have sent you a mountain of forms and a lengthy letter dealing with my illness, which is ovarian cancer, I am surprised that you are not aware that I am a woman. I realize that it is unusual for a woman to have a man's first name, but I have signed my correspondence to you with my middle name of Ann. Also we have spoken by phone within the last month. Combined with the fact that my claim has been pending for five months, I am forced to wonder whether it is receiving proper attention.

In mid-August, CIGNA denied Ann's claim on the basis of her visit to the New York gynecologist two and a half months before she started work in Jakarta. Shortle's office notes had indicated that she had formed a working hypothesis of uterine cancer, though Ann said Shortle never discussed that hypothesis with her. When I spoke with Shortle, she said it was quite possible that she had not told Ann of her suspicions. "Whenever you do a D and C on any woman who has bleeding on and off, you're always doing it to rule out uterine cancer," she said. But, she said, the procedure can be therapeutic as well as diagnostic. She might not, at that point, tell a patient her thinking.

Ann requested a review of the denial and informed CIGNA that she was turning over the case to "my son and attorney, Barack Obama." Years later, during the presidential campaign and even after his election, Obama would allude to his mother's experience, albeit in an abbreviated form, when making the case for health care reform. Though he often suggested that she was denied health coverage because of a preexisting condition, it appears from her correspondence that she was only denied disability coverage.

Ann, characteristically, had hoped for the best. If all went well, the chemotherapy would be completed by the end of August, after which it would take two months for the side effects to abate. "Then, assuming that I go into remission and there is no recurrence of the disease, I should be able to return to work in November," she had written to CIGNA in May. Because she would need monitoring and regular blood tests, it would be difficult to take a long-term overseas assignment again. "Instead, I plan to do short-term assignments for DAI which will allow me to return to Hawaii for checkups in between," she wrote.

When friends called on the telephone, Ann often sidestepped the subject of her illness. In a series of conversations with Madelyn's youngest brother, Jon Payne, they sparred jokingly for the title of black sheep of the family, wondering why they had allowed themselves to fall so far out of touch. To Made Suarjana, calling from Bali, Ann insisted she was fine. He began to notice, however, that her voice sounded different. Slamet Riyadi, a colleague from Bank Rakyat Indonesia, was uncomfortable even asking about her health. Instead, he told her he would pray for her. Dick Patten came away from one telephone conversation believing that Ann had beaten the cancer. Julia Suryakusuma received a letter from Ann, which she allowed herself to understand, only later, had been intended to let her know that her friend was dying. When Rens Heringa called from Los Angeles on a visit from the Netherlands, Ann implored her to fly to Hawaii, but Heringa could not. Ann made it clear to Heringa that she knew she would never get better. Why was she forcing herself to continue with chemotherapy? Heringa wondered. Ann refused to give up hope. "Even when she knew she was seriously ill, it was probably not a matter of denial but really believing she was not ready to die," Suryakusuma said.

Ann Hawkins, whom Ann had first met fifteen years earlier in the mountains above Semarang on the north coast of Java, understood that Ann was extremely ill. With some people, Ann seemed to keep the conversation light so she could think about happier things, Hawkins told me. But she spoke honestly with Hawkins. "She didn't really talk about her life," Hawkins remembered. "Except that I always had the sense that Ann felt very privileged. She felt, yeah, of course her life was cut short. But at the same time she had an extraordinary life. . . . And I think she knew that. I think she *showed* it, in how she treated other people. She felt such abundance— that's the word—in not only her own life but life all around."

Hawkins extended her arms out in front of her, palms turned upward.

"I see Ann sort of like this, with her hands out, giving," she said. It was a gesture, she said, of generosity, perceptiveness, and compassion.

In early September, Ann said good-bye to her friend Georgia McCauley, whom she had known since her days at the Ford Foundation with McCauley's husband, David. In their weekly visits over the previous months, the two women had talked often about their children, rarely about Ann's illness. Now the McCauleys were moving. "It was difficult, because we both sort of knew that we wouldn't be seeing each other," Georgia McCauley remembered. Ann indicated that she believed Barack would be fine: He was happy, and Ann thought Michelle would be a good partner. "She was just worried about Maya," McCauley remembered. "'Will you take care of Maya? Keep an eye out for Maya.'

"She was saying something pretty profound," McCauley told me. "But it was sort of like the end of a conversation, as you're leaving. Nobody wants to face the obvious."

Ann had told McCauley many times that she did not want her children to see her in the state she was in. But in the weeks that followed, McCauley said, "I often wondered, maybe I should have called Barry and bugged him. I asked Maya to talk to him. I said, 'You all need to realize that it's going to happen fairly soon.' But I didn't know him well enough. I just thought it was kind of presumptuous for me to tell him what to do. I know they spoke. It's a difficult issue to deal with."

In mid-September, Ann and Madelyn flew to New York City for a series of appointments at Memorial Sloan-Kettering Cancer Center, widely considered the most respected cancer center in the country. An oncologist at Sloan-Kettering had agreed to give Ann a second opinion. Maya, working full-time as a student teacher while in graduate school, met her mother and grandmother at La-

Guardia Airport. Ann emerged from the terminal in a wheelchair, looking dazed and startled. Madelyn, a month away from her seventy-third birthday, was suffering from severe back pain. They were carrying with them Ann's medical records, X-rays, and tumor slides. They settled into the Barbizon Hotel on the East Side of Manhattan, near the hospital. Barack, back from his book tour and one week away from announcing his candidacy for the Illinois State Senate, arrived from Chicago with Michelle. At the first of two appointments at Sloan-Kettering, Ann was given a physical examination; she turned over the records to the doctor and the tumor slides for reevaluation by the pathology department. Then she returned to the hotel to wait.

Maya and Ann walked in Central Park, bought frozen yogurt, wandered among the glittering displays of smoked fish and cheeses at Zabar's, the legendary food store on Broadway on the Upper West Side. They watched a movie of no particular interest to either one of them, Maya sitting next to her mother, holding her hand. When it was over, Maya asked Ann what she thought of the movie. It was a good distraction, she said, from the turmoil inside. Years later, Maya would remember her uncertainty about how best to help her mother—whether to encourage her to talk about what she was feeling or simply to be with her. If she could just get through the semester at New York University and at the school where she was teaching, Maya thought, she could fly home to Hawaii and stay with her mother as long as she was needed.

On September 15, 1995, the oncologist saw Ann for a second time. On the basis of the reevaluation of the tumor cells and the pattern of the illness, he believed Ann's cancer was uterine, not ovarian, and stage four, not stage three. He recommended that Ann's physician in Honolulu switch to a chemotherapy regimen based on a different drug, Adriamycin, or doxorubicin. The survival rate for women in Ann's condition was poor, he said, and sixty percent of patients did not respond positively to the drug he was suggesting. But if it worked, Ann might hope for a delay in recurrence and a period relatively free of symptoms.

Back in Honolulu, the new treatment proved grueling. Arlene Payne's conversations with her niece became shorter and shorter. Ann had never been inclined toward regrets. If she regretted anything now, it was not having left Indonesia sooner to get medical care, Payne told me. "But she fought it for as long as she could. Then she sort of gave up and just sort of lived out the rest of her life." The United Nations Fourth World Conference on Women in Beijing came and went. From the point of view of Women's World Banking, it had gone well. Much of the language hammered out in the report of the expert group on women and finance, in which Ann had played a central role, had been incorporated into the action plan endorsed by the delegates in Beijing. Hillary Rodham Clinton, then the First Lady, had spoken on a panel on microfinance that Women's World Banking had helped organize. For the first time, microfinance seemed to have emerged front and center in the world's attention. Nina Nayar, Ann's young protégée from Women's World Banking, returned from China via India, then flew to Honolulu to see Ann. Ann's mane of dark hair was gone. But she was ornamented, as always, for the occasion. "The turban becomes you," Nayar marvelled affectionately. "I think it's even more majestic." As Nayar recalled that visit, she and Garrett Solyom hoisted Ann into a wheelchair and set off on one last field trip. After all, it was Nayar's first visit to Hawaii. They picnicked at sunset and tried Ann's favorite Hawaiian foods. At Ann's insistence, they made their way up to the Nuʻuanu Pali State Wayside, where the trade winds climb the windward cliff of what remains of the Koʻolau volcano and roar through the Pali Pass as though through a funnel. There, not far from the tunnels that carry traffic through the mountain and from one side of Oʻahu to the other, there is a panoramic view of the green Nuʻuanu Valley, Kaneohe Bay, and the beach town of Kailua. Struggling with the wheelchair against the wind and trying to keep Ann's headgear from taking flight, Nayar remembered, she and Solyom maneuvered Ann into the optimal spot. "It was the same feeling as we had on top of the pyramid," Nayar said. "It was probably a parting gift for both of us."

In early November, during a collect call to her mother on a pay phone near the NYU campus, Maya noticed that Ann sounded momentarily confused.

"You know what, Mom?" she later recalled saying. "I'm coming. I'll work it out. I'll do whatever papers I have left. I'm coming. I'll see you there very soon.'

"She said, 'Okay,'" Maya remembered. "And I told her I was scared. And she said, 'Me, too.' And then, 'I love you.'

"And that was it."

On November 7, Maya flew to Honolulu, unsure of what she would find. Ann was unconscious and emaciated. To Maya, she appeared to be starving. But she was alive, as though she had waited. Maya took Madelyn's place by Ann's bed in the hospital room so that her grandmother could go home. Then she talked— about all that Ann had given her, about how she would be remembered with love. Maya had brought with her a book of Creole folktales, which she had been reading with her students as part of a study of origin myths. She began reading aloud. In one story, a person was transformed into a bird. Then the bird took flight.

"I told her finally that she should go, that I didn't want to see her like that," Maya remembered. "And she was gone about fifteen minutes later."

For Barack, not being at his mother's bedside when she died was the biggest mistake he made, he would say later. He was at home in Chicago when he got word. He had last seen Ann in New York City in September, and had last spoken to her, he told me, several days before her death, before she lost consciousness. "She was in Hawaii in a hospital, and we didn't know how fast it was going to take, and I didn't get there in time," he told the *Chicago Sun-Times* in 2004.

Word spread quickly. Dick Patten got the news in Burma, where he was working on a project for the United Nations Development Programme—trying to help the Burmese people, as he would later put it, without helping the Burmese government. Don Johnston, whom Ann had discreetly nudged into domestic happiness, got the news in Indonesia in the field. Made Suarjana, at his typewriter in his office in Bali, wept when Maya called. In a private ceremony, he told me, his family offered prayers to help deliver Ann's spirit to the next world. In Colorado, Jon Payne asked the priest in his church to include his niece in the congregation's prayers. After all, as far as Payne could tell, Ann had been doing what Christians always said saints did—helping people. "She wasn't a particularly religious person, if at all," Payne said. "But she did more things for people than a lot of Christians do."

In Jakarta, Julia Suryakusuma made an impromptu altar out of a table and a Balinese mirror in the living room of Gillie Brown's house on Jalan Gaharu in Cilandak. She placed a photograph of Ann in the center, along with candles, flowers, wood carvings, ikat, and traditional Indonesian cookies and cakes. Like an offering, Suryakusuma told me. She sent around flyers announcing a memorial gathering for Ann. On the afternoon of November 13, two dozen friends turned out. There was a period of silence, followed by a guided meditation, with music, led by an Australian yogi ("a lot of stuff that Ann privately laughed at," Don Johnston told me, chuckling). Wahyono Martowikrido, the archaeologist who had helped introduce Ann to the mysteries and meaning of the patterns in Javanese textiles and the shapes of silver jewelry, and Johnston, the Southern Baptist from Little Rock, Arkansas, were there. So was Ong Hok Ham, the historian, and Yang Suwan, the anthropologist, and several Indonesian women who had tried to start an Indonesian affiliate of Women's World Banking. There were women from Ann's team at the Ministry for the Role of Women. There were messages sent by Bruce Harker; Sabaruddin, Ann's driver; and others. After the guided meditation, Ann's friends regaled one another with memories of and stories about her. When everyone had drifted away, Gillie Brown sat down and wrote a letter to Madelyn, Barack, and Maya in Hawaii, listing everyone who had turned out in Jakarta. "The spirits of all these people will be with you in Hawaii today, as you say your farewells to Ann," she wrote.

In Honolulu, they gathered in the Japanese garden behind the East-West Center, the institution that embodied, more than any other, the spirit of the time in which Ann had come of age and the values by which she had lived. They convened near the stream, whose rambling course beneath the monkeypod trees was intended to signify the progress of a life. The group of several dozen included Madelyn Dunham, Maya and Barack, Michelle, Alice Dewey, the Solyoms, Nancy Peluso, Ann Hawkins, Michael Dove, Benji Bennington, and others—close friends from graduate school, the East-West Center, Jakarta, Yogyakarta, Semarang, Pakistan, and New York. They, too, recounted recollections of Ann. Then they drove east out of Honolulu to the Kalaniana'ole Highway, the road that winds along the wind-whipped southeastern coast of the island of O'ahu. They followed it, past the turnoff for Hanauma

Bay, to where the coastline turns wilder and great slabs of rock tilt toward the indigo water. At a scenic lookout, they parked and got out. Beyond a low wall built of volcanic rock, the ledges descended toward a distant point the shape of an ironing board jutting into the surf. There, gripping each other against the wind, Barack and Maya carried the ashes of their fifty-two-year-old mother across the water-slicked rocks and delivered them into the rough embrace of the sea.

Epilogue

I n the aftermath of her death, the heirs of Bu Ann set their sights on the horizon.

Kellee Tsai, who had left Women's World Banking for graduate school with Ann's encouragement, spent two years doing fieldwork in China. She wrote a five-hundred-page dissertation and became a professor of political science and director of East Asian Studies at Johns Hopkins University. But she prided herself on being a closet anthropologist, combining in her work large statistical analyses with hundreds of interviews in the field; she had learned from Ann the impossibility of understanding the numbers before talking to and knowing the people. In China, she met an American whom she married and with whom she now has two children. In her dissertation, she wrote that the memory of Ann, along with that of another friend, "followed me into the field and back. Both would have scrutinized every page, footnote, and table in this dissertation."

For Nina Nayar, Ann's assistant at Women's World Banking, it was time to break out of the role of the good Indian daughter. "Losing Ann was a big moment where you say, 'Well, life is short,'" Nayar remembered. "'You have to do what you want to do now.'" After nearly twenty years abroad, Nayar decided—against the advice of her family, she told me—to base her life in Asia, not in the United States. It was not easy to return to India as a single woman of marrying age with relatives around. "This is the influence that Ann had," Nayar said. "She didn't do the stuff that her parents or community thought was appropriate." Nayar spent two years in Bangladesh, working on building a virtual microfinance network, and much of the next three years in Cambodia as a consultant in microfinance sector development. When she and I first spoke in 2008, Nayar was in Kabul, having turned her attention to the role of microfinance in countries recovering from conflict. By mid-2010, she had worked in nearly thirty countries, mostly in Africa and Asia. She had also abandoned her resolve to remain single. Instead, she had married a man whose values reminded her of Ann's. She was certain, she said, that Ann would have approved.

Gillie Brown, Ann's colleague in Jakarta, was hired by the World Bank in 1996 on the strength of the work she had done as Ann's replacement on the project to strengthen the State Ministry for the Role of Women. By the time Suharto fell in 1998 and the World Bank staff was evacuated from Indonesia, Brown was already planning to resign and rejoin her husband and children, who had returned earlier to Great Britain. But when the bank offered her a job in Washington, she surprised herself by accepting. She left her children in Britain with her husband. She would never have considered a step like that, she told me, if she had not known Ann.

Maybe there was more than one way to be a good mother after all, she thought. Ann's children seemed to have done okay.

Maya, who was twenty-five when her mother died, immersed herself in the profession of her Kansas forebears. She went to work in a new school on the Lower East Side of Manhattan that served a largely poor and Latino population. The staff was young, the work demanding, the learning curve steep. She accompanied her students to museums in upper Manhattan to widen their horizons, and to the city jail on Rikers Island, in a few cases, to visit their parents. Near the end of each pay period, she would rummage through her coat pockets for money to cover her commute. Immediately after Ann's death, Maya had wondered fleetingly if she should remain in Hawaii and help her grandmother. "Then I thought, 'Oh, gosh, Mom wouldn't have wanted that,'" she told me. "'I'm twenty-five years old. It's time for me to really grow up.'"

Several years earlier, Maya had told Ann that she was thinking of getting married. At the time, she was five years older than Ann had been when she had married Barack Obama Sr. Maya was working toward a master's degree, but she had barely begun a career. According to Maya, Ann advised her to wait. If marriage was what she really wanted, she should do it, Ann said. But she should know herself well enough to know who would satisfy her for the duration. Women have choices, Ann reminded her. They had gone through the women's movement, she said, yet they continued to act as if they had no options. They needed to ask themselves what they really wanted, then go out and get it.

"She was reminding me that it was okay to want to do things differently," Maya told me. "Which was, I thought, very enlightened."

In 2002, Maya met her future husband at the East-West Center.

Konrad Ng, a Chinese-Canadian graduate student in political science, shared an office at the center with Maya's martial-arts instructor. Maya, who had moved back to Honolulu several years earlier to help her grandmother, was teaching at a charter school and at the university while working toward a Ph.D. The following year, Maya and Konrad Ng married. After the birth of their first child, Maya dispatched her own dissertation—writing between the hours of ten p.m. and two a.m., she told me—and received her Ph.D. She began teaching history and doing curriculum development at a girls' school, where she developed a class in peace education. She started writing books, including one for children, *Ladder to the Moon,* in which Ann appears one night to Maya's elder daughter, Suhaila, and takes her up a golden ladder to the moon.

"What was Grandma Annie like?" Suhaila asks her mother in the story.

"She was like the moon," her mother replies. "Full, soft, and curious."

Barack, meanwhile, was elected to the Illinois State Senate in November 1996, one year after his mother's death. The original edition of *Dreams from My Father,* which was published in 1995 and sold approximately nine thousand copies in hardcover, came out in paperback the following year and went out of print. Obama ran unsuccessfully for Congress in 2000, then won the Democratic primary for the U.S. Senate in March 2004. Four months later, he gave the keynote speech at the Democratic National Convention in Boston—the speech that laid out, for millions of Americans for the first time, his father and mother's story and made him into a national political sensation almost overnight.

The news traveled swiftly among people who had once known Ann.

"Did you watch the Democratic convention?" a former student

of Alice Dewey's wrote in an e-mail to Nancy Cooper, an anthropologist and former Dewey student herself.

"Yes, I did," Cooper answered.

"Did you see that guy who gave the keynote speech?"

"Yes."

"You know who that is?"

"No, I don't."

"It's Barry. Ann's Barry."

Ann's friend from Mercer Island, John Hunt, had happened on the connection years earlier in the frequent-flyer lounge at Los Angeles International Airport on the day the *Los Angeles Times* published its two-thousand-word profile of the first black president of the *Harvard Law Review.* In Yogyakarta, Djaka Waluja and Sumarni, Ann's former field assistants, had no idea what had become of Barry until a photograph of him with Ann, Lolo, and Maya turned up on Indonesian television in a report on Obama during the presidential campaign in 2008. When Linda Wylie, another Mercer Island classmate of Ann's, had the connection pointed out by a friend after the 2004 convention speech, she went looking for a copy of Obama's book. The resemblance between Obama and his mother seemed unmistakable.

"The minute I saw the picture, I felt like crying," Wylie said.

Beyond the physical resemblance, people who had known Ann well were certain they recognized the imprint of her values, her confidence, her intelligence, on her son. There were even traces of her dry humor. Many remembered her pride in him and wished she could have seen his success. Some wondered what she would have made of his choice to go into politics. Nancy Cooper remembered, sometime later, an exchange between herself and Ann during the 1988 presidential election campaign. The Reverend Jesse Jackson, running for the Democratic nomination, had given a speech at the University of Hawai'i —a speech that Cooper had attended. When she and Ann talked about it, Cooper was struck by Ann's excitement about Jackson and his multiracial Rainbow Coalition. Ann seemed, Cooper told me, "to have some sort of insider knowledge." When Cooper asked her about it, Ann told Cooper, for the first time, that her son's father was African. "Then, for me, it was as if a light went on," Cooper told me. "Up till that point, everything I knew about her was associated with Java. . . . In that moment, she was just really enthusiastic about Jackson's campaign. It was almost as if she knew Jesse Jackson."

Two months after Obama's 2004 speech in Boston, the Crown Publishing Group reissued *Dreams from My Father,* and it became an instant bestseller. The editor of the new edition had asked Obama to write a short preface, bringing his story up to date. In it, Obama briskly summarized what had happened in his life and in the world in the years since the book had first appeared in the summer of 1995, while Ann was dying. He ended the preface on the memory of his mother, "the single constant in my life."

> In my daughters I see her every day, her joy, her capacity for wonder. I won't try to describe how deeply I mourn her passing still. I know that she was the kindest, most generous spirit I have ever known, and that what is best in me I owe to her.

When we met in July 2010, Obama was eighteen months into his term as president. It had been a scorching summer. The administration had been taken up with the war in Afghanistan, the biggest oil spill in history, an economic recovery that felt fitful at best. That morning, however, Obama had signed into law a major overhaul of the financial regulatory system, the product of a series of reforms he had proposed thirteen months earlier. By the time he settled into a chair in the Oval Office that afternoon, he seemed downright buoyant. He spoke about his mother with fondness, humor, and a degree of candor that I had not expected. There was also in his tone at times a hint of gentle forbearance. Perhaps it was the tone of someone whose patience had been tested, by a person he loved, to the point where he had stepped back to a safer distance. Or perhaps it was the knowingness of a grown child seeing his parent as irredeemably human.

"She was a very strong person in her own way," Obama said, when I asked about Ann's limitations as a mother. "Resilient, able to bounce back from setbacks, persistent—the fact that she ended up finishing her dissertation. But despite all those strengths, she was not a well-organized person. And that disorganization, you know, spilled over. Had it not been for my grandparents, I think, providing some sort of safety net financially, being able to take me and my sister on at certain spots, I think my mother would have had to make some different decisions. And I think that sometimes she took for granted that, 'Well, it'll all work out and it'll be fine.' But the fact is, it might not always have been fine, had it not been for my grandmother, who was a much more orderly and much more conservative—I don't mean politically but conservative in terms of how you structure your life—a much more conventional person. Had she not been there to provide that floor, I think our young lives could have been much more chaotic than they were."

Disorganized, I observed, could mean almost anything—from a messy house to a messy life.

"All of the above," he said.

As a child, the president went on to say, he did not care that his mother was uninterested in housekeeping or cooking or traditional homemaker activities. In fact, she used to joke about that. But in her handling of financial matters, he said, she put herself in vulnerable positions and was "always at the margins." He ascribed the struggle over her insurance at the end of her life to "the fact that she'd never make a decision about a job based on did it provide health insurance benefits that were stable and secure, or a pension, or savings or things like that." Her neglect of those details was a source of tension between her and her parents, "because they always felt they had to kind of come in and provide assistance to smooth over some of her choices."

But he did not, he said, hold his mother's choices against her. Part of being an adult is seeing your parents in the round, "as people who have their own strengths, weaknesses, quirks, longings." He did not believe, he said, that parents served their children well by being unhappy. If his mother had cramped her spirit, it would not have given him a happier childhood. As it was, she gave him the single most important gift a parent can give—"a sense of unconditional love that was big enough that, with all the surface disturbances of our lives, it sustained me, entirely." People wonder about his calm and even-keeled manner, the president observed. He credited the temperament he was born with and the fact that "from a very early age, I always felt I was loved and that my mother thought I was special."

Looking back, he said, many of his life choices were informed by her example. His decision to go into public service, he said, grew out of values she instilled—"a sense that the greatest thing you can do in the world is to help somebody else, be kind, think about issues like poverty and how can you give people a greater opportunity? . . . So I have no doubt that a lot of my career choices are rooted in her and what she thought was important." On the other hand, his decision to settle in Chicago, to marry a woman with roots in the city, and to place a premium on giving stability to his children was in part a reaction to "the constant motion that was my childhood. And some of it wasn't necessarily a rejection of her, it was just an observation about me and how I fit in, or didn't fit in, in certain environments.

"My mother lived a classic expatriate life, and there are aspects of that life that are very appealing," Obama said, going on to characterize his mother's life in a way that seemed perhaps to understate the depth and seriousness of her commitment to Indonesia. "Both my sister and I, I think, to one degree or another, wrestle with the fact that it's fun to just take off and live in a new culture and meet interesting people and learn new languages and eat strange foods. You know, it's a life full of adventure. So the appeal of that is very powerful to me. Now, the flip side of that is that you're always a little bit of an outsider, you're always a little bit of an observer. There's an element of you're not fully committed to this place and this thing. It's not so much, I think, me rejecting what she did; I understood the appeal of it, and I still do. But it was a conscious choice, I think, on my part, that the idea of being a citizen of the world, but without any real anchor, had both its benefits but also its own limits.

"Either way, you were giving something up. And I chose to give up this other thing—partly because I'd gotten what my mother had provided when I was young, which was a lot of adventure and a great view of the world."

Was there a moment during the campaign or the election, I wondered, when his mind turned to his mother—the person who had given him the values, the self-confidence, and the life story that became the foundation of his extraordinary political rise?

"I'm sure there were a number of moments," he said. "But there was one. . . ."

It was January 3, 2008, the night of the Iowa caucuses, the first major step in the nominating process for the presidency.

"We had been thirty points down in the national polls," he said. "Everybody was doubting that we could pull something off. And our whole theory in the Iowa caucuses was that we could create this whole new group of caucus-goers—people who hadn't been involved in politics before, people who had become cynical and disaffected about politics. There were doubts, obviously, that an African-American candidate would get the votes in an overwhelmingly white state. And so, caucus night, you go to this caucus site and you see just these people sort of streaming in. And they're all kinds of folks, right? Young, old, black, white, Hispanic—this is Des Moines."

Obama began to chuckle at the memory of that night, his face breaking into a broad smile.

"There was one guy who looked like Gandalf," he continued. "He had a staff. He had installed a little video monitor—I still don't know how he did this—that looped one of my TV commercials on this thing. You know, had a long white beard and stuff? But the mood and the atmosphere was one of hope and this sense that we can overcome a lot of the old baggage. So it was a wonderful moment. At that point, we figured we were going to win that night.

"But I remember driving away from that caucus and thinking not, 'Wouldn't my mother be proud of me,' but rather, 'Wouldn't she have enjoyed *being in* this caucus.' It would have just felt like she was right at home. It was imbued with her spirit in a way that was very touching to me. I teared up at that point, in a way that I didn't in most of the campaign. Because it just seemed to somehow capture something that she had given to me as a young person—and here it was manifest in a really big way. It seemed to vindicate what she had believed in and who she was."

Could he say what it was about that evening that seemed so consistent with her spirit? I asked.

"It was a sense that beneath our surface differences, we're all the same, and that there's more good than bad in each of us. And that, you know, we can reach across the void and touch each other and believe in each other and work together.

"That's precisely the naiveté and idealism that was part of her," he added. "And that's, I suppose, the naive idealism in me."

Acknowledgments

I began working on this book in the late spring of 2008, before Barack Obama was the Democratic presidential nominee. At a time when it might not have seemed reasonable to do so, many people trusted me and gave me the benefit of the doubt. In the text and the endnotes, I've credited the nearly two hundred people who took the time to help me understand my subject. To some of them, I owe an extra debt of gratitude for additional acts of generosity and kindness; there are other people, too, who helped me in different ways. I wish to thank them here.

First and foremost, there is Ann Dunham's family. I could not have begun to understand her childhood and the lives of her parents without the cooperation and openness of Charles Payne, Arlene Payne, Jon Payne, and Ralph Dunham. I do not underestimate the magnitude of what I asked of Maya Soetoro-Ng, whose memories and insights were a gift, bestowed with a graceful balance of candor, loyalty, and discretion. I am indebted, too, to her brother for having made the time to talk with me in the White House and for the frankness and feeling with which he did it.

In Hawaii, Alice Dewey, an inspiration to generations of anthropologists, shared with me her infectious passion for Java, her wide-ranging wisdom, and countless letters and papers. Garrett and Bron Solyom gave me access to Ann's field notebooks and other papers, meticulously archived by Bron. They fed me, gave me a place to work, and explained mysteries of Java that they surely doubted I would ever comprehend. Marguerite Robinson, in Brookline, Massachusetts, gave me a brilliant tutorial in the development of microfinance in Indonesia, as well as invaluable introductions to her former colleagues at Bank Rakyat Indonesia.

In Jakarta, I am especially thankful to Agus Rachmadi of Bank Rakyat Indonesia for serving as my guide to the bank, and to Kamardy Arief, the former chief executive officer. Made Suarjana took time away from his job to travel from East Kalimantan to Yogyakarta and spend several days with me there and in Kajar and other villages where Ann worked. Julia Suryakusuma shared with me her wonderfully illuminating correspondence with Ann. John McGlynn, the American writer and translator of Indonesian literature, took me on an unforgettable walk through one of the last neighborhoods that resemble Jakarta as Ann found it in 1967. Taluki Sasmitarsi accompanied me to villages and markets, and took me all over Yogyakarta on the backseat of her motorbike.

Kris Hartadi, pressed into service at the last minute after another translator was quarantined in Singapore during the H1N1 pandemic, did two consecutive days of simultaneous interpreting in Yogyakarta. Tita Suhartono and Yan Matius in Jakarta helped with research and gave me invaluable practical advice. In the United States, Alan M. Stevens, one of the two coauthors of *A*

Comprehensive Indonesian-English Dictionary, generously translated documents, proofread my manuscript, and enlightened me about such things as Indonesian orthography and honorifics.

At the Ford Foundation in New York, Tony Maloney and Marcy Goldstein made it possible for me to read dozens of grant files in the foundation's archives. In Kansas, Kim Baker combed the public record for clues to the lives of Ann Dunham's forebears. Michael J. Rosenfeld, author of *The Age of Independence: Interracial Unions, Same-Sex Unions, and the Changing American Family* (Harvard University Press, 2007), supplied me with statistics on interracial marriage. In New York, Steven Rattazzi kept my computer running and made my manuscript look flawless. Catherine Talese secured permission to use certain photographs. Jill Bokor and Sandy Smith made available a serene and sunlit aerie in which to write.

At *The New York Times,* Bill Keller, Jill Abramson, and Dick Stevenson gave me the opportunity to write at length about Barack Obama, starting in the spring of 2007, not long after he declared his candidacy, and continuing for a year. Rebecca Corbett, who edited those articles, did not flinch when I proposed a detour to consider the candidate's mom. On the basis of that article, Sarah McGrath at Riverhead Books proposed a book on Ann, and Riverhead gave me the time and the means to research her life in depth. Sarah proved to be as incisive and supportive an editor as one could possibly hope. I am grateful to Geoff Kloske at Riverhead, and to Sarah Stein. Scott Moyers of the Wylie Agency inspired utter confidence that nothing could go awry. Arthur Gelb, the former managing editor of *The New York Times,* encouraged the project from its very beginning.

Mia and Owen Ritter, who have taught me much of what little

I understand about being a mother, tolerated my absences, took an interest in my work, and provided joy and comic relief. As for Joe Lelyveld, to whom I am indebted in too many ways to count, I will say here simply that he gave me unfailingly wise advice, perfectly grilled sardines, great happiness, and best of all, himself.

Notes

Works cited in brief in the Notes are cited in full in the Bibliography.

PROLOGUE

Page

6 *modernized the spelling:* The spelling of certain Indonesian words changed after Indonesia gained its independence from the Dutch in 1949, and again under a 1972 agreement between Indonesia and Malaysia. *Dj,* as in Djakarta, was replaced with *J,* as in Jakarta. The letter *J,* as in Jogjakarta, became *Y,* as in Yogyakarta. Names containing *oe,* such as Soeharto, are now often spelled with a *u,* as in Suharto. However, older spellings are still used in some personal names. Both "Soeharto" and "Suharto" are used for the name of the former president of Indonesia. After her divorce from Lolo Soetoro, Ann Dunham Soetoro kept his last name for a number of years while she was still working in Indonesia, but she changed the spelling to Sutoro. Their daughter, Maya Soetoro-Ng, chose to keep the traditional spelling of her Indonesian surname.

7 *"the single constant":* Barack Obama, *Dreams from My Father,* xii.

7 *put those values to work:* Barack Obama, *The Audacity of Hope,* 205–206.

8 *"I gave you an interesting life":* Interview with President Obama, July 21, 2010.

CHAPTER ONE. DREAMS FROM THE PRAIRIE

For the history of Kansas, I am indebted to Craig Miner, a professor of history at Wichita State University, and to his book, *Kansas: The History of the Sunflower State, 1854–2000.* For the history of Butler County, I received invaluable help from Lisa Cooley, the curator of education at the Butler County History Center and Kansas Oil Museum in El Dorado, and from Jay M. Price, an associate professor of history at Wichita State University and the author of *El Dorado: Legacy of an Oil Boom.* I benefited by reading *Augusta, Kansas 1868–1990,* by Burl Allison

Jr., in the Augusta public library, and an unpublished paper, "The Klan in Butler County," by Roxie Olmstead, on file in the Butler County History Center library. Kim Baker, a researcher based in Topeka, combed newspaper archives and public records for the history of the Dunham and Payne families. Most of what I have written about the early lives of Stanley Dunham and Madelyn Payne came from long interviews with his brother, Ralph Dunham, and her siblings, Charles, Arlene, and Jon Payne. A cousin of the Paynes, Margaret McCurry Wolf, also helped me with family history. Clarence Kerns, Mack Gilkeson, and Virginia Ewalt, contemporaries of Stanley Dunham and Madelyn Payne, helped me understand the place and time in which they grew up. Ian Dunham, the grandson of Ralph Dunham, gave me valuable guidance.

17 *grasshoppers blanketed the ground:* Burl Allison Jr., *Augusta, Kansas 1868–1990* (Hillsboro, KS: Multi Business Press, 1993).

18 *planted with kaffir corn:* Jay M. Price, *El Dorado: Legacy of an Oil Boom.*

26 *"dabbling in moonshine, cards, and women":* Barack Obama, *Dreams from My Father*, 14.

30 *campaign weakened the Klan:* Jack Wayne Traylor, "William Allen White's 1924 Gubernatorial Campaign," *Kansas Historical Quarterly,* 42, no. 2, 180–191.

37 *"'He looks like a wop'":* Obama, *Dreams from My Father,* 14.

41 *The transformation had begun:* Martin Shingler, "Bette Davis Made Over in Wartime: The Feminization of an Androgynous Star in *Now, Voyager* (1942)," *Film History,* 20 (2008), 269–280.

42 *"One of Gramps's less judicious ideas":* Obama, *Dreams from My Father,* 19.

CHAPTER TWO. COMING OF AGE IN SEATTLE

This chapter is based largely on interviews and correspondence with Marilyn McMeekin Bauer, Susan Botkin Blake, Maxine Hanson Box, Bill Byers, John Hunt, Elaine Bowe Johnson, Stephen McCord, Jane Waddell Morris, Marilyn O'Neill, Raleigh Roark, Iona Stenhouse, Jim Sullivan, Kathy Powell Sullivan, Chip Wall, Jim Wichterman, and Linda Hall Wylie. I also interviewed Thomas Farner and Judy Farner Ware, whose late sister, Jackie Farner, was a friend of Stanley Ann's. On the subject of Madelyn and Stanley Dunham during this period, I am again indebted to their siblings Charles Payne, Arlene Payne, Jon Payne, and Ralph Dunham. The Reverend Dr. Peter J. Luton, senior minister at East Shore Unitarian Church, helped me with the history of the church, as did Judy Ware. The account of the case against John Stenhouse is based on information from his daughter, Iona, and on contemporaneous reporting in *The Seattle Times.*

71 *"my grandfather forbade her":* Obama, *Dreams from My Father,* 16.

CHAPTER THREE. EAST-WEST

For statistics on Hawaii in 1960, I relied on the *State of Hawaii Data Book,* published in 1967 by the Department of Planning and Economic Development. On the University of Hawai'i and the East-West Center, I read several years' worth of issues of the student newspaper, *Ka Leo O Hawai'i,* and back issues of *Impulse,* a magazine published later by East-West Center grant recipients. At the East-West Center, I received help from Karen Knudsen, director of the Office of External Affairs; Derek Ferrar, a media relations specialist; and Phyllis Tabusa, a research information specialist. Jeannette "Benji" Bennington, now retired from the center, provided invaluable insight and stories. Mia Noguchi, director of public relations for the university, and Stuart Lau, the registrar, helped me with statistics and facts. I benefited from interviews with former students, including Bill Collier, Gerald Krausse, Sylvia Krausse, Jeanette Takamura, Mark Wimbush and Pake Zane. On the subject of the Dunham family, I drew on interviews with Charles, Arlene, and Jon Payne; Ralph Dunham, and Maya Soetoro-Ng. I also used information from interviews with Marilyn Bauer, Maxine Box, Bill Byers, Takeshi Harada, Renske Heringa, Richard Hook, John Hunt, Kay Ikranagara, Kadi Warner, and Linda Hall Wylie. On the subject of Lolo Soetoro, I spoke with Benji Bennington, Bill Collier, Gerald and Sylvia Krausse, Kismardhani S-Roni, Maya Soetoro-Ng, Trisulo, Sonny Trisulo, and Pete Vayda. For the account of the events of September 30, 1965, and afterward in Indonesia, I am indebted to Adam Schwarz's *A Nation in Waiting: Indonesia's Search for Stability* and Adrian Vickers's *A History of Modern Indonesia.*

80 *"Gramps's relationship with my mother":* Obama, *Dreams from My Father,* 21.
81 *Russian language class:* Ibid., 9.
81 *He had been flown to the United States:* Michael Dobbs, "Obama Overstates Kennedys' Role in Helping His Father," *The Washington Post,* March 30, 2008, A1.
81 *received "invitations to campus":* Ka Leo O Hawai'i, October 8, 1959, 3.
82 *interview in the* Honolulu Star-Bulletin: *Honolulu Star-Bulletin,* November 28, 1959, 5.
82 *"If the people cannot rule themselves":* "First African Enrolled in Hawaii Studied Two Years by Mail," *Ka Leo O Hawai'i,* October 8, 1959, 3.
85 *"many things I didn't understand":* Obama, *Dreams from My Father,* 10.
86 *"There's no record of a real wedding":* Ibid., 22.
86 *left in late June:* Honolulu Star-Bulletin, June 20, 1962, 7.
86 *"No mention is made":* Obama, *Dreams from My Father,* 26–27.
89 *little thought to black people:* Ibid., 18.
89 *encountered race hatred:* Ibid., 19–20.
90 *"the condition of the black race":* Ibid., 21.
90 *Obama only imagines their reaction:* Ibid., 17–18.

91 *"I am a little dubious"*: David Mendell, *Obama: From Promise to Power* (New York: Amistad, 2007), 29.

91 *"weren't happy with the idea"*: Obama, *Dreams from My Father,* 125.

92 *"he didn't want the Obama blood sullied"*: Ibid., 126.

93 *"grande dame of escrow"*: Dan Nakaso, "Obama's Tutu a Hawaii Banking Female Pioneer," *Honolulu Advertiser,* March 30, 2008.

99 *Like some Javanese:* Indonesians are addressed by their first name, usually preceded by a title—never by their last name, if they have one. The Indonesian equivalent of *Mr.* is *Bapak,* meaning "father," or its abbreviated form, *Pak,* as in Pak Soetoro. The title is an expression of respect for age, position, and other attributes. Sometimes the name is shortened, as in Pak Harto for Soeharto. The equivalent of *Mrs.* is *Ibu,* meaning "mother" or "married woman," or *Bu,* as in Bu Ann. However, because I have written this book in English and many of the names are Western, I have tended to use, for consistency's sake and where possible, surnames on subsequent references. For family members of Ann Dunham, I have often used first names.

100 *"beyond her parents' reach"*: Obama, *Dreams from My Father,* 42.

102 *"choked with bodies"*: Adam Schwarz, *A Nation in Waiting,* 21.

102 *"one of the worst mass murders"*: Ibid., 20.

103 *married on March 5, 1964:* Date given on passport application filled out by Ann Dunham in early 1980s, from her personal papers.

CHAPTER FOUR. INITIATION IN JAVA

The description of Jakarta and Indonesia in the late 1960s and early 1970s and details of Ann's life there come from interviews with Halimah Bellows, Halimah Brugger, Elizabeth Bryant, Bill Collier, Stephen des Tombes, Michael Dove, Rens Heringa, Ikranagara, Kay Ikranagara, Samardal Manan, Wahyono Martowikrido, John McGlynn, Saman, Garrett and Bronwen Solyom, Sumastuti Sumukti, and Yang Suwan. I also relied on *A History of Modern Indonesia* by Adrian Vickers and *A Nation in Waiting* by Adam Schwarz. On the subject of Ann's employment, I am indebted to Irwan Holmes, Kay Ikranagara, Trusti Jarwadi, Leonard Kibble, Samardal Manan, Felina Pramono, Joseph Sigit, Sudibyo Siyam, and Stephen des Tombes. Information on the Institute for Management Education and Development also came from the archives of the Ford Foundation. For the facts of Lolo's work, I relied on his brother-in-law, Trisulo, and on Sonny Trisulo, Lolo's nephew. Insight into Ann as a parent came from her children as well as from Richard Hook, Kay Ikranagara, Don Johnston, Saman, Julia Suryakusuma, and Kadi Warner, among others.

108 *"join in the killings"*: Adrian Vickers, *A History of Modern Indonesia,* 158.

111 *Indonesia's Prague Spring:* Schwarz, *A Nation in Waiting,* 33.

115 *"The Indonesian businessmen"*: Obama, *Dreams from My Father*, 43.

124 *"They are not my people"*: Ibid., 47.

124 *Ann's loneliness was a constant:* Ibid., 42–43.

126 *"power had taken Lolo"*: Ibid., 45.

128 *"She loved to take children"*: Obama, *The Audacity of Hope,* 205.

129 *"you're going to need some values"*: Obama, *Dreams from My Father,* 49.

129 *ideal human virtues:* Koentjaraningrat, *Javanese Culture,* 122.

133 *"I was an American, she decided"*: Obama, *Dreams from My Father,* 47.

133 *"no picnic for me either, buster"*: Ibid., 48.

134 *"in Hawaii very soon —a year, tops"*: Ibid., 54.

134 *"never would have made the trip"*: Obama, *The Audacity of Hope,* 273.

CHAPTER FIVE. TRESPASSERS WILL BE EATEN

For the details of Ann's 1973 bus trip, I relied on her letter to Bill Byers and interviews with Jon Payne and Arlene Payne. The information on Ann's life as a graduate student came from Benji Bennington, Evelyn Caballero, Alice Dewey, Mendl Djunaidy, Ben Finney, Jean Kennedy, John Raintree, Garrett and Bronwen Solyom, Kadi Warner, and Brent Watanabe. For the sections on her experiences in Jakarta and Yogyakarta in the mid-1970s, I spoke with Rens Heringa, Terence Hull, Kay Ikranagara, Wahyono Martowikrido, Nancy Peluso, and Maya Soetoro-Ng. I also had access to some of Ann's academic records and correspondence with Alice Dewey.

143 *"'You two will become great friends'"*: Obama, *Dreams from My Father,* 64.

143 *Obama's account of his father's Christmas visit:* Ibid., 67–69.

146 *baking cookies was not at the top:* Ibid., 75.

149 *Her most important market informants:* Alice G. Dewey, *Peasant Marketing in Java,* xiv.

150 *"the best and most comprehensive study"*: Koentjaraningrat, *Javanese Culture,* 176.

154 *Her interest was function:* Bronwen Solyom, Symposium on Ann Dunham, University of Hawai'i at Mānoa, September 12, 2008.

155 *"was interested in the place where vision meets execution"*: Maya Soetoro-Ng, foreword to S. Ann Dunham, *Surviving Against the Odds: Village Industry in Indonesia,* ix–x.

156 *course in entrepreneurship:* Interview with Mendl W. Djunaidy, associate dean, East-West Center, October 7, 2008.

157 *"I immediately said no"*: Obama, *Dreams from My Father,* 76–77.

CHAPTER SIX. IN THE FIELD

Most of the material in this chapter comes from Ann Dunham's field notes, proposals, papers, and drafts, and the unpublished version of her dissertation, "Peasant Blacksmithing in Indonesia: Surviving and Thriving Against All Odds." I also drew on Garrett and Bronwen Solyom's writings on the Javanese kris; correspondence between Ann Dunham and Alice Dewey, and a 1974 edition of *Guide to Java* by Peter Hutton and Hans Hoefer. I used material from interviews with Clare Blenkinsop, Nancy Cooper, Alice Dewey, Michael Dove, Maggie Norobangun, President Obama, John Raintree, Khismardani S-Roni, Taluki Sasmitarsi, Maya Soetoro-Ng, the Solyoms, Sumarni and Djaka Waluja, and from e-mails written by Haryo Soetendro.

172 *Clifford Geertz confessed:* Richard Bernstein, "Anthropologist, Retracing Steps After 3 Decades, Is Shocked by Change," *The New York Times*, May 11, 1988.

173 *part-time unpaid cottage-industry workers:* S. Ann Dunham, "Women's Work in Village Industries on Java," unpublished paper from the 1980s.

175 *But Ann intended to expand the concept:* Ann Dunham, "Occupational Multiplicity as a Peasant Strategy," early draft of dissertation.

176 *sounds of forging:* S. Ann Dunham, "Peasant Blacksmithing in Indonesia: Surviving and Thriving Against All Odds," unpublished dissertation, 1992, 499.

183 *One scene of Pak Sastro and his wife:* Ibid., 556–560.

184 *"men of Kajar are fated":* Ibid., 495.

185 *"Whenever villagers have a problem":* Ibid., 533.

185 *"There are numerous stories of kerises rattling about":* Dunham, "Women's Work in Village Industries on Java," 41.

187 *In the acknowledgments:* Dunham, unpublished dissertation, vii–viii.

193 *In a haunting scene:* Obama, *Dreams from My Father,* 94–96.

CHAPTER SEVEN. COMMUNITY ORGANIZING

The account of Ann's years in Semarang and her work on the Provincial Development Project is based on interviews with Clare Blenkinsop, Alice Dewey, Carl Dutto, Don Flickinger, Bruce Harker, Ann Hawkins, Richard Holloway, Sidney Jones, Dick Patten, Nancy Peluso, John Raintree, Jerry Mark Silverman, Maya Soetoro-Ng, Kadi Warner, and Glen Williams. For the brief history of early credit programs, I also drew on *The Microfinance Revolution: Lessons from Indonesia* by Marguerite S. Robinson and on *Progress with Profits: The Development of Rural Banking in Indonesia* by Richard H. Patten and Jay K. Rosengard. The final paragraph, about the Ford Foundation, is based on documents in the Ford Foundation archives.

209 *"they believed that poor village women":* Letter from Ann Sutoro to Hanna Papanek, July 2, 1981.

211 *one-third of the 486 units:* Robinson, *The Microfinance Revolution: Lessons from Indonesia*, 115–118; Patten and Rosengard, *Progress with Profits*, 22–30.

212 *providing not only capital but training:* Ibid., 31–35.

215 *"Many hours of my childhood":* Maya Soetoro-Ng, foreword to S. Ann Dunham, *Surviving Against the Odds: Village Industry in Indonesia*, ix.

216 *"would be superb":* Memorandum to the File from Sidney Jones, March 10, 1980, PA 800-0893, Ford Foundation Archives.

CHAPTER EIGHT. THE FOUNDATION

This chapter draws heavily on information from grant files in the Ford Foundation archives. In addition, I had access to some of Ann Sutoro's personal papers, field notes, and correspondence from this period. I've also relied on interviews with Terry Bigalke, Halimah Brugger, Bill Carmichael, Carol Colfer, Bill Collier, Alice Dewey, Michael Dove, Jim Fox, Adrienne Germain, Ann Hawkins, Rens Heringa, Richard Holloway, Kay Ikranagara, Tim Jessup, Sidney Jones, Tom Kessinger, David Korten, Frances Korten, David McCauley, Georgia McCauley, John McGlynn, Paschetta Sarmidi, Adi Sasono, Suzanne Siskel, Maya Soetoro-Ng, Saraswati Sunindyo, Julia Suryakusuma, Frank Thomas, Pete Vayda, Yang Suwan, and Mary Zurbuchen. Some information on the history of the Ford office in Jakarta came from *Celebrating Indonesia: Fifty Years with the Ford Foundation 1953–2003,* published by the Ford Foundation in 2003.

220 *"Life in the bubble":* Interview with Mary Zurbuchen, September 30, 2008.

225 *William Carmichael, Ford's vice president:* "Recommendation for Grant Action," April 18, 1985, PA 800-0893, Ford Foundation Archives, 4–5.

226 *Ann wrote in 1981 to Carol Colfer:* Letter from Ann Sutoro to Carol Colfer, February 2, 1981, PA 800-0893, Ford Foundation Archives.

227 *"With all this complexity":* Memorandum to the files from Ann D. Sutoro, November 3, 1981, PA 800-0893, Ford Foundation Archives.

228 *"a country of 'smiling' or gentle oppression":* Memorandum to participants, Delhi Conference on Women's Programming, from Ann Dunham Soetoro, April 18, 1982, PA 809-0878, Ford Foundation Archives.

230 *"our best reference on the condition":* Memorandum to the files from Ann D. Sutoro, March 16, 1984, PA 835-0145, Ford Foundation Archives, 2.

231 *"Okay, sport":* Interview with Sidney Jones, July 1, 2009.

231 *"How do you think she felt?":* Interview with Saraswati Sunindyo, February 17, 2009.

231 *"a lonely witness for secular humanism":* Obama, *Dreams from My Father,* 50.

231 *her chin trembles:* Ibid., 126.

231 *"the unreflective heart of her youth":* Ibid., 124.

231 *"helping women buy a sewing machine":* Ibid., xi.

253 *"looked like a black ball surrounded by a brilliant white light":* Ward Keeler, "Sharp Rays: Javanese Responses to a Solar Eclipse," *Indonesia,* 46 (October 1988), 91–101.

259 *helped shift the government's focus:* Memorandum to the files from Mary S. Zurbuchen, October 29, 1998, PA 800-0893, Ford Foundation Archives, 6.

CHAPTER NINE. "SURVIVING AND THRIVING AGAINST ALL ODDS"

Material in this chapter came from interviews with Jim Boomgard, Alice Dewey, Michael Dove, Ralph Dunham, Ben Finney, Jim Fox, Rens Heringa, Dick Hook, Mary Houghton, John Hunt, Don Johnston, Nina Nayar, Barack Obama, Dick Patten, Sarah Patten, Marguerite Robinson, Sabaruddin, Maya Soetoro-Ng, Garrett and Bronwen Solyom, Eric Stone, Made Suarjana, Julia Suryakusuma, Trisulo, Sonny Trisulo, and Yang Suwan. In connection with Bank Rakyat Indonesia, I spoke with Sulaiman Arif Arianto, Kamardy Arief, Ch. Oktiva Susi E., Cut Indriani, Sriwiyono Joyomartono, Agus Rachmadi, Slamet Riyadi,Tomy Sugianto, Flora Sugondo, and Widayanti and Retno Wijayanti. I also drew on personal papers and field notes of Ann Dunham's, her letters to Dewey and Suryakusuma, her reports to the bank, her unpublished dissertation, and her curriculum vitae.

263 *helped make up the difference:* Interview with Maya Soetoro-Ng.
265 *"spir. develop (ilmu batin)":* This appears to refer to spiritual development. *Ilmu batin* is an Indonesian phrase referring to esoteric learning or mysticism.
267 *Madelyn would rent a hotel room:* Interview with Adi Sasono, January 22, 2009.
269 *first credit project for women and artisan-caste members:* Ann Dunham, curriculum vitae, 1993.
269 *In the Punjab:* Dunham, "Peasant Blacksmithing in Indonesia: Surviving and Thriving Against All Odds," 877–879.
272 *"in many ways the most spiritually awakened person":* Obama, *The Audacity of Hope,* 205.
273 *Though Ann had been led to believe:* Interviews with Alice Dewey.
274 *a rate of 120,000 a month:* James J. Fox, "Banking on the People: The Creation of General Rural Credit in Indonesia," in Sandy Toussaint and Jim Taylor, eds., *Applied Anthropology in Australasia* (Perth: University of Western Australia Press, 1999).
276 *"probably the single largest and most successful credit program":* For the history of the microfinance program of Bank Rakyat Indonesia, I have relied on *The Microfinance Revolution,* vol. 2: *Lessons from Indonesia,* by Marguerite S. Robinson; "Banking on the People," by James J. Fox; and *Progress with Profits: The Development of Rural Banking in Indonesia,* by Richard H. Patten and Jay K. Rosengard. Additional information came from a long interview with Kamardy Arief, the former chief executive officer of Bank Rakyat Indonesia.

277 *115,000 loans a month:* James J. Boomgard and Kenneth J. Angell, "Bank Rakyat Indonesia's Unit Desa System: Achievements and Replicability," in Maria Otero and Elisabeth Rhyne, eds., *The New World of Microenterprise Finance: Building Healthy Financial Institutions for the Poor* (West Hartford, CT: Kumarian Press, 1994).

277 *helped the bank weather the crisis:* Richard H. Patten, Jay K. Rosengard, and Don E. Johnston Jr., "Microfinance Success Amidst Macroeconomic Failure: The Experience of Bank Rakyat Indonesia During the East Asian Crisis," *World Development,* 29, no. 6 (2001), 1057–1069.

277 *more than four thousand microbanking outlets:* Interview with Sulaiman Arif Arianto, managing director, Bank Rakyat Indonesia, January 14, 2009.

278 *"the finest development worker":* Interview with Mary Houghton, November 14, 2008.

282 *"a little of his magical power had managed to rub off":* Dunham, unpublished dissertation, 285.

293 *"is one of the richest ethnographic studies":* Michael R. Dove, *Anthropological Quarterly,* 83, no. 2 (Spring 2010), 449–454.

CHAPTER TEN. MANHATTAN CHILL

This chapter is based largely on interviews with Niki Armacost, Nancy Barry, Brinley Bruton, Donald Creedon, Susan Davis, Sri R. Dwianto, Ruth Goodwin Groen, Dewiany Gunawan, Sarita Gupta, Bruce Harker, Mary Houghton, Don Johnston, Celina Kawas, Dinny Jusuf, Wanjiku Kibui, Nina Nayar, Brigitta Rahayoe, Barbara Shortle, Maya Soetoro-Ng, Garrett and Bronwen Solyom, Made Suarjana, Monica Tanuhandaru, Kellee Tsai, Pete Vayda, and Lawrence Yanovitch. I also had access to some of Ann Dunham's correspondence and personal papers dating from this period. Amy Rosmarin made available to me a videotape of a professional presentation made by Ann.

311 *microfinance institutions were reaching only a tiny fraction: What's New in Women's World Banking,* 2, no. 2 (May 1994).

317 *"I am now going further into credit card debt":* Memo from Ann Dunham Sutoro to Nancy Barry, September 8, 1993.

322 *"except the D and C, which I postponed":* Letter from Ann Sutoro to Barbara E. Shortle, July 18, 1995.

CHAPTER ELEVEN. COMING HOME

This chapter relies on interviews with James Boomgard, Gillie Brown, Alice Dewey, Michael Dove, Bruce Harker, Ann Hawkins, Rens Heringa, Don Johnston, Georgia McCauley, Ferne Mele, Nina Nayar, Mayling Oey-Gardiner, Dick Patten, Arlene Payne, Jon Payne, Nancy Peluso, Slamet Riyadi, Sabaruddin, Barbara Shortle, Maya Soetoro-Ng, Garrett and Bronwen Solyom, Made Suarjana,

Julia Suryakusuma, Tanya Torres, Pete Vayda, and Yang Suwan. I also had access to some of Ann Dunham's personal papers and correspondence.

344 *biggest mistake he made:* Scott Fornek, "Stanley Ann Dunham: 'Most Generous Spirit,'" *Chicago Sun Times,* Sept. 9, 2007. In response to a question from me, President Obama, through a spokesman on Dec. 16, 2010, confirmed the *Sun-Times* account and said he had last spoken with his mother several days before her death.

EPILOGUE

This epilogue includes material from conversations with Gillie Brown, Nancy Cooper, John Hunt, Nina Nayar, President Obama, Maya Soetoro-Ng, Sumarni, Kellee Tsai, Djaka Waluja, and Linda Wylie.

350 *approximately nine thousand copies:* Interview with Peter Osnos, former publisher of Times Books, March 2, 2008.
350 *in paperback the following year:* Interview with Philip Turner, former editor in chief of *Kodansha Globe,* March 4, 2008.
352 *"best in me I owe to her":* Obama, *Dreams from My Father,* xii.

Bibliography

Bresnan, John. *At Home Abroad: A Memoir of the Ford Foundation in Indonesia, 1953–1973*. Jakarta: Equinox, 2006.

Dewey, Alice G. *Peasant Marketing in Java*. New York: Free Press of Glencoe, 1962.

Dunham, S. Ann. *Peasant Blacksmithing in Indonesia: Surviving and Thriving Against All Odds*. Honolulu: University of Hawai'i, 1992.

Dunham, S. Ann. *Surviving Against the Odds: Village Industry in Indonesia*. Durham, NC: Duke University Press, 2009.

Ford Foundation. *Celebrating Indonesia: Fifty Years with the Ford Foundation 1953–2003*. New York: Ford Foundation, 2003.

Hutton, Peter, and Hans Hoefer. *Guide to Java*. Hong Kong: Apa Productions, 1974.

Koentjaraningrat. *Javanese Culture*. Oxford: Oxford University Press, 1985.

Miner, Craig. *Kansas: The History of the Sunflower State, 1854–2000*. Lawrence: University Press of Kansas, 2002.

Obama, Barack. *The Audacity of Hope*. New York: Crown, 2006.

———. *Dreams from My Father*. New York: Three Rivers Press, 1995.

Patten, Richard H., and Jay K. Rosengard. *Progress with Profits: The Development of Rural Banking in Indonesia*. San Francisco: ICS Press for the International Center for Economic Growth and the Harvard Institute for International Development, 1991.

Price, Jay M. *El Dorado: Legacy of an Oil Boom*. Charleston, SC: Arcadia, 2005.

Robinson, Marguerite S. *The Microfinance Revolution,* vol. 2: *Lessons from Indonesia*. Washington, DC: The World Bank, 2002.

Schwarz, Adam. *A Nation in Waiting: Indonesia's Search for Stability*. Oxford: Westview Press, 2000.

Solyom, Garrett, and Bronwen Solyom. *The World of the Javanese Keris*. Honolulu: Asian Arts Press, 1988.

Vickers, Adrian. *A History of Modern Indonesia*. Cambridge, England: Cambridge University Press, 2005.

A Note on Photos

Over the past three years, people surprised me repeatedly with photographs of Ann Dunham. There was the photo of Ann, at forty-four, on a Manhattan rooftop—the photo that left me wondering about her in the first place. There was the photo of Ann, in a borrowed sarong and *kebaya,* at the University of Hawai'i at age twenty-one. Over a dish of crisp fried cow's lung in a Jakarta restaurant in 2009, Samardal Manan pulled out a black-and-white snapshot dating back to 1969. When I met Bill Byers, he showed me a photo, of Ann in a dashiki, which he had held on to for thirty-five years. Classmates, colleagues, field assistants, a driver, a professor, protégées, family members, and friends unearthed images in old albums, stuffed in envelopes, bent at the corners. Ann kept photos, too. For years, she documented in photographs as well as writing the working lives of the blacksmiths and other craftspeople she studied. She took her camera on field trips with teams of younger colleagues to places like Sulawesi and Bali. Some of those pictures became part of her dissertation. After her death, many were kept by her close friends. Some of the images in this book were made public during the 2008 presidential campaign by Obama for America, the campaign organization. But most were made available to me by family members and friends of Ann Dunham, some of whom chose not to be credited by name.

Photo Credits

Page 27: Courtesy Margaret McCurry Wolf
Page 54: Linnet Dunden Botkin
Page 61; photo insert page 5: Polaris
Pages 94, 144, 145; photo insert page 2, middle: AP Photo/Obama for America
Page 98: Gerald and Sylvia Krausse

A NOTE ON PHOTOS

Page 135: AP Photo/Obama Presidential Campaign
Page 141: Bill Byers
Pages 164, 166: Nancy Peluso
Page 247: Collection of Julia Suryakusuma, reproduced with permission of Julia
Suryakusuma